THE WEATHER AND ITS SECRETS

THE EARTH, ITS WONDERS, ITS SECRETS

THE WEATHER AND ITS SECRETS

Reader's Digest

PUBLISHED BY

THE READER'S DIGEST ASSOCIATION LIMITED

LONDON NEW YORK MONTREAL SYDNEY CAPE TOWN

THE WEATHER AND ITS SECRETS
Edited and designed by Toucan Books Limited
with Bradbury and Williams
Written by Philip Eden
Edited by Helen Douglas-Cooper and Andrew Kerr-Jarrett
Picture Research by Marian Pullen

FOR THE READER'S DIGEST, U.K.
Series Editor Christine Noble
Editorial Assistant Alison Candlin

FOR THE READER'S DIGEST, U.S.
Series Editor Gayla Visalli
Series Art Editor Martha Grossman
Assistant Editors Mary Jo McLean, Valerie Sylvester

The picture credits that appear on page 160 are hereby made a part of this
copyright page.

Printed in the United States of America
1998

Address any comments about THE WEATHER AND ITS SECRETS to
U.S. Editor, General Books, 260 Madison Avenue, New York, NY 10016

Library of Congress Cataloging in Publication Data
The weather and its secrets
            p.   cm.—(The earth, its wonders, its secrets)
        Includes index.
        ISBN 0-7621-0084-2
        1. Weather. 2. Climatology..   I. Reader's Digest Association.
    QC981   1998
    551.5—dc21   97-52721
                                                                      CIP

FRONT COVER *Altocumulus clouds appear at sunset over the
southern Namib Desert. Inset: Lightning strikes over Arizona, USA.*

PAGE 3 *A distant cumulonimbus, typical of tropical latitudes, gives
a heavy downpour near the horizon, while the pinks and golds of the
sunset promise a fine night.*

CONTENTS

THE POWER OF THE ELEMENTS

From earliest times people have tried to accurately predict the weather. Thanks to modern science that dream has largely become a reality – though daily weather conditions still occasionally confound the experts' best forecasts.

Two days after Christmas in 1831, the *Beagle,* a 240-ton brig belonging to the British Royal Navy, set sail from Portsmouth on the south coast of England and traveled to South America, the Galápagos Islands, New Zealand, Australia and Mauritius. The voyage, which lasted until 1836, became famous eventually because of a civilian passenger aboard – the naturalist Charles Darwin. His now widely accepted theory of evolution developed from the astute observations he made during the trip. Coincidentally, there was another man on board who also had a considerable impact on the way we see the world today. He was the captain, Robert Fitzroy, who later set up one of the world's first national storm-forecasting systems, issuing warnings of severe weather to ships around the British coastline. His system was the forerunner of the modern daily weather forecast.

A keen student of the weather, he made thoughtful observations during the *Beagle's* voyage and on later journeys. He also invented a special seaworthy barometer for

COMING THUNDER *The top edge of this thundercloud is turning fibrous. Within an hour, thunder and lightning will probably occur.*

WEATHER-WISE *Admiral Robert Fitzroy, the first head of the British Meteorological Office, pioneered gale warnings around the coasts of the British Isles.*

mariners and was the author of comments known as 'Remarks', often inscribed on barometers. The Remarks were based on Fitzroy's observation that rising or falling air pressure was frequently followed by particular kinds of weather: for example, 'A fall when the thermometer is low indicates snow or rain.' The principles behind many of these observations are still regarded as reasonably reliable. Then, in 1854, having served as a member of Parliament and the governor of New Zealand, he retired from the Navy as a rear-admiral and became chief of the Meteorological Department for the British Board of Trade.

Using the newly invented telegraph, Fitzroy gathered weather reports from 40 weather stations around the British Isles and from this information drew maps showing weather conditions simultaneously – the first ever 'synoptic' maps. In February 1861 he began issuing storm warnings by telegraphing ports and harbours about the country, which relayed the news to passing ships by semaphore. Before long, he became more ambitious, publishing weather forecasts for Britain as a whole in *The Times* (London). However, meteorology was still a primitive science, and Fitzroy's forecasts were far from infallible. His predictions were received with scepticism by the general public and some scientists. More importantly – the editor of *The Times* lost faith, so this forecasting service ended early in 1865, shortly before Fitzroy took his own life. The warnings for mariners, though, continue today.

THE WEATHER IN OUR LIVES

This early experiment with general forecasts failed to convince. Eventually, however, as accuracy improved, ordinary people started to take them seriously, until they became, as they are today, an essential part of the paraphernalia of everyday life. The trend was hardly surprising. Our lives are bound up with the weather. Crops – the food we eat – depend on favourable weather. We are all vulnerable to natural disasters – storms, mudslides, floods – brought on by weather. Heavy snowfall disrupts our routines. Sunny weather can make the difference between a good holiday and a bad one.

Admittedly, people nowadays in prosperous Western countries are more protected from the weather and its milder vagaries than their forebears were. Their homes and workplaces are centrally heated in winter and often air-conditioned in summer, so that extremes of temperature have less affect on them. They have sophisticated systems that usually manage to take away excess water after rainstorms and deliver domestic supplies during droughts. The weather affects work less because far fewer people work outdoors than used to be the case. However, even in Western countries, the weather, in one of its extreme moods, can still seriously disrupt the delicate balance between nature and civilisation. Hurricanes, tornadoes, and other windstorms wreck homes, block roadways, and disrupt power and water sources. Severe floods also leave many houses uninhabitable. Paradoxically, high-tech societies have become so dependent on their reliable supplies of power, food, and water that they are sometimes more vulnerable to extremes in weather, which interrupt these supplies, than their lower-tech predecessors of 100 or 200 years ago.

Moreover, even though fewer people work out of doors nowadays, many modern leisure pursuits expose us to the weather. Most organised sports are affected by the

BATTLING THROUGH *A sailing boat ploughs through rough seas. In open waters, the height of the waves depends on the strength of the wind and the length of time it has been blowing from one direction.*

WASHED OUT *Wimbledon fortnight, one of the highlights of the tennis year, is frequently disrupted by rain.*

weather, liable to be disrupted or abandoned because of snow or ice or waterlogging in winter, or because of rain or storms in summer. Every year hundreds of people across the world lose their lives while engaged in activities such as mountaineering and hiking, sailing and skiing, most often because of extreme weather. Even tamer sports have their dangers: in Britain, for example, five

people on average are killed each year by lightning; many are fatally struck while playing soccer, cricket, or golf, some even while fishing.

The weather has shown its dangerous side in practically every country on the planet in recent years. Take 1994, for instance. The year began with floods in north-western Europe and the British Isles, with thousands of people evacuated from their homes for several weeks. At the same time bush fires raged through New South Wales including some of the wealthier suburbs of Sydney, leaving five people dead and hundreds homeless. On January 30, after copious snowfalls in the Alps, an avalanche hit the mountain slopes near the French winter-sports resort of Tignes, killing five British doctors and their French guide. By the end

of the winter, not a particularly severe one in Britain, 15 walkers and climbers had died in the Scottish Highlands, having underestimated the dramatic weather changes that can occur there almost instantaneously.

TRAIL OF DESTRUCTION

In February an intense depression located south of Ireland whipped up violent storms, severe gales, and heavy seas. In the midst of this tempest, the Greek cargo vessel *Christinaki* sank, losing 27 members of its crew. On March 27 tornadoes in the southeastern region of the U.S. caused 42 deaths and destroyed hundreds of houses. On May 3 a major catastrophe was averted when a severe cyclone heading for the middle of Bangladesh changed course and landed in the sparsely populated region near the border with Myanmar (formerly Burma); only 100 people died. Water followed wind: June floods in southern and eastern China drowned 700 people. There were 580 fatalities as monsoon floods swept parts of India between July 14 and 20, and China suffered again when torrential downpours hit Zhejiang province on August 23, drowning 750 people. Further floods hit northern Italy on November 5 and 6 leading to 64 deaths. Drought followed by strong winds kindled bush fires in Colorado in July. Twenty-six people were injured by explosions at an oil refinery at Milford Haven in Wales following a lightning strike on July 24, and on November 2 a similar bolt of lightning at a fuel depot in Egypt had catastrophic results – fires raced through a neighbouring village in a matter of minutes, killing 460 inhabitants.

The weather is a force that will not permit us to ignore it.

BATTERED BY WIND *Chaos reigns in the streets of St Thomas, Virgin Islands, following a battering from Hurricane Marilyn in September 1995.*

For our distant forebears it was a mystery, like so much else in life, controlled by the gods. In the Old Testament book of Jonah, the Bible describes how 'the Lord hurled a great wind upon the sea, and there was a mighty tempest on the sea...' This particular storm, according to the Bible story, was a result of the disobedience of the prophet Jonah. Only when the sailors of a ship caught up in the storm took Jonah, who was hiding on board, and threw him into the sea did it 'cease from its raging'. The story continues: 'Then the men feared the Lord exceedingly, and they offered a sacrifice to the Lord and made vows.' Jonah, meanwhile, was miraculously saved, so the story goes, by being swallowed by a whale and later regurgitated.

But even among our forebears there were the glimmerings, at least, of a more scientific view of the weather. A huge amount of weather lore has come down to us, from many different cultures across the world, most of it about predicting what the weather will do. Amongst it, there is much that is based on superstition and therefore useless for forecasting. On the other hand, there is also much that is clearly based on experience and precise observation. The 'weather machine' as modern science understands it is a complex three-dimensional mechanism involving the different levels of the atmosphere and its winds, water vapour in the atmosphere and heat energy radiating from both the Sun and the surface of the Earth. The interworkings of these different influences are played out in the atmosphere, and so much of the most reliable weather lore relates, not surprisingly, to observations of the sky. It is true, for example, that a red sky in the morning is often, though by no means always, a sign of bad weather to come. Often the effect of a red sky is created when the rising Sun shines on the undersides of the oncoming clouds of a warm or cold front bringing rain.

'Every wind has its weather,' noted the Elizabethan English scholar Francis Bacon. This is another truth, supported by the findings of modern science, that has long been recognised by weather prophets. The ancient Greeks associated the different winds with specific wind gods, but by the time the world's first-known weather vane was erected on top of the Tower of the Winds in 1st century BC Athens, they also clearly recognised that different winds brought different kinds of weather. The Tower of the Winds, which still stands, is an eight-sided structure, and each of the eight sides features a sculpture representing the characteristics of the wind originating from that direction. The south-east wind Euros, for example, is depicted as an elderly man wrapped up against damp, squally weather. Farmers and sailors alike were, of necessity, keen observers of the wind, anxious about their crops or to determine the chances of a safe voyage. During the Middle Ages, weather vanes became a common feature in European towns and villages, and were often seen perched atop church towers or castle keeps.

FLOODED *Torrential rainstorms caused serious flooding over a large part of Piedmont in November 1994. Turin was badly affected, but the floods were worst in and around Asti and Alessandria.*

The ancient Greeks were, in fact, among the first people who attempted to explain aspects of the weather scientifically. In the 4th century BC the philosopher Aristotle wrote a treatise on weather entitled *Meteorologica*. In this he shows, among other things, some understanding of the hydrological cycle – the cycle in which water evaporates into the atmosphere from seas, lakes and rivers and then condenses into rain, sleet or snow which returns to the surface of the Earth. He noted that by the action of the Sun's heat 'the finest and sweetest water is every day carried up and is dissolved into vapour and rises to the upper region, where it is condensed again by the cold and so returns to the Earth.... So the sea will never dry up; for before that can happen the water that has gone up beforehand will return to it.' Later, one of his pupils, Theophrastus, wrote *On Weather Signs* in which he observed, correctly, that winds blowing off the sea often bring rain, and clouds often drop rain when they pass over mountains.

After that, few advances were made in the science of meteorology until much more modern times – the 18th-century English man of letters Dr Samuel Johnson was able to comment of his countrymen, with some

SPARK ACROSS THE SKY *A rare picture shows a single lightning discharge arcing across open sky from one cloud to another. Discharges within clouds, and from cloud to ground, are much more frequent.*

justice, that whenever two of them met, 'they begin to talk about the weather, each trying to inform the other of that which they know nothing about'. Even as Johnson made his comment, however, people in a number of countries were doing their best to rectify their ignorance. By 1793, the Societas Meteorologica Palatine in Germany had 70 weather observers in places as far afield as New York and Stockholm, St Petersburg and Baghdad. This and other similar societies in France and Britain encouraged observers to keep detailed weather diaries. In this way they hoped to build up a body of reliable information that would enable scientists to speculate more authoritatively about the workings of the weather. Another keen observer was the American statesman Thomas

Jefferson who for a year kept a daily weather diary at his country house Monticello in Virginia, comparing results with a fellow enthusiast James Madison in Williamsburg.

FLYING HIGH

An event that took place in Paris in October 1783, just a few years before the French Revolution, was to have a marked impact on the study of meteorology. It was the first manned flight in a hot-air balloon. The hot-air balloon had been invented by the brothers Joseph-Michel and Jacques-Etienne Montgolfier, and in September there had been a demonstration flight at Versailles in the presence of the French king Louis XVI. On that occasion the 'car' or basket underneath the balloon had carried a sheep, a cock and

THE HAYMAKERS *The shadows in this painting by John Linnell (1792-1882) tell us that it is the middle of the day, probably in June or July.*

a duck. Then the physicist Jean-François Pilâtre de Rozier volunteered to become the first human passenger. He went up in a tethered balloon on October 15 and a few days later embarked on the first-ever free, untethered flight. On October 21, 'this bold adventurer,' in the words of the scientist and chronicler of early ballooning, Camille Flammarion, 'accompanied by his friend the Marquis d'Arlandes, actually rose from the Chateau de la Muette in the car of a magnificent Montgolfier, and after passing over the capital, to the astonishment of the whole of Paris, they descended in the country near the Butte aux Cailles. This bold experiment opened out a new path, which was not long untrodden.'

Scientists interested in the weather were quick to spot the potential of this invention. Within years intrepid meteorologists were mounting to the skies, carrying aloft instruments for measuring pressure, temperature, humidity and wind at different altitudes. For the first time, they could systematically study the workings of the weather in three dimensions rather than just two. In particular, they could study the composition and movement of the atmosphere. In one flight in 1804 the French chemist Louis-Joseph Gay-Lussac ascended to 23 018 ft (7016 m), analysing air samples at each level. As a result of such experiments scientists discovered that most of the water vapour in the atmosphere is concentrated in the bottom 20 000 ft (6000 m). An American balloonist John Wise discovered to his cost the sheer power of the updraughts of air in a thunderstorm when he got caught in one in 1843. He was violently tossed around and when he eventually made it back to the ground his beard had a mantle of hoarfrost on it.

Then, in the middle of the 19th century, came the invention of the electric telegraph,

HIGH IN THE SKY *Balloons, then aircraft, encouraged the study of conditions in the upper air. Early aircraft were very sensitive to wind and weather.*

and with it the ability to exchange and collate weather observations from many different places in a matter of hours. Experts were now able to build up a much better picture of weather patterns. In the United States, the physicist Joseph Henry of the Smithsonian Institution in Washington made a deal with the expanding telegraph companies whereby they gathered weather information for him and he sent them the resulting summaries – unlike his British

SPACE VIEW *New generations of satellites stay above the same point on the Earth's surface and provide more information than ever about the weather.*

World War and civilian aviators in the years that followed – were voracious consumers of weather forecasts; it is difficult to imagine a more weather-sensitive occupation. Not only did they need a reliable picture of the wind and cloud conditions during their flights, but they also needed predictions of the weather at their expected destinations, and at alternative destinations in case they were diverted. At the same time, planes and airships were also able to provide new information about atmospheric conditions aloft. In the 1930s unmanned balloon flights carried meteorological instruments into the far reaches of the upper atmosphere and the measurements were transmitted back to ground stations by radio. After the Second

World War a worldwide network of radio-sonde stations was established – radiosondes are lightweight transmitters able to send back pressure, temperature, humidity and wind readings. For the first time this gave weather forecasters regular daily information about upper-air weather patterns.

INTO THE FUTURE

In the last 50 years, technological advances have followed hard on the heels of one another. The advent of satellite images, growing computer power, satellite sensing of temperature and wind, and radar measurements of rainfall intensity and wind velocity have all helped to improve the accuracy of our forecasts. Thus we now have huge amounts of information about the atmosphere, updated at frequent intervals throughout the day. Computers are big enough to handle it all, and the theoretical scientific knowledge is available to predict what will happen in the next few days. The fact that weather forecasts still occasionally go wrong just shows what a hugely complex machine the atmosphere is.

The business of forecasting has been transformed out of all recognition since Fitzroy offered his first predictions in the mid 19th century. Scientists' understanding of the weather and what causes it continues to grow, and in the years to come they should be able to give accurate forecasts for up to 10 or 12 days ahead. At the same time, there will probably be a shift of emphasis in scientific research from weather – day-to-day conditions – to climate – prevailing conditions over the long term. The prospect of man-induced climate change – as a result, for example, of damage to the ozone layer – and the potential impact of such change on the global economy means that meteorology, once a relative backwater among the sciences, is becoming ever more vital to our very survival. The task that now faces atmospheric scientists is the attempt to predict what will happen to the patchwork of different climates that cover the planet over the coming decades and centuries.

contemporary Robert Fitzroy, however, he did not attempt forecasts. Across the Atlantic, meanwhile, the Crimean War gave an impetus to European weather services. In 1854 some French and British warships were wrecked in the Black Sea off Balaclava when they got caught in an unexpected storm. It transpired that a warning could easily have been telegraphed to Balaclava and the disaster would probably have been averted. In response to that, the French government set up a storm-warning service. A few years later, in 1863, the Paris Observatory started issuing weather maps. Experts' knowledge of weather patterns was still rudimentary and they were able to formulate only the simplest forecasting rules, such as those laid down by Fitzroy in his *Weather Book*, published in 1863. Even so, the American national weather service, within a decade of its founding in 1871, claimed a 74 per cent accuracy rate in its forecasts of coming rain and snow and temperature changes – though these claims are, in fact, open to some doubt.

The coming of aviation in the early 20th century gave another huge prod to the development of meteorological science. The early aviators – the flying aces of the First

ARCTIC HOLE, MARCH 1995
Ozone depletion (blue and mauve areas) is most evident over the Russian Arctic and over north-west Europe.

How the Weather Works

1

NORTHERN LIGHTS *The aurora borealis brings displays of coloured lights to Arctic skies.*

THE ATMOSPHERE IS A SORT OF MACHINE, AN ENGINE OPERATING ON A VAST SCALE. THE ENERGY WHICH DRIVES THE MACHINE COMES FROM THE SUN. THE ENGINE RUNS ON AIR AND WATER, AND THE POWER IT PRODUCES MANIFESTS ITSELF IN THE FORM OF THE WEATHER WE EXPERIENCE: THE WINDSTORMS, RAINSTORMS, SNOWSTORMS, THUNDERSTORMS AND SANDSTORMS WHICH ARE RAGING SOMEWHERE OR OTHER IN THE WORLD AT EVERY MOMENT OF EVERY DAY OF THE YEAR. THIS POWER IS ESSENTIAL TO LIFE AS WE KNOW IT, PROVIDING THE MOISTURE AND WARMTH TO NURTURE PLANTS AND ANIMALS. THE CYCLE OF THE SEASONS, ANOTHER ASPECT OF THE WEATHER MACHINE, ALLOWS THE PROPAGATION OF LIFE FROM YEAR TO YEAR.

SUN SPOTS *Dark red patches are cooler spots on the Sun's surface.*

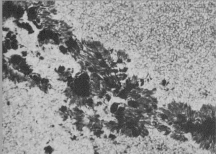

AIR, FIRE, EARTH AND WATER

Heat energy from the Sun drives the 'weather machine'. It warms the Earth's surface, which warms the air above it. The winds circulate and moisture is exchanged between the atmosphere and the surface below in a never-ending cycle.

Viewed from space, the Earth presents a peaceful picture, its hues of blue, green, white and brown combining in slowly changing patterns. The influence of mankind is invisible from this distant viewpoint. Equally, there is little sense of the power of the air around us and the destructive forces it can unleash. In fact, the white swirls spread across the blue-green disc that appear decorative from afar are huge cloud systems, sometimes covering thousands of square miles. They mark areas where atmospheric processes are at their most turbulent.

The atmosphere is sometimes the source of extreme violence, as in a tropical hurricane; at other times it creates scenes of utter serenity, as on a clear autumn day. The weather is the state of the atmosphere at a particular place and time, and the weather, as we all know, has a vital impact on our lives. It affects the sorts of houses we live in, the character of the towns and cities we inhabit, the types of animals and plants with which we share our particular corner of the planet, the sort of food we eat and the agricultural methods we have devised over the millennia to produce that food. Our lives and lifestyles are so intricately interwoven with the behaviour of the weather that it is hardly surprising that we try so hard to predict what it is going to do next.

Weather follows certain patterns, a few of which have been understood for centuries,

SATELLITE VIEW *This image shows an active depression over the Atlantic between Brazil and South Africa and heavy storms over equatorial Africa.*

enabling the first 'weather prophets' to offer elementary predictions. Modern meteorologists, however, have built up a much more comprehensive knowledge of these patterns and what causes them, so that they are able to make detailed and usually accurate forecasts for several days ahead.

The ancient Greeks believed that four 'elements' – air, fire, earth and water – were the foundation of all things. Modern scientists have a much more complex view of things, but as far as the basic processes that cause the weather are concerned the Greeks were surprisingly close to the mark. Scientists nowadays compare the workings of the atmosphere to those of a vast heat engine, powered by the heat coming from the Sun and running on air and water. Today, we would represent the four basic 'elements' as the atmosphere, heat energy from the Sun, heat energy from the Earth's surface and water vapour. Without any of these four constituents, our planet would be incapable of supporting life as we know it.

THE LAYERS OF THE ATMOSPHERE

What is the atmosphere? Not that long ago – in the 1950s and 1960s – it was common to describe it as the envelope of life-giving gases that surrounds the Earth, extending to a height of some 100 to 200 miles (160 to 320 km) above the planet's surface. Scientists now know that there is no definable upper limit to the atmosphere. It just becomes more and more tenuous the farther one gets from the Earth's surface. The air molecules per unit of volume become fewer and

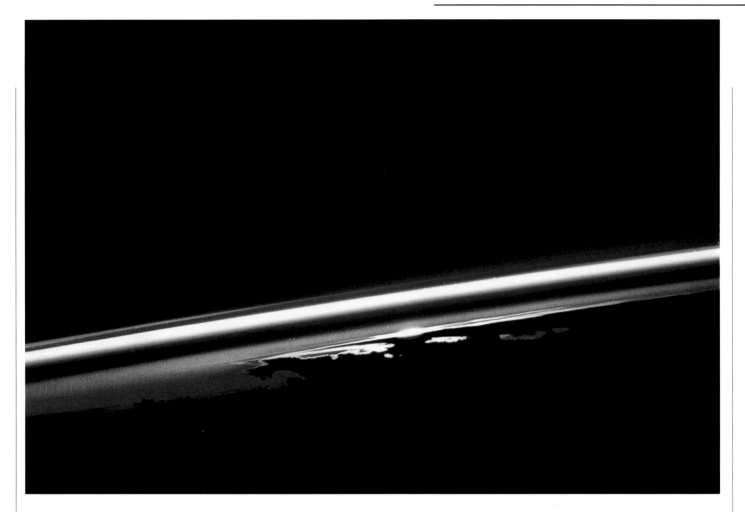

THE ATMOSPHERE SIDEWAYS
This view of the Earth's atmos-
phere was taken from the space
shuttle Endeavor *in 1992.*
The dense air of the lower
atmosphere refracts mainly red
light, while the thin upper
atmosphere refracts blue light.

fewer; in other words, the air becomes less and less dense and its pressure – the weight of air resting on a particular area – drops.

The total mass of air in the atmosphere is estimated at 5.6 quadrillion – 5600 million million – tons. Although this sounds like a lot, it represents barely a millionth of the mass of the Earth itself. Some 95 per cent of the mass of the atmosphere lies in the lowest 30 to 35 miles (48 to 56 km), with about 75 per cent in the lowest 7 to 8 miles (11 to 13 km). This is where the air pressure is highest. It has been estimated that an average person standing at sea level carries about a quarter of a ton of air on his or her head.

The different gases that comprise the atmosphere include nitrogen (just over 75 per

cent by weight), oxygen (about 23 per cent) and small quantities of argon, helium, carbon monoxide, sulphur dioxide, nitrogen dioxide and methane. Water vapour is another component, comprising some 2.5 per cent by volume at any one time. The proportions of the gases vary with altitude. Nearly all the water vapour is in the lowest 5 miles (8 km), while hydrogen and helium are the dominant gases at the highest altitudes. 'Aerosols' are another significant element. They are suspended particles of dust, smoke, organic matter and sea salt, coming from a variety of natural sources – sea spray, volcanic activity, dust raised by the wind – as well as being a result of man-made industrial and agricultural pollution.

LOW PRESSURE *Air pressure at*
the summit of Mount Everest is
roughly 30 per cent of what it is
at sea level. Thus mountaineers
need to carry extra oxygen.

The atmosphere can be divided into a number of distinct layers, called spheres, defined by the variation in temperature at different altitudes above the Earth's surface. Inevitably, the air's pressure declines with altitude since the column of air weighing down on any one place is smaller and less dense the higher you go. By contrast, the temperature of the air fluctuates very

EQUATORIAL SNOW *In the troposphere, temperature drops with altitude. Thus Mount Uhuru (Kilimanjaro) is snow-capped even though it rises close to the Equator.*

markedly and in different directions from sphere to sphere.

The lowest layer is the troposphere which extends from the Earth's surface to an average height that ranges from roughly 5 miles (8 km) at the poles to some 10 miles (16 km) at the Equator, although these figures vary from season to season – differing levels of atmospheric activity due to the Sun's heating of the Earth's surface account for the variations. Except during long-distance aircraft journeys or when engaged in underwater activity, we live out our lives in the troposphere, and all our weather happens here.

The distinctive feature of the troposphere is that the temperature drops with altitude. There are occasional exceptions to this rule over limited areas – notably over landmasses in winter when a shallow layer of cold air often collects near the Earth's surface – but these are all purely temporary. At the top of the troposphere is the tropopause where the temperature ceases to fall with height. The drop in temperature with altitude inside the troposphere is usually called the 'lapse rate', and it averages roughly 1°C per 500 ft/150 m (1°F per 300 ft/90 m).

Even the summit of Mount Everest lies within the troposphere, albeit in the upper reaches. Generally, there is not enough air for us to breathe at these high altitudes, while the temperature there is rarely any higher than –30°C (–22°F) – it has even been known to drop below –70°C (–94°F). This upper region of the troposphere is truly inhospitable, so that only the lowest 3 to 4 miles (5 to 6.5 km) of Earth's atmosphere can really be regarded as an 'envelope of life-giving gases'.

BEYOND THE TROPOSPHERE

The stratosphere extends upwards from the tropopause to a height of about 50 miles (80 km) above the ground. Between about 10 and 20 miles (16 and

THROUGH THE STRATOSPHERE *Jumbo jets on long-haul flights carry their passengers above the weather at heights of about 6 miles (10 km).*

32 km) up, the temperature is more or less static at about –50°C (–58°F). But a relatively warmer layer exists beyond that, about 30 miles (48 km) up, where the temperature climbs to about 0°C (32°F), and this marks the top of the region. A few very thin clouds made of ice crystals are found in the stratosphere from time to time, but generally it is cloudless with little water vapour present. For most of us, our closest contact with this realm of deep blue sky, brilliant sunlight and rasping winds is through the window of a jet. The stratosphere also contains the ozone layer which protects the Earth's surface from harmful ultraviolet rays coming from the Sun.

Next comes the mesosphere, a deep layer where the air is extremely tenuous. It

stretches upwards from the top of the stratosphere to about 50 miles (80 km) above the surface of the Earth. This is a zone where temperature again declines with height; the coldest part of the entire atmosphere lies between 50 and 60 miles (80 and 97 km) up where the temperature of the air – what there is of it – is around –90°C (–130°F). Occasional 'noctilucent' – night-shining – clouds form in this sphere, a result probably of meteoric dust that gathers to it a few stray traces of water vapour.

NIGHT-SHINING *Tenuous 'noctilucent' clouds form high in the mesosphere where they can reflect the Sun's rays even in the middle of the night.*

Above the mesosphere, the next layer, the thermosphere, stretches upwards many hundreds of miles until it reaches the point at which the density of the air surrounding the

INTREPID EXPLORERS OF THE UPPER ATMOSPHERE

The upper air was a new frontier for 19th-century meteorologists, as a few remarkable individuals came to understand that it held the key to a more complete understanding of the behaviour of the atmosphere. To pursue their studies, some established observatories on mountain tops; others experimented with balloons.

Observatories were set up on Mount Washington in New Hampshire, Zugspitze in the Bavarian Alps, and Mont Aigoual in France's Massif Central. In Britain, one was established on the summit of Ben Nevis in the 1880s. In Paris, weather-recording equipment was fixed to the summit of the Eiffel Tower on its completion in 1889.

Before that, the British Association, a scientific body, had sponsored a series of manned hot-air balloon flights, with a weather observer making meteorological readings at regular intervals throughout the voyage. These flights took place between 1862 and 1866; another series of observations was made from a tethered balloon at Chelsea in

PERILS ON HIGH *The Victorian meteorologist James Glaisher loses consciousness during a balloon ascent in 1862.*

London during 1869. The man entrusted with recording information while the balloon was airborne was James Glaisher, Superintendent of the Meteorological Department at the Greenwich Royal Observatory in London. Although nearly 60 years old, he jumped at the opportunity of a fresh challenge. However, the project almost came to a grisly end before it had started, as one of the earliest flights nearly proved fatal. The flight started from Wolverhampton in the English Midlands on the morning of

SCOTTISH AIR *Dedicated meteorologists measured weather changes on Ben Nevis.*

September 5, 1862, and it reached a record height of over 7 miles (11 km). But the temperature had fallen to below –40°C (–40°F), and the air pressure had dropped to a fifth of its sea-level value without the occupants of the basket realizing that they were in danger.

It appears that Glaisher himself lost consciousness at about 29 000 ft (8800 m). His companion, Henry Coxwell, was flying the balloon. He tried frantically to operate the release valve but was unable to do so, because his hands had become completely numb from the cold. In a last desperate attempt as he, too, drifted in and out of consciousness, Coxwell gripped the cord between his teeth and jerked his head several times as hard as he could. Eventually he was successful. The valve opened, and the balloon began very gradually to lose height.

A lesser man might have been put off by this experience, but Glaisher was undaunted and continued on to complete the series of upper-air investigations. Indeed he lived a long and active life; Glaisher was 94 years old when he died in 1902.

LIGHTS OF THE IONOSPHERE
Electrically charged particles
from the Sun interact with the
Earth's magnetic field to create
the light displays of the aurora
borealis – seen here (left and
above) over Alaska.

Earth is so minute that it is indistinguishable from the density of interplanetary gas. In this sector of the atmosphere, as height above the ground increases, temperatures rise rather than fall.

Somewhere between 200 and 500 miles (320 and 800 km) above the ground lies the limit beyond which air molecules are no longer bound by gravity. The region above this limit used to be dubbed the 'exosphere', because it was thought that air molecules here, freed from gravity, could escape into space. However, experts now believe that the motion of air particles at this height is controlled by the Earth's magnetic field rather than by gravity, so in practice this critical level does not exist.

Straddling the mesosphere and thermosphere is a broad zone – stretching from about 35 to 250 miles (55 to 400 km) above the Earth's surface – which is usually called the ionosphere, although it is not a separate sphere as far as temperature is concerned.

and other material suspended in the atmosphere; 26 per cent is absorbed by clouds or reflected by them back out to space; 4 per cent is reflected by land and sea surfaces, and 47 per cent is absorbed by the Earth's surface. For shorter periods and at a local level, however, when the Sun shines powerfully from a clear sky, between 70 and 80 per cent of the incoming radiation may go towards heating up the ground.

At the same time, heat energy is lost to outer space. This is not just the small proportion reflected by clouds, land, sea and ice, but includes energy, originally absorbed from the Sun, that the Earth itself radiates back out again. In the end, the incoming and outgoing radiation balance out. The white swirls of cloud seen against

Even so, it is an important region where the interaction of radiation from the Sun and tiny air particles produces an electrical charge – a process called ionisation. Certain layers in the ionosphere reflect radio waves and allow radio transmissions to be made over long distances. It is also the zone where the aurora borealis and the aurora australis (northern and southern lights) are born.

HEAT AND WATER

The interplay between heat energy and water vapour creates much of our weather. Surprisingly perhaps, the air is not significantly heated by the Sun, as days of strong sunshine when the air is crisp and fresh, or hot and sultry days when the Sun is nowhere to be seen, all testify. It is the Earth's surface that absorbs heat energy directly from the Sun. The lowest layer of the atmosphere is then warmed by contact with the Sun-heated ground – a process known as 'conduction' – and this warmth gradually spreads upwards and outwards with the movement of the air.

Not all of the solar energy that strikes the atmosphere gets through to the ground. Averaged over the whole planet during a long period, just 7 per cent of solar energy is taken up by the air itself; 16 per cent is absorbed by water vapour, dust, salt particles

ENERGY BALANCE *Incoming heat energy supplied by the Sun is balanced by outgoing heat energy, either reflected back into space or re-radiated by the Earth's surface.*

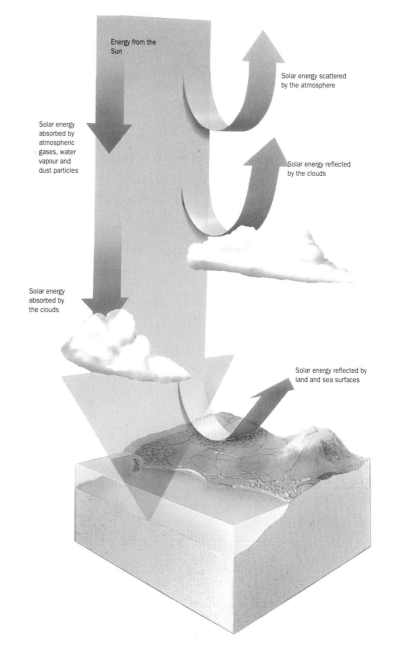

Energy from the Sun

Solar energy scattered by the atmosphere

Solar energy absorbed by atmospheric gases, water vapour and dust particles

Solar energy reflected by the clouds

Solar energy absorbed by the clouds

Solar energy reflected by land and sea surfaces

the blue-green sphere of the Earth from a spacecraft are travelling storms that redistribute heat energy from the tropics towards the poles. If they did not, the tropics, receiving the brunt of the Sun's radiation, would get hotter and hotter, and the poles colder and colder.

MOISTURE EXCHANGE

The source of heat energy, the Sun, is external to the Earth and its atmosphere. By contrast, the moisture is supplied 'in house'; that is, no significant water is gained from or lost to outer space. Water in its various forms moves between the Earth and the atmosphere in a never-ending two-way traffic. The downward traffic takes the form of precipitation – not just rain, but snow and hail as well. Some of this falls directly over the oceans; a substantial proportion of the precipitation that falls over the land also finds its way back to the oceans via river systems.

The upward traffic is a result of evaporation from the oceans, seas and lakes, and also from rain-soaked land. This evaporation is supplemented by transpiration – the process by which a plant loses water vapour from its surface. Over the vast forested areas of the equatorial zone the contribution

WATER IN THE SKY *Liquid water is found in the air as well as seas and rivers. Clouds are millions of tiny water droplets held aloft by air currents.*

of transpiration is considerable, and this is also true of the high-latitude forests of Canada and Siberia.

Moisture in the atmosphere has only a limited direct impact on our everyday lives – when it is raining, for instance, or in foggy weather, or when humidity levels are uncomfortably high. What we do not readily perceive is that there is always moisture in the atmosphere even when the weather is dry and sunny – in the form of invisible water vapour. To prove this, you have only to take an iced drink into the sunshine on a hot day; the outside of the glass soon becomes fogged with tiny water droplets. The air in contact with the glass is cooled to such an extent that it can no longer hold all its natural moisture in the form of water *continued on page 24*

CONSTANT TRAFFIC *The traffic of water between land, air and sea – the so-called water cycle – involves exchanges of moisture, often happening in different directions at the same time.*

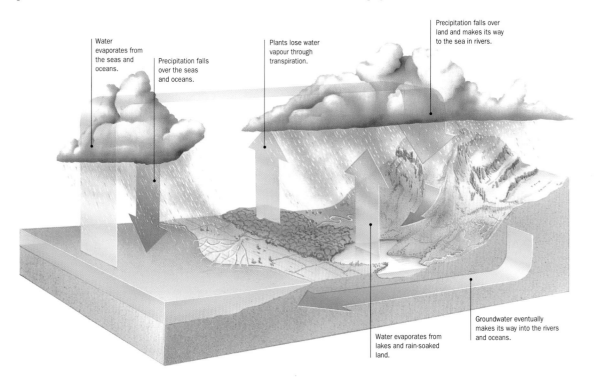

Water evaporates from the seas and oceans.

Precipitation falls over the seas and oceans.

Plants lose water vapour through transpiration.

Precipitation falls over land and makes its way to the sea in rivers.

Water evaporates from lakes and rain-soaked land.

Groundwater eventually makes its way into the rivers and oceans.

HOW THE OCEANS FLOW

The great wind patterns of the atmosphere are mirrored in similar patterns in the oceans. Indeed, it is the prolonged action of prevailing winds that drives the major currents of the oceans' surfaces.

However, water and air behave very differently. In particular, it takes much more energy to move a volume of water at, say, 5 mph (8 km/h) than it does to move a similar volume of air at the same speed. Thus an ocean current will carry on regardless, even though the winds above may reverse direction for weeks at a time. Ocean currents are also restricted by geography in a way that winds are not. Most notably, the shape of the world's oceans forces their currents to go round in distorted circles or ellipses – ocean 'gyres' that are found in the North and South Atlantic, the North and South Pacific and the Indian Ocean.

Among the best-known currents are the warm ones of the Northern Hemisphere, driven from south-west to north-east by the mid-latitude westerlies. In the Atlantic Ocean this current is called the Gulf Stream (after its source in the Gulf of Mexico) while it flows adjacent to the eastern seaboard of the USA and then becomes the North Atlantic Drift as it crosses the ocean towards north-western Europe. In the northern Pacific Ocean, the main warm current is known as the Kuroshio off the Japanese coast; it becomes the North Pacific Current as it travels eastwards towards North America. South of the Equator, equivalent warm currents lap the east coasts of South America (the Brazil Current), southern Africa (the Agulhas Current) and Australia.

Complementing these warm currents and completing the ocean gyres or ellipses are cold southward-flowing currents. The shape of the North Atlantic, for example, is such that the warm oceanic waters of the North Atlantic Drift flood the coasts of western Europe as far north as northern Norway. On the other side of the ocean, outside the North Atlantic gyre, the cold Labrador current is free to flow from the Greenland coast southwards to Newfoundland.

The patterns created by such currents play a vital part in redistributing heat energy from the tropics towards the poles. This is seen in their effect on coastal climates, especially in winter. At roughly 70°N, the town of Tromsø in Norway has a mean January temperature of −3.8°C (25°F); at about the same latitude Clyde on Baffin Island in Canada has a mean January temperature of −27.4°C (−17.3°F). At 60°N, the figure for Bergen in Norway is 1.3°C (34.3°F) which contrasts with −18°C (−0.4°F) on Canada's Resolution Island. Close to the 50th parallel, St Mary's in the Isles of Scilly has a mean January temperature of 7.8°C (46°F) compared with −6.2°C (20.8°F) at Gander Airport in Newfoundland. Just south of the

OCEAN GYRES *Ocean currents (warm ones shown red, cold ones blue) are driven by the prevailing winds above. The main features are the so-called gyres in the North Atlantic and North Pacific.*

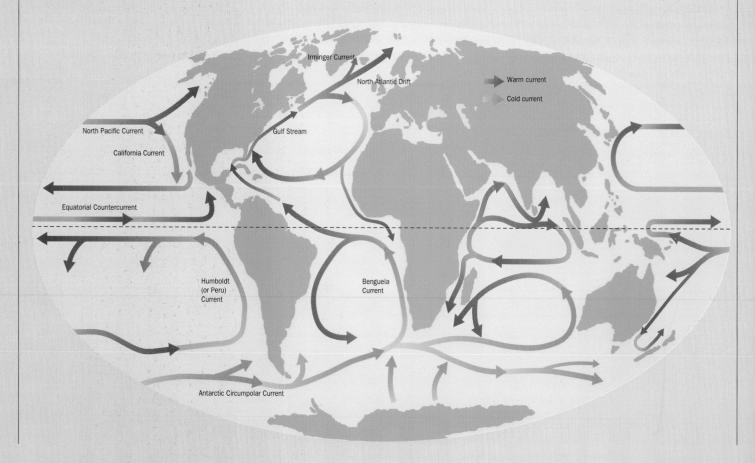

Irminger Current

North Atlantic Drift

Warm current

Cold current

North Pacific Current

California Current

Gulf Stream

Equatorial Countercurrent

Humboldt (or Peru) Current

Benguela Current

Antarctic Circumpolar Current

WARMED BY THE SEA The mean January temperature on Baffin Island (above left) is almost 23°C (41°F) lower than in Tromsø (above right) where the North Atlantic Drift keeps winters warmer.

40th parallel, the figures are 10.8°C (51.4°F) at Lisbon and 2.9°C (37.2°F) at Washington DC. Similar contrasts exist across the North Pacific, with a January mean temperature of 4.1°C (39.4°F) at Victoria in British Columbia and −18.2°C (−0.7°F) at Poronaysk on Sakhalin Island, in south-east Russia.

On reaching the eastern side of their oceans, the warm currents split, one arm turning north and the other south. The southward-flowing currents gradually become cold for their latitude as they reach the subtropics (although the actual water temperature may not change much). Relatively cool currents like these affect all subtropical western seaboards, including California (the California Current), Morocco (the Canaries Current), northern Chile and Peru (the Humboldt Current) and Namibia (the Benguela Current).

Not only does this cold offshore water keep the coastal climates comparatively cool, especially during summer, but it also inhibits rainfall. Cool air in the lowest part

HOT STREAM Warm water from the Gulf of Mexico streams past Florida's southern tip. On this coloured image, the warmest surface water is shown in dark orange.

of the atmosphere prevents rising air currents from developing, and these rising currents are necessary for clouds and rain to develop. Thus the Atacama Desert in northern Chile and southern Peru, and the Namib Desert in south-western Africa are the driest places on Earth. At Walvis Bay, which lies at

latitude 22°S on the Namibian coast, the mean January (midsummer) temperature is 18.9°C (66°F), and the average annual rainfall is just 9/10 in (22 mm). The equivalent figures on the opposite coast of southern Africa, at Beira in Mozambique, are 28°C (82.4°F), and 60 in (1524 mm).

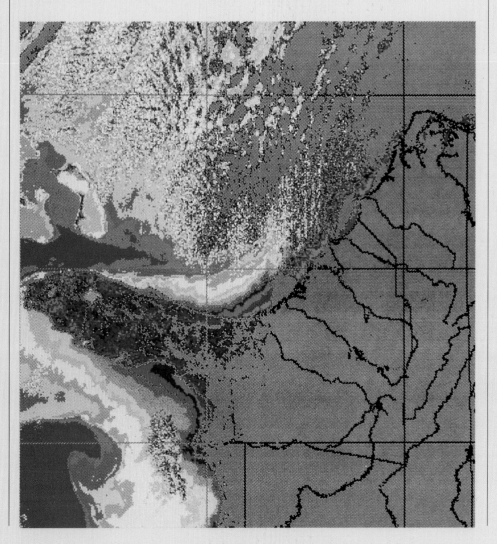

OCEAN MISTS *Sea fog shrouds Baccalieu Island off Canada's Atlantic coast. Warm, moist air drifting across cold water is cooled, and some of the moisture condenses as fog and low clouds.*

vapour. Consequently, some of it condenses into small but visible water particles on the cold outside surface of the glass. The same process happens in other ways. Eyeglasses become opaque with water droplets when you come indoors on a cold day – the warm indoor air is cooled on contact with the cold eyeglasses and releases moisture. Similarly, a car's windshield sometimes steams up on the inside when it is taken out of the garage in cold weather. Again, the warmer air inside the car is releasing moisture through contact with the cold windshield. This process illustrates an important fact:

WARM AIR RISING *Fair-weather clouds are formed by gentle currents of rising air, warmed over hot land or, in this case, sea.*

warm air is able to hold more water vapour than cold air. There is another rule of physics that helps to explain the workings of the weather: warm air rises, and as it rises it expands, and as it expands it cools.

These two rules can be linked. When a bubble of air is warmed by contact with the sun-heated ground, it rises, expanding and cooling while it does so. As it cools, it approaches the point at which it can no

WEATHER LORE: ST SWITHIN'S AND OTHER SAINTS' DAYS

Before the mid-19th century, our forebears were unaware that the weather they experienced in their own towns or villages was part of a bigger pattern. They did not know that their wet Sunday morning might be related to a wet Monday morning 1000 miles (1600 km) away. But people have always watched the weather. From prehistoric times, farmers, hunters, travellers and mariners have studied the vagaries of the clouds and winds and seas, and the better observers gained enough useful knowledge to be regarded in their communities as 'weather wise'. In Europe a large body of weather lore developed over the centuries, and when Europeans colonised other parts of the world they had to learn as much about the weather patterns in their adopted surroundings as quickly as possible. Thus even a comparatively young nation such as the USA also has an abundance of weather sayings.

Often an item of weather lore took the form of rhyming couplets, making it easier to remember. Many were linked to saints' days. They indicated a tendency for a particular kind of weather to occur at roughly that time of the year. The saint's day was a useful 'hook' on which to hang the relevant scrap of knowledge. One of the best-known pieces of weather lore in the English language concerns St Swithin's Day, July 15. Although the saying takes many forms, the thrust

WHAT THE WEATHER DOES *A 19th-century drawing shows a variety of weather conditions.*

is always the same, as in this Scottish version:

St Swithin's Day, if ye do rain,
For 40 days it will remain;
St Swithin's Day, and ye be fair,
For 40 days 'twill rain nae mair.

Modern research confirms the general accuracy of this observation. By the middle of July in Britain, the summer weather has usually established a fairly settled pattern, whether rainy or sunny, that lasts

until the last week or so of August. It relates to prevailing atmospheric cycles in the Northern Hemisphere.

Another adage is:

He who shears his sheep before
St Servatius' Day
Loves his wool more than his
sheep.

The feast of St Servatius (or St Gervase) falls on May 13, and along with St Mamertus' Day (May 11) and St Pancras' Day (May 12) it formed part of the traditional festival of the 'ice saints'. Mid May is still regarded as a period when sudden sharp frosts can cause damage to crops.

There is also a mass of weather lore that addresses day-to-day changes, relying on observation of the sky and wind. Many of these are appropriate to all mid-latitude zones of westerly winds, so that sayings originating in Britain will still work in Seattle or Vancouver or Wellington:

Rain before seven,
Fine by eleven.

Rain long foretold, long last;
Short notice, soon past.

All can be explained by depressions and their frontal systems that sweep in from the ocean at regular intervals, separated by ridges of high pressure.

longer hold all its moisture. Eventually, the bubble of air has cooled so much that excess water vapour begins to condense into visible water droplets. In the free atmosphere there is no glass of iced water or pair of spectacles where the droplets can form, but there are tiny fragments of dust and soot and, especially above the oceans, of salt. These are known as 'condensation nuclei'. The water droplets gather on the condensation nuclei, forming an embryonic cloud. Depending on how buoyant the bubble of air is, these small clouds may continue to

grow until they form rain clouds, or they may remain as broken fair-weather clouds, or they may dissipate again almost as soon as they form.

WIND AND THE MOVEMENT OF THE EARTH

Another vital cog in the weather machine is motion. Even if the Earth did not rotate at all, air currents would still be established in the atmosphere, simply because warm air is less dense than cool air. Pockets of warmed air rise – creating areas of low air

pressure – to be replaced by surrounding cooler air. This, in its simplest form, is what wind is – the air in motion.

However, the rotation of the Earth about its axis complicates things by supplying the world's weather system with huge additional quantities of energy. To see what rotation does to the atmosphere, it is best to visualise an imaginary Earth that is a simple sphere, completely covered with oceans, spinning on a vertical axis. The area of maximum heating is the zone that straddles the Equator. The warmth of the

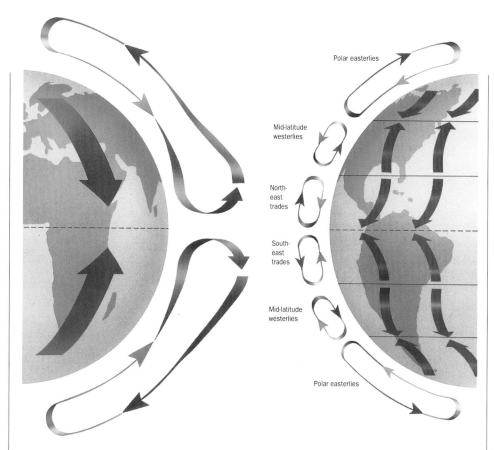

Polar easterlies

Mid-latitude
westerlies

North-
east
trades

South-
east
trades

Mid-latitude
westerlies

Polar easterlies

CELLS OF AIR *Early theories about the circulation of the atmosphere proposed a single rotating cell in each hemisphere (far left). Later theories suggested a series of adjacent circulation cells (left) to explain the world's wind belts.*

equatorial sea is transmitted to the air in contact with it, and this warmed air rises, to be replaced by cooler air coming from the direction of the poles – which is then also warmed and so rises in its turn.

If the world were not spinning on its axis, this rising equatorial air would be evenly balanced by descending cold air coming from the North and South Poles. The result would be a single system or 'cell' of circulating air in each of the Northern and Southern Hemispheres, with the wind blowing from the poles to the Equator at low levels of the atmosphere, and from the Equator to the poles in the upper atmosphere. This circulation pattern is known as the 'Hadley cell', after an 18th-century British scientist, George Hadley, who first proposed the idea.

The Earth's rotation alters this basic pattern by skewing the direction of the winds from a straightforward north-south axis. It affects things in a number of ways. In the first place, a point on the Earth's surface in lower latitudes – the latitudes on either side of the Equator – has farther to move in a complete rotation, because of the planet's girth in this region, than a point in higher latitudes – those closer to the poles. The Kenyan capital Nairobi, for instance, moves

farther in 24 hours than, say, the Norwegian capital Oslo. Thus a point close to the Equator moves faster than a point that is closer to the poles. At the same time, although the Earth and its atmosphere rotate together,

RECORDING THE WEATHER

The first-known weather journal comes from medieval England. On most days from 1337 to 1344, the clergyman William Merle made a note of the weather in Lincolnshire, where his parish was, or Oxford, where he was a don. From his diary it is clear that England endured a severe winter in 1338-9, while notable heatwaves occurred in the summers of 1337, 1339 and 1340. Much later, the Danish astronomer Tycho Brahe kept a weather journal for about 16 years, ending in 1597. Around the same time mariners from several countries started to note the wind and weather during their voyages.

the air is not physically attached to the ground. In fact, the surface of the Earth and the air above it rotate at different speeds.

Taking these factors into account experts came up with a model of the prevailing wind

patterns across the globe that has three cells of circulating air in each hemisphere. In the first, between the Equator and about 35°N and S, the Earth moves faster than the air above it. As the planet is moving west to east, this means that the surface winds are skewed in a broadly east-to-west ('easterly') direction in relation to the ground beneath – hence the north-east trade winds of the Northern Hemisphere and the south-east trades of the Southern Hemisphere. In the next cell, located between about 35°N and S and 60°, the Earth's surface moves more slowly than the air in contact with it, hence the prevailing 'westerlies' of the mid-latitude temperate regions in both hemispheres.

The polar regions, meanwhile, have very cold, dense air which produces areas of high pressure in both the Arctic and Antarctic. The cold outflows from these high-latitude 'highs' (high-pressure areas) are known as the polar easterlies – the dense air rotates more slowly than the ground beneath.

Between these cells are belts of alternating low and high pressure. Around the Equator itself, where the wind systems of the two hemispheres meet, lies a broad belt of low pressure, created by the constantly rising warm air of the equatorial region. Here, the winds are light and variable. This is often referred to as the 'doldrums' but is more technically called the inter-tropical convergence zone (or ITCZ).

Separating the trade winds from the mid-latitude westerlies in each hemisphere is another belt of light and variable winds, sometimes known as the 'horse latitudes'. Unlike the doldrums, however, this is a belt with high pressure. Some of the air that was warmed around the Equator and rose into the upper atmosphere has by now cooled down. It becomes denser as it cools and therefore sinks towards the surface of the

CLOUD AROUND THE MIDDLE
The trade wind belts of both hemispheres converge on the Equator, where rising air creates thick bands of cloud.

Earth. The name 'horse latitudes' apparently dates from the era when sailing ships, transporting animals from Europe to the Americas or the Caribbean, occasionally became becalmed for long periods in these latitudes. Food ran short, and horses and other creatures were thrown overboard or eaten to relieve the pressure on supplies.

Finally, there is another zone of low pressure in each hemisphere, located near 60°N and S, where the polar easterlies converge with the mid-latitude westerlies.

In reality, of course, the winds do not always conform to these patterns. This is because the real Earth is not a simple, ocean-covered sphere spinning on a vertical axis.

It is a much more complex chunk of rock, tilted on its axis relative to the Sun at an angle of some 23.5°, its surface composed of a complex patchwork of land and sea. There are also a number of substantial mountain ranges, some of which straddle the main wind-belts of the world, and there are ice caps of variable extent at the poles. All of these deflect and divert the winds to create the varying weather patterns that we experience from day to day.

DAY AND NIGHT, SUMMER AND WINTER

The Earth tilts in its orbit. For half the year, the Northern Hemisphere is tilted towards the Sun; for the other half, it is the Southern Hemisphere that receives more heat – the source of our seasons and the different lengths of day and night.

The tilt in the axis of the Earth complicates the world's weather patterns. It means that the length of daylight varies at different times of the year and in different parts of the globe. Since each hemisphere in turn is tilted towards the Sun, it also means that, from our point of view on the Earth's surface, the Sun climbs higher in the sky and then retreats again in an annual cycle, providing seasonal changes.

The irregular patchwork of continents and oceans complicates matters still further. This is because land and sea react differently when heat energy beams onto them from the Sun. The land heats up more quickly than the sea, but also loses its heat more quickly. The sea takes longer to heat up but, once heated, retains its heat more effectively. There is a higher proportion of land to sea north of the Equator than there is south of it – another complicating factor. Mountain ranges and broad plains, the permanent ice caps around the poles, and the seasonal snow and ice cover in the Arctic and Antarctic regions, all make their contributions to the varied brew. At a more local scale, weather and climate are further influenced by local relief, soil-types and vegetation cover, by lakes and marshes, and by towns and cities.

The Sun is the Earth's sole source of heat energy. It is a relatively small star when

HOT SEAS, COLD SEAS *A computer-generated map shows ocean temperatures across the globe – the warmest waters around the Equator, the coldest around the poles.*

Sun; winter when it is tilted away from it.

Because of the Earth's tilt, the regions at the top and bottom of the globe experience the greatest contrasts in the amount of daylight they receive. In places north of 66.5°N – the Arctic Circle – in the Northern Hemisphere and south of 66.5°S – the Antarctic Circle – in the Southern Hemisphere, the Sun is above the horizon for 24 hours a day in midsummer, while at midwinter it remains permanently below the horizon. At the poles themselves, the year is divided into six months of constant daylight and six months of darkness. By contrast, the equatorial belt receives roughly 12 hours of daylight throughout the year.

In the Northern Hemisphere, the period from March to September is the summer half of the year, when this part of the globe is tilted towards the Sun. It reaches a maximum tilt on or around June 21, when the midday Sun is overhead at latitude 23.5°N – the Tropic of Cancer. Between October and February the Southern Hemisphere is tilted towards the Sun, reaching its maximum tilt on or around December 21, when the Sun is overhead at the Tropic of Capricorn – 23.5°S. These moments of maximum tilt are known as the solstices. Between the solstices are the equinoxes – around March 21 and September 22 – when the Equator is the nearest part of the Earth to the Sun.

The word 'equinox' comes from the Latin *aequi*, 'equal', and *nox*, 'night'. At this point in the yearly cycle, no part of the globe is tilted towards the Sun, and as a result no part receives more daylight than any other. In theory at least, day and night are of equal length the world over, with the Sun above the horizon everywhere for 12 hours. (The exceptions to this rule are the points

SEASONAL SUN *At the December solstice the midday Sun appears to be directly overhead at the Tropic of Capricorn; at the June solstice at the Tropic of Cancer. At the equinoxes it appears to be directly overhead at the Equator.*

compared with some others, but its statistics are still mind-boggling by human standards. Its diameter is approximately 865 000 miles (nearly 1.4 million km). Its surface temperature is some 5500°C (10 000°F), while the temperature at its centre is believed to be more than 15 million°C (approaching 30 million°F). The Earth, which is orbiting roughly 93 million miles (150 million km) away, intercepts a tiny part of the heat radiating from it – about one two-billionth part – but this is still enough to maintain a world teeming with life.

THE EARTH'S TILTED AXIS

Our position in relation to the Sun is what dictates the cycles of day and night, summer and winter. The Earth rotates on its axis once every 24 hours, approximately, resulting in the cycle of day and night as each point on its surface moves from the sunlit side of the planet to the darkened side facing away from the Sun. At the same time, the Earth's axis tilts at 23.5° from the vertical. Summer is the time of year when our portion of the planet is tilted towards the

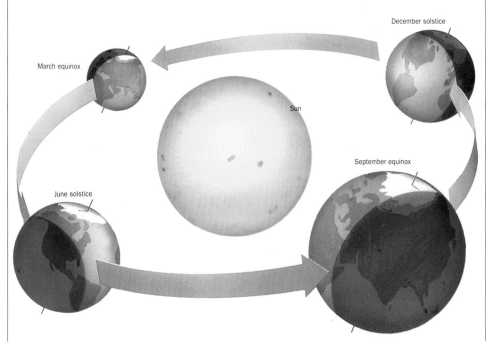

March equinox

December solstice

Sun

September equinox

June solstice

ASLEEP IN THE SUN *Huskies nap in the midnight Sun. Even though the Sun never sets in summer in polar regions, it never gets higher than 47° above the horizon either.*

lying at the very top and very bottom of the planet – the poles – where the Sun should travel around the rim of the horizon.) In practice things do not quite work out like this. Slight irregularities occur around the horizon in most places, thanks to neighbouring hills and valleys, while the fact that the Earth is not quite spherical also has a very small effect.

More importantly, the rays of the Sun are refracted (they are bent slightly) as they pass through the Earth's atmosphere. Thus we actually see the sun rising a few minutes before, strictly speaking, it is there, and we see it setting for a few minutes after it has gone. In middle latitudes this gives us six or seven minutes of added daylight throughout the year.

At the North and South Poles this phenomenon presents an interesting paradox. Although the spring equinox should be the date, following the six-month winter night, on which the Sun travels around the rim of the horizon, this does not happen. Thanks to refraction, the Sun appears to be just above the horizon, rather than on the rim, during the spring and autumn equinoxes at both poles.

HEAT AND THE SEASONS

The amount of heat energy received from the Sun is the most important factor in determining seasonal changes in our weather and climate. At the top of the atmosphere this depends on two things – how high in the sky the Sun is, and how long it remains above the horizon. At the equinoxes, when day length is roughly equal across the planet, the greatest heating occurs above the Equator where the Sun is overhead at midday. At the June solstice, with the Northern Hemisphere tilted towards the Sun, it occurs above the North Pole; at the December solstice, with the Southern Hemisphere tilted towards the Sun, it occurs above the South Pole. The 24-hour daylight that the polar regions receive during their hemispheres' summer solstice more than compensates at the top of the atmosphere for the relatively low angle of sunshine.

These are the facts – yet they are clearly at odds with our experience. How can it be that at certain seasons the frozen wastes of the Arctic and Antarctic receive more energy than the sun-scorched Sahara? The answer lies in what happens to the heat energy from the sun during its journey from the top of the atmosphere to the ground. When the sun is overhead, its energy passes directly through the atmosphere by the shortest route, allowing the maximum possible amount of energy to reach the surface of the Earth. At the Arctic and Antarctic Circles even at the summer solstice the midday Sun is only 47° above the horizon – barely halfway between the horizon and overhead – while at the North and South Poles at midsummer the Sun circles the sky only 23.5° above the horizon.

DAYLIGHT HOURS *A composite photograph, taken from the Lofoten Islands off north-west Norway, shows hourly images of the Sun's position and also shows the entire visible horizon.*

Around the Equator the Sun shines at right angles to the Earth's surface. In polar regions the same amount of energy passes through a greater thickness of atmosphere and is spread across a larger area of ground.

In polar regions, therefore, the Sun's rays pass obliquely through the atmosphere. This relatively long journey allows a substantial proportion of the solar energy to be absorbed by air molecules and dust particles, and to be reflected by clouds. At the Northern Hemisphere's summer solstice, when the latitude of maximum heating is the Tropic of Cancer, there is a 63 per cent loss of energy at the Equator, a 60 per cent loss at the Tropic of Cancer, a 75 per cent loss at the Arctic Circle and at the North Pole an 83 per cent loss. The same figures apply for the Tropic of Capricorn, Antarctic Circle and South Pole at the Southern Hemisphere's summer solstice. Thus the energy loss is least at the Tropics of Cancer and Capricorn at their respective summer solstices.

This affects the climate across the entire globe. During the Northern Hemisphere's summer, the zone of maximum heating – the area where the Sun's rays beam most directly and intensely onto the surface of the

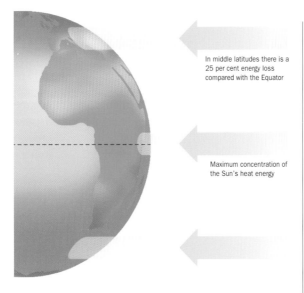

In middle latitudes there is a 25 per cent energy loss compared with the Equator

Maximum concentration of the Sun's heat energy

Earth – migrates several degrees of latitude northwards towards the Tropic of Cancer; then it travels a similar distance southwards towards the Tropic of Capricorn during the Southern Hemisphere's summer. How far the zone moves depends upon the efficiency with which the planet's surface responds to the solar heating. Areas covered with oceans respond very slowly, so the seasonal migration is comparatively small. Areas with no oceans respond more rapidly, resulting in a relatively large seasonal migration.

This migration has considerable effects. The zone of maximum heating corresponds to the zone of low pressure, marked by hot rising air, that acts as a kind of axis for the various climatic bands of the two

hemispheres – to its north lie the north-east trades, the horse latitudes, and then the mid-latitude westerlies of the Northern Hemisphere; to its south, the south-east trades, the horse latitudes, and then the mid-latitude westerlies of the Southern Hemisphere. In the hemisphere that is experiencing summer at the time, each of these various wind and pressure belts is pushed slightly towards its pole. Each belt is also squeezed somewhat. The opposite, meanwhile, happens in the winter hemisphere where the zones are stretched.

LAND AND SEA

It takes more energy to heat up a particular volume of water than the same volume of rock. Heat is more quickly and effectively distributed through water than it is through soil and rock, and where the water is in constant motion, as in the world's oceans, this process is all the more effective. That is why the oceans warm up and cool down much more slowly than the landmasses. It means that the contrast between summer and winter temperatures is much smaller over the oceans than over the continents. Furthermore, over any large body of water there is much less variation between day and night-time temperatures than there is over land.

The result is further complications in the world's weather systems. During spring, for example, the landmasses warm up faster than the oceans, and by late spring there is a

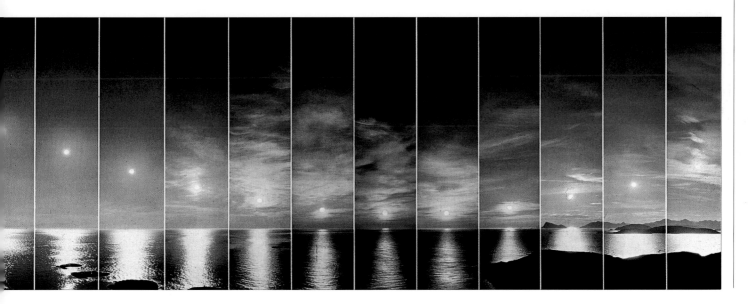

JANUARY

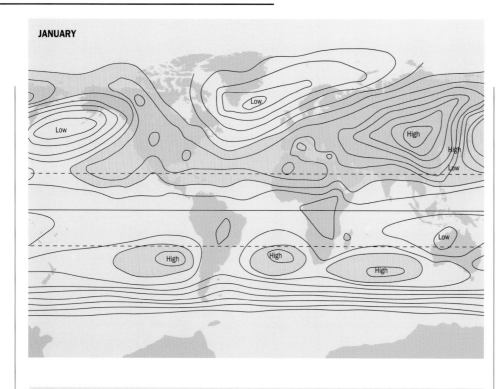

JULY

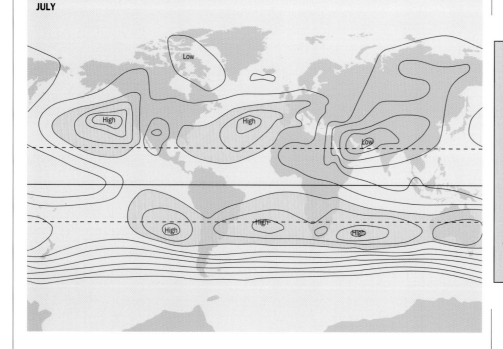

HIGHS AND LOWS *In January low pressure is prominent over Northern Hemisphere oceans while high pressure dominates the continental interiors; in July the pattern is reversed. In the Southern Hemisphere the contrast between summer and winter is less marked.*

mid-latitude westerlies. Over the oceans of the Northern Hemisphere, this creates areas where light, variable winds prevail. Over the huge landmasses of North America, Europe and Asia, however, this pattern is completely obliterated by the winter high-pressure and summer low-pressure cycle with its accompanying winds. In the Southern Hemisphere, on the other hand, where comparatively small landmasses penetrate southwards from

BLOCKED BY THE ANDES

South America's narrow southern tip presents some remarkable contrasts in temperature range. This is due to its great mountain chain, the Andes. This high barrier straddles the prevailing westerly airflow and prevents maritime air on the west coast from getting as far as the eastern side of the landmass. At Los Evangelistas in southern Chile the yearly temperature range is just 4°C (7°F), while at Victoria just the other side of the Andes in central Argentina the equivalent figure is 18°C (32°F).

the tropics, there is much less to interfere with the light winds of the horse latitudes which have a much greater influence on the climate of the land as well as the sea.

CONTINENTAL V. MARITIME

The annual range of temperature is a good measure of the contrasting influences of the continents and oceans on the places where we live. In the middle of a large continent in the middle latitudes, the range between deep midwinter cold and high summer heat is enormous, while over the oceans the differences between the mild moist winter and the cool humid summer is quite modest.

marked difference in temperature between the two. The hot landmass warms the air in contact with it which becomes less dense. As a consequence, the air pressure – the weight of air resting on any particular place – falls over the continental interior. Over the oceans the air remains relatively cool and dense, and therefore the air pressure is comparatively high. The area of low pressure over the continent will draw in air from the high-pressure area over the ocean. During the autumn, by contrast, the land cools

more rapidly than the ocean, and from late autumn high pressure forms over the continental interior, with the air pressure relatively low over the neighbouring seas. Air will flow out to sea from the continental interior.

It is the interaction of effects like these with the prevailing winds and air pressures at different latitudes that creates much of the variety in the world's weather. Take, for example, the horse latitude belt of high pressure that lies in both hemispheres between the zones of the trade winds and the

BY THE SEA *São Miguel in the Azores (above left) and St Mary's in the Isles of Scilly (above right) enjoy typically maritime climates with a small temperature range between summer and winter.*

Maritime climates also have a relatively small daily range of temperature, with mild nights and cool days, while the degree of variation from day to day is normally damped down.

The most maritime climates are those of islands and peninsulas on windward coasts. In Ponta Delgada in the Azores, for example, the difference between the mean monthly temperatures for February and August is no more than 8°C (14°F). At St Mary's in the Isles of Scilly (off England's south-western tip) the mean annual range is also 8°C. At Vestmannaeyjar, an island off the south coast of Iceland, the equivalent figure is 9°C (16°F). Around the Pacific fringes, Estevan Point on Vancouver Island has an annual range of 9.5°C (17°F), while at Eureka where the north Californian coast bulges out into the Pacific the range is just 5°C (9°F).

In fact, Eureka has one of the most pronounced maritime climates in the world. In winter, strong westerly and south-westerly winds bring warm oceanic air from distant regions of the north Pacific. In summer, gentler oceanic breezes originate over the cool southward-flowing California Current just off the coastline, and grey misty weather with frequent fogs prevails.

By contrast, Ulan Bator, capital of Mongolia, has a range of 41°C (74°F), while at Verchojansk in Siberia the range is still more impressive. The mean January temperature here is –51°C (–60°F) and the mean July temperature 14°C (57°F), giving a mean annual range of 65°C (117°F). The North American interior is not quite as extreme, but Edmonton in Alberta has a range of 31°C (56°F) and Yellowknife in the Canadian North-west Territories has one of 44°C (79°F). In the USA, Devil's Lake in North Dakota has an annual range of 36°C (65°F).

Close to the Equator, land and sea temperatures are less at odds with one another. Tropical climates are hot throughout the

CLIMATES OF EXTREMES
Sheltered from the moderating influence of Pacific airstreams by the Rockies, Edmonton (below left) and Yellowknife (below right) experience highly continental climates.

EL NIÑO: THE 'BOY CHILD' CURRENT OF THE PACIFIC

One of the most dramatic instances of maritime influence affecting weather patterns on land is the ocean current known as El Niño, which recurs every few years in the equatorial Pacific. *El Niño* means 'the boy child' in Spanish; it refers here to the Christ child, because it normally sets in during the Christmas season.

In the Pacific Ocean, the north-east and south-east trade winds drive currents both north and south of the Equator. To the north, they drive cold water from the northern Pacific down the coast of North America, then westwards across the open Pacific. To the south, they drive cold water up the coast of South America, then

up the coast of South America is reversed, so that warm equatorial water is driven southwards down the coasts of Ecuador and northern Peru. This is what is known officially as ENSO (El Niño Southern Oscillation).

The repercussions along the coasts of Ecuador and Peru are dramatic. The normal flow of plankton-rich water originating in the Antarctic is cut off and local fish stocks are decimated as a result. This in turn has a catastrophic effect on bird life and the

LETHAL CURRENT *The onset of El Niño along the coast of Peru and Ecuador causes a huge drop in fish stocks (below).*

local fishing industry. The warm current warms the adjacent coast, bringing excessive amounts of rain, flash floods and mudslides.

Until recently, these ENSO 'events' have taken place every three or four years, lasting several months at a time, before the more normal pattern resumes. Major El Niños occurred in 1972-3, 1976-7, 1982-4, 1986-7 and 1991-5. Those of 1982-4 and 1991-5, however, were so long-lasting that meteorologists now think the old pattern may be changing. Some have even speculated that, thanks to global warming, an era may be beginning in which the Niño pattern becomes the norm. This is very important, as it is now recognised that the effects are felt far afield. For example, the warm water flowing into the eastern Pacific induces a countercurrent of cold water flowing into the western Pacific. This affects eastern Indonesia, New Guinea and north-eastern Australia, where the resulting cool air prevents the rising air currents needed for clouds and rain to form. A drop in rainfall levels follows.

RSMAS/NESDIS/RL
SEA SURFACE TEMPERATURE DEG C
01-JUL-1982   100KM MCSST

RSMAS/NESDIS/RL
SEA SURFACE TEMPERATURE DEG C
01-JUL-1984   100KM MCSST

WATER BANDS *Normally, cool water (shown in yellow and green) flows through the Pacific at the Equator. In 1982 (top), the onset of El Niño disturbed this pattern. By 1984 (above), it had re-established itself.*

westwards. Any current will induce a countercurrent to maintain water levels. In this case the countercurrent runs between the two westward-flowing currents along the line of the Equator – the warm eastward-flowing Equatorial Countercurrent. Every few years, weather conditions strengthen the Equatorial Countercurrent, reorganising the currents of the east Pacific. In particular, part of the current bringing cold water northwards

DROUGHT *El Niño's effects on climate are believed to extend far afield: for example, bringing drought to South Africa.*

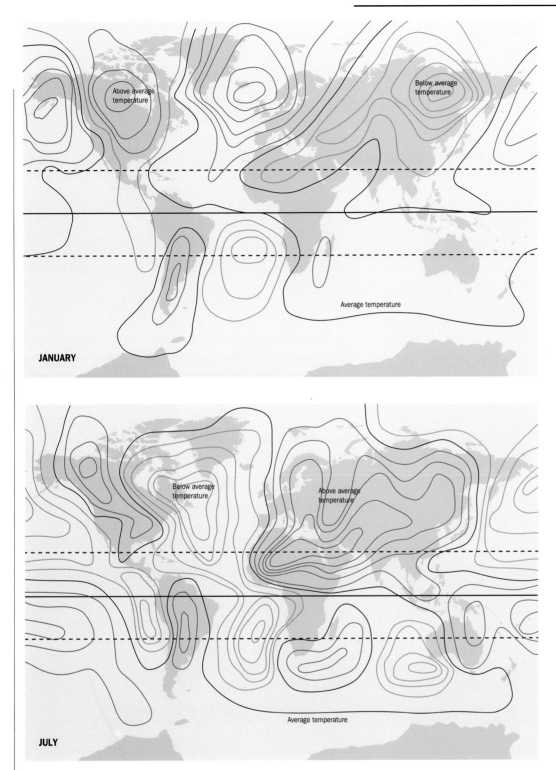

JANUARY

JULY

COMPARED WITH AVERAGE
In January, parts of the North Atlantic are almost 20°C (36°F) warmer than average, while Siberia is up to 20°C colder than average. In July the patterns are largely reversed.

cool down, there is a marked lag between the summer solstice – the moment of maximum solar heating – and the warmest time of the year, and between the winter solstice and the lowest temperatures. The Northern Hemisphere's summer solstice comes in June but in its islands and coastal regions August is usually the warmest month. Its winter solstice comes in December but February is usually the coldest month. Such a lag also exists in continental climates, but in these areas the warmest and coldest times rarely occur more than two or three weeks after the solstices.

THE CHARACTER OF THE LAND

At a more local level, the lay of the land, the type of soil and vegetation, and the proximity of large urban areas all influence temperature patterns. Nearby lakes and marshes, along with snow and ice cover, also play their part. These effects are most noticeable when large-scale air movement is sluggish. Local conditions are less important in parts of the world where the prevailing winds are strong and persistent enough to give warm and cold air masses coming from afar more impact than any originating in the immediate region.

Waterlogged soils, marshes and land bordering lakes and rivers, all share some of the characteristics of bodies of water, though to a lesser degree. The water in the soil carries the heat or cold downwards and outwards, so these types of land surface warm up and

year, so there is less chance for contrasts to build up over the continents and oceans. Even so, small contrasts are still evident. For instance, at Malacca on the Malay coast, the mean annual range is a mere 0.5°C (1°F), whereas in Nairobi, high in the African interior, it is 4°C (7°F).

Leeward coasts – east-facing coasts in the mid-latitude belt of westerly winds – have a greater temperature range than west-facing

coasts, simply because the prevailing winds blow from the interior of the landmass rather than the ocean. Thus there is a greater continental influence on their climate than on windward coasts. In New York, for example, the annual range averages 24°C (43°F).

The oceans exercise other influences on the ups and downs of temperature in areas with a strongly maritime climate. Because oceans take a long time to heat up and

HEAT SENSIBLE AND HEAT LATENT

If you put a pan of water to boil on a stove, you can watch the temperature rising by means of a thermometer. Until it gets too hot you can even feel the water heating up by inserting a finger. This sort of heat is known as 'sensible heat' because we can detect it with our sense of touch.

But when the water begins to boil, the temperature stops rising, even though heat is still being supplied to the pan of water. The heat energy is now being used to transform the water into steam – the scientific name for this is a 'change of phase' from liquid to water vapour – and this sort of heat energy is known as 'latent heat'. It is absorbed in the process of vaporisation and carried away by the steam.

The same happens at the change of phase from ice to liquid. A thermometer placed in a bucket of ice taken from the deep freeze will

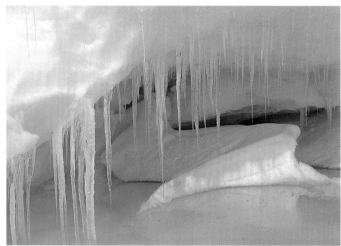

HEAT AND THE AIR *When snow melts, latent heat is absorbed from the surrounding air. When water freezes, latent heat is released into the air.*

show a steady rise in temperature at first, but when it reaches 0°C (32°F) it will stop climbing while the ice melts. Not until the last chunk of ice has gone will the temperature of the water start to climb again.

Latent heat, then, is absorbed while ice turns to liquid and while liquid turns to water vapour; it is released into the air while water vapour condenses into liquid, and while liquid freezes. These very special processes are important in the atmosphere during the formation and dissipation of clouds, during the melting of snowflakes and hailstones, and during the formation of frost and the disappearance of a snow-cover.

cool down comparatively slowly. Latent heat, the heat absorbed or released when a substance changes its state, as when ice changes to water or water to vapour, also plays its part in regions with waterlogged soil. During the daytime, some of the heat energy is used up as latent heat as the surface moisture evaporates, while on very cold nights heat energy is emitted as the water freezes.

Grass, trees and crops also have a moderating influence on extreme temperatures, although the degree to which this happens depends on how closely spaced the plants are, and how much heat from the Sun gets through to the soil below. Thickly growing woodland is notably effective in moderating the temperatures on the ground. This is

ISLAND LAKE, WYOMING
Lakes and rivers tend to be warmer at night and cooler by day, compared with the surrounding dry land.

MODERATING INFLUENCES
*In dense woodland, the shaded
area between the ground and
the canopy acts as a kind of
insulator. Marshlands are like
lakes, with relatively mild
nights and cool days.*

mainly because a thick leaf canopy prevents
a proportion of incoming energy from reaching the ground, and also makes it harder for
outgoing radiation from the land surface to
escape upwards – which is necessary for rapid
night-time cooling. However, clearings in a
forested area will heat up rapidly by day and
cool down rapidly at night. This effect is
exacerbated because the surrounding woodland prevents much air movement.

ENCLOSED HEAT *A winter Sun shines over Death Valley in California. In summer, temperatures in this enclosed valley can exceed 50°C (122°F).*

Different kinds of land, often quite close to each other, react very differently to heat from the Sun. At one extreme, dark-coloured soil produces both very high and very low temperatures. The dark colour of the soil means that it absorbs rather than re-flects the heat. Sandy soils also produce ex-treme temperatures, though for different reasons. The comparatively large particles of sand are poor conductors of heat, so the heat energy is transmitted very inefficiently downwards into the soil. Furthermore, the relatively large air pockets trapped between the grains of sand hold the heat and so in-crease this inefficiency. The heat is absorbed readily at the surface of the soil and it builds up because it is not transmitted downwards. At night, however, with the source of heat – the Sun – gone, the heat at the surface is equally readily lost into the air above.

In this way, sand-surface temperatures in the Sahara, in the Australian interior and in the Arizona desert occasionally reach 80° to 90°C (176° to 194°F) in mid-summer. By contrast, December and January nights occasionally see sand-surface temperatures plunging to between –10° and –5°C (14° to 23°F) in the northern Sahara. Even in the equable climate of the British Isles, dry sandy soils are well-known for their extreme temperatures, producing unexpected and damaging frosts on still spring nights.

Solid rock and compacted clay soils are much better conductors of heat than sand. Heat from the Sun is therefore transmitted more easily downwards to layers below the surface, so temperatures above these types of soil are much less extreme.

SNOW AND ICE – HEAT REFLECTORS

A deep cover of snow and ice prevents much warming, even in strong sunshine, for two reasons. Latent heat again plays a role. The sunshine may melt a thin surface layer of snow, but even as the snow changes to water, latent heat is absorbed from the layer of air immediately above the melting snow. This reduces the temperature of the air above the surface to close to 0°C (32°F), which in turn slows down any melting. Sec-ondly, ice and especially snow reflect a large proportion of incoming radiation; a dry powdery snow-cover, in particular, is known to reflect up to 80 per cent of heat energy. Dry powdery snow is also a very poor con-ductor, so night-time cooling is concentrat-ed in the surface layer of the snow which therefore becomes intensely cold on clear calm nights.

Human beings, meanwhile, have creat-ed their own climates – by building cities.

URBAN CLIMATES *Cities, such as New York, create their own climatic conditions. Buildings and streets, shown green here, generate the greatest heat.*

DO SUNSPOTS INFLUENCE OUR CLIMATE?

Long before the modern science of meteorology had been established, people interested in the weather sought to forecast it weeks or months ahead. Some have even tried to predict climate fluctuations over a period of years, which is impossible even with today's sophisticated equipment. The most persistent attempts at this sort of extra-long-range forecasting have involved trying to indentify regular cycles of droughts, hot summers or severe winters.

There are darker patches – sunspots – visible on the surface of the Sun, which mark the existence of 'cooler' areas where the temperature is a mere 4200°C (7590°F) compared with the 5500°C (9930°F) of the brightest parts of the Sun's disc. What causes them is still very poorly understood, but we do know that the number of these spots varies over a roughly 11 year cycle.

In the vast collection of weather statistics that has built up over the last 300 years, many people, whether research scientists or amateur dabblers, have identified apparent weather cycles. When these cycles repeat themselves once every 10, 11 or 12 years on average, attempts are often made to link them to the sunspot cycle.

Reputable scientists in the United States in the 1970s demonstrated a 22 year cycle in the occurrence of drought in the High Plains, while several less rigorous studies in Britain found an approximate 11 year repetition in severe winters. This cycle appeared to be impressive, linking the winters of 1894-5, 1906-7, 1916-17, 1928-9, 1939-40, 1950-1 and 1962-3. The mean temperature over central England during these seven winters averaged 2.3°C (4.1°F) below the long-term norm, and it seemed reasonable to expect another very cold winter during the early to middle 1970s. Unfortunately for the theory's proponents, 1972-3 was 0.9°C (1.6°F) warmer than average, 1973-4 was 1.4°C (2.5°F)

SNOW CYCLE? *Snowy winters occured in England at roughly 11 year intervals between 1895 and 1963, but the cycle failed in the 1970s and 1980s.*

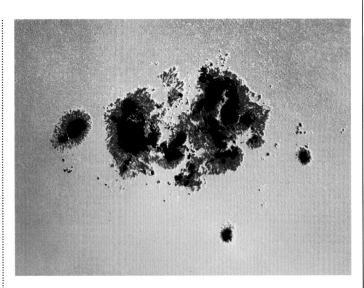

warmer, and 1974-5 was 2.4°C (4.3°F) warmer.

Astronomers have been aware of sunspots for centuries – the ancient Chinese referred to them as 'flying birds'. It is known that there was a period between 1645 and 1715 when there were hardly any sunspots at all. Many researchers during the earlier part of the 20th century pointed to an apparent correlation between this period and the long cold period commonly known as the Little Ice Age. More recent analysis, however, has

SUN STORM *Sunspots mark relatively cool areas on the Sun and are like giant storms in the solar atmosphere.*

shown that the Little Ice Age began long before 1645 and ended some time after 1715, and the coldest decades did not correlate with the smallest number of sunspots.

The trouble is that no one has yet produced a viable theory explaining why the variation in the numbers of sunspots should affect the climate on any particular part of the Earth. All cycles are likely to break down at times, and if there is no basic underlying scientific theory, then the broken cycle, however compelling the figures may have looked for a time, must be regarded as a coincidence.

Scientists have shown that the variation in energy output from the Sun caused by the sunspot cycle is less than 0.1 per cent. They have also calculated that the average temperature variation on Earth in response to this is approximately 0.03°C (0.05°F) – so small a change as to be virtually undetectable. The conventional wisdom amongst climate experts is that no reliable cause-and-effect mechanism has been identified linking sunspot cycles and variations in climate.

FROST POCKET *On clear calm nights, cold air collects in valley bottoms, often leading to damaging frosts.*

The materials from which towns and cities are made – stone, brick, tarmac, concrete and slate – are usually very different from those of the surrounding countryside. Moreover, the irregularity of the city surface also makes the movement of air more difficult.

The air therefore becomes stagnant in the city's streets and squares when there is not enough wind to penetrate to street level. Most building blocks are, like solid rock, good at absorbing heat energy from the Sun, and the darker the colour of the material the less energy is reflected and the hotter it becomes. Tarmac therefore becomes especially hot on sunny afternoons. The heat absorbed during the day is released at night, rather like a giant night-storage heater. As a

result, cities are warmer than neighbouring districts, especially at night, and especially when there is no wind to spread the warmth around. Under the right atmospheric conditions, city centres have been known to be more than 10°C (18°F) warmer than the outermost suburbs at night.

HILLS, VALLEYS AND FROST POCKETS

Normally, temperature falls steadily the higher you get above sea level. This means that mountainous areas have large temperature variations within short distances, most of them a result of the ups and downs of the terrain. However, another process is also sometimes at work. Night-time cooling in still air produces a layer of very cold air close to the ground. The colder the air is, the denser it is, so if there is no wind to redistribute it, the cold air will drift downhill, collecting in valleys and basins rather as water would. Even in gently rolling country, cloudless and windless nights produce lakes of cold air in low-lying districts. Places that are particularly prone to this effect are often known as frost pockets or frost hollows.

One such frost pocket at Gstettneralm, in the foothills of the Austrian Alps south-west of Vienna, regularly has temperature differences of 20°C (36°F) between the valley bottom and the hillsides 300 ft (90 m) above. On the morning of March 31, 1931, a valley bottom temperature of –43°C (–45°F) contrasted with –16°C (3°F) higher up – a range of 27°C (48°F). Another frost hollow is at Rickmansworth on London's north-western fringe. This has been known to record temperatures 15°C (27°F) lower than in central London, just 15 miles (24 km) away.

WHAT THE WEATHER MACHINE DOES

2

CLOUD STREETS *Patterns like this indicate undulating motion in the windflow at cloud level.*

NEARLY ALL OUR WEATHER IS THE RESULT OF THE INTERACTION OF HEAT, AIR AND WATER. THE CONSTANTLY MOVING AIR WE EXPERIENCE AS WIND RANGES FROM GENTLE BREEZES TO CATASTROPHIC HURRICANES AND TYPHOONS. WATER MANIFESTS ITSELF AS DRIZZLE AND DOWNPOURS, AS GENTLE SHOWERS, MIST AND FOG AND DEW, AND OF COURSE THE EVER-CHANGING CLOUDS. WHEN IT IS COLD ENOUGH WE GET SNOW AND SLEET AND HAIL, FROST AND ICE, AND SOME CLOUDS ARE MADE OF ICE PARTICLES, TOO. A FEW WEATHER PHENOMENA REQUIRE AN ADDITIONAL INPUT — DUST TO CREATE A DUST STORM OR DUST HAZE, ELECTRICITY TO CREATE A THUNDERSTORM, AND LIGHT FROM THE SUN TO CREATE A RAINBOW OR HALO.

CITY SKYLINE *Forked lightning during a storm in Arizona.*

WINDSTORMS GREAT AND SMALL

The wind is always there. Sometimes it is near-imperceptible, as gentle zephyrs rustle the leaves on a summer's afternoon. At other times, it is raised to ire, unleashing the fury and destruction of full-blooded tornadoes and hurricanes.

Winds can be good news or bad news. Violent winds are to be feared with their power to damage homes, wreak havoc in woods and forests and disrupt our everyday routine. A brisk breeze may be gladly received in summer when it relieves heat and humidity; on the other hand, it may be decidedly unwelcome in winter when it brings an additional 'chill factor' making the weather feel much colder than the temperature recorded by the thermometer would suggest. The same fresh wind can be described as 'nagging' or 'bracing' according to mood or circumstances.

The wind can be regarded as 'blowing away the cobwebs' on one day and 'going right through you' on another.

The wind is virtually always there because the atmosphere is always in motion. Even on calm days there is usually a very faint breeze. Rarely, a sheltered spot such as an enclosed valley or hollow may experience periods with no wind at all. These occasions can give an odd feeling. Countryside sounds and smells are magnified and we may even have the sensation of being interlopers in our environment.

Wind is all around us and throughout history people have tended to endow it with human or personal qualities – from the ancient Greeks with their wind gods, such as Aeolus, mythical ruler of the floating island of Aeolia and controller of the winds, to the modern habit of giving hurricanes and typhoons human names. This extends to the words we use to describe the wind – rough, gentle, wild, soft, fierce, boisterous, vigorous, frantic, whistling, moaning. Wind is also associated with our own breathing, as in 'hardly a breath of wind'.

THE POWER OF MOVING AIR

Wind is simply air in motion, created when air from an area of high pressure flows into an area of low pressure. Driving the whole system is the Sun's energy, warming different parts of the Earth's surface at different rates. Concentrations of warm air form and, since warm air is less dense than cold air, they create areas of low pressure. The tropics receive more

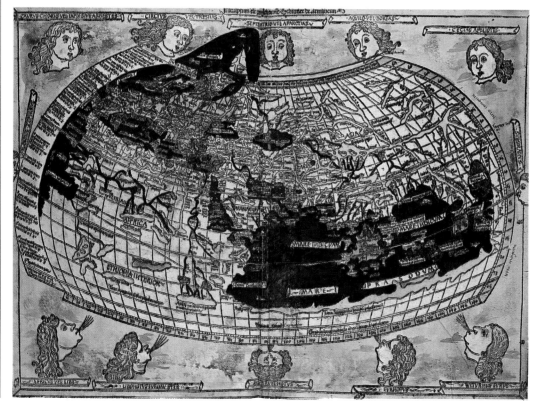

WINDS AROUND THE WORLD
Ptolemy's map of the world, dating from the 2nd century AD, is reproduced in a 15th-century woodcut. The different winds are illustrated around the fringes of the map.

AIR POWER *Hurricanes are among the most ferocious of windstorms. In September 1988 Hurricane Gilbert struck Jamaica with sustained winds of 170 mph (274 km/h) or more.*

Some regions have well-known winds that regularly blow across them, such as the cold, dry *mistral* of France's Rhône Valley and Mediterranean coast or the hot, dry, dust-carrying *sirocco* of North Africa. These are shaped by particular local conditions. The *sirocco*, for example, forms ahead of areas of low pressure that from time to time travel west to east across the southern Mediterranean. It picks up moisture as it crosses the Mediterranean, bringing rain and fog to its northern shores. Similar winds in the Mediterranean

heat than the poles; land and sea heat up and cool down at different rates. Both are factors that help to create areas with varying pressure, as does the passage of the seasons with its alternation of heat and cold.

Winds range in power from the destructive furies of hurricanes, which can gust at speeds of 200 mph (320 km/h) or more, to light airs not even perceptible to the human face, though smoke from a bonfire or chimney will generally indicate tiny amounts of drift. They include 'general' winds prevailing over large areas of the globe, such as the north-east and south-east trades. They also include 'local' winds such as the night-time land breezes of tropical coasts, a result of temperature contrasts between land and sea when the land cools more rapidly at night than the sea.

HIGH WINDS AT SEA *Wind speeds over the sea are, on average, stronger than over land. The 'roughness' of the land surface creates friction which reduces wind speed.*

WHERE WINDS BLOW *Farmers in the Rhône Valley (left) plant cypress barriers to protect their crops from the* mistral. *The* sirocco *can originate as far south as the Hoggar Mountains of southern Algeria (above).*

region are the *leveche* of south-eastern Spain and the *khamsin* of Egypt.

There are also winds that blow at different layers of the Earth's atmosphere. These include the mid-latitude 'jet streams', gigantic conveyor belts of wind in the upper atmosphere, usually 5 to 6 miles (8 to 10 km) above the ground. These are the concentration at high altitudes of the prevailing westerlies of the mid-latitudes – the bands of the Earth's surface lying between 30° and 60° in each hemisphere, that is roughly between the latitudes of southern Morocco and Oslo in the Northern Hemisphere and between Durban in South Africa and a point some 400 miles (600 km) south of Cape Horn in the Southern Hemisphere.

The jet streams can blow at speeds of 300 mph (480 km/h) or more. They are familiar to air travellers as the 'head winds' that occasionally slow down transatlantic flights from Europe to North America or

SKY STREAM *A satellite picture of Egypt and the Red Sea shows a streak of cloud about 6 miles (10 km) above ground level, marking the path of a subtropical jet stream.*

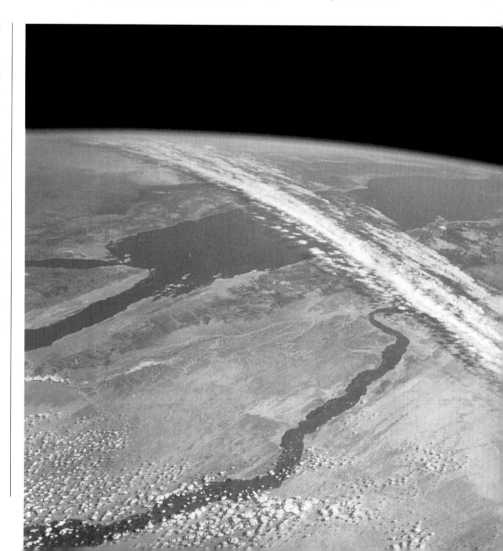

the 'tail winds' that speed up flights in the opposite direction.

Winds are a vital element in the planetary weather machine. Without them, energy would not be transferred from one part of the atmosphere to the other. The most effective wind systems in this respect are travelling storms, huge whirls of energy moving across the surface of the globe, usually accompanied by complex patterns of clouds that deposit rain and snow. These, too, range vastly in power and extent, some storms covering almost a million square miles (2.6 million km²), others, such as tornadoes, only a few hundred square yards.

LOWS IN MID-LATITUDES

The largest atmospheric whirls are mid-latitude depressions or 'lows' (also known as cyclones), huge spiralling weather systems that form around an area of low pressure. They chase each other at irregular intervals

across the Pacific and Atlantic oceans in the Northern Hemisphere, and in the Southern Hemisphere race frantically around the Southern Ocean with scarcely a break.

The biggest can measure more than 2000 miles (3200 km) across, and may take several days to pass over a particular point on the Earth's surface. They are far too large for the detail of how they work to be detected by an observer on the ground, but they are clearly defined on weather charts and are often magnificently displayed on satellite images. Their development and movement is controlled by the mid-latitude jet streams.

Even before the advent of satellites, meteorologists had learnt enough about mid-latitude depressions to devise a good 'model' of the way they work. This model dates from the time of the First World War and the Bergen school of meteorology in Norway. The physicist Vilhelm Bjerknes and his son Jakob investigated the behaviour of a large number of Atlantic depressions as they approached the Norwegian coast. They discovered that the sequence of events fell into a recognisable pattern.

The typical depression starts with two contrasting air masses flowing side by side.

HEAVY WEATHER IN THE OFFING
A huge bank of threatening-looking clouds marks the approach of a cold front.

One is of subtropical origin and is warm and very moist; the other is of polar origin and is very much colder and clearer. The boundary between these two masses of air is often very sharp, bringing abrupt changes in temperature, wind and weather as it passes over any particular place.

In wartime Europe it was natural to liken the air masses to two huge armies advancing and retreating, and the boundaries between them to battle fronts. The Bjerknes es named the atmospheric battle front between the two air masses the 'polar front'. Particular sections along the polar front where warm air is advancing became 'warm fronts', and those where cold air is advancing became 'cold fronts'.

Sometimes a kink forms on the polar front. On one side of the kink, the cold air advances, creating a cold front; on the other side, the warm air advances, creating a warm front. The pressure drops rapidly at the tip of the kink as air is drawn upwards and outwards by the jet streams in the

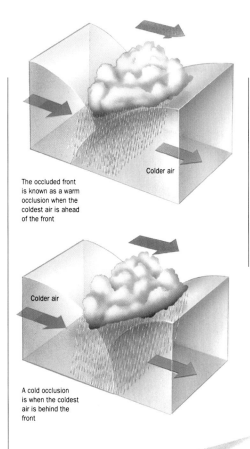

The occluded front is known as a warm occlusion when the coldest air is ahead of the front

Colder air

Colder air

A cold occlusion is when the coldest air is behind the front

atmosphere far above. Winds circulate around this centre point, swinging in a counterclockwise direction in the Northern Hemisphere and in a clockwise direction in the Southern.

The different directions of the circulation are an effect of the Earth's rotation which can best be understood by imagining a disc of white card placed on the turntable of a record player. Imagine first that the disc is a flattened version of the Northern Hemisphere, with the centre point as the North Pole. The Earth rotates west to east and so imagine the turntable revolving counterclockwise. If you try to draw a straight line from the centre to the rim as the turntable is moving, you will in fact end up with a counterclockwise spiral. Even if you do not start at the centre, the line will still swerve in a counterclockwise direction. Then imagine the disc as the Southern Hemisphere, with the centre as the South Pole. Now you will have to imagine the turntable revolving clockwise. If you try to

HOISTED ALOFT *At the Earth's surface, cold fronts nearly always catch up with warm fronts, a process known as occlusion, lifting the warm air mass aloft.*

Rising warm air

Rising warm air

Warm front

Cold front

Cool air

SKY FRONTS *Warm and cold fronts are three-dimensional features, separating air masses with contrasting characteristics. These 'frontal boundaries' usually bring rain or snow, or both, and sometimes thunderstorms.*

draw a similar straight line, you will end up with a clockwise spiral.

As the depression 'matures', the pressure at the tip of the kink sinks lower and the depression is said to be 'deepening'. The winds circulating within it grow correspondingly stronger. The kink becomes more marked, with a slice of warm air sandwiched between the cold air circulating ahead of it and the cold air behind it. The jet streams drive the system as a whole in a general west-to-east direction – many of the

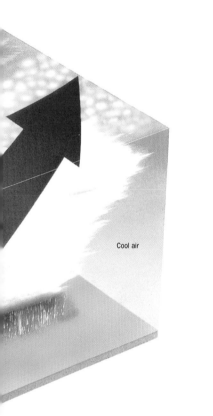

Cool air

depressions that hit Europe form on or near North America's Atlantic seaboard.

For the observer on the ground, the noticeable effects of a depression as it passes over are the approach, arrival and moving on of the fronts – the warm front first, followed by the cold one.

FRONT AFTER FRONT

No two depressions are exactly alike. In a 'classic' one, however, the first sign of the approaching warm front is a layer of high-level cloud. At this point, the less dense warm air is sliding over the denser cold air

beneath it. Where the two air-masses meet high above the Earth's surface, the water vapour in the warm air cools slightly as it is forced upwards and condenses to form tiny water particles – clouds. The clouds gradually get thicker and lower as the warm front draws nearer, displacing the cold air ahead of it closer and closer to ground level. This leads to a period of steady rain or snow.

Eventually, the warm front arrives at ground level. For a while, the warm air reigns supreme. The rain or snow stops and the temperature rises. Then the mass of cold air that follows behind the warm air in the whirl of the depression approaches: the cold front. Once again, the clash between the two air masses creates unsettled weather – sudden, sometimes thundery downpours and a squally wind. Then, as the cold air displaces the warm air, the weather settles down again. Overhead, the skies clear rapidly and there is a sharp drop in temperature.

The depression weakens because the cold front, driven by stronger winds in the upper air, travels slightly faster than the warm front ahead of it. The gap between the two fronts narrows, and eventually the cold front catches up with the warm front, forcing the warm air aloft so that none is left at the Earth's surface. At this point the warm front is said to be 'occluded' – from the Latin *claudere*, 'to close' – having been squeezed out at ground level between the cold air ahead of it and the cold air behind. The continuous supply of warm, tropical air is now reduced or cut off completely. There is no longer a sharp contrast between masses of cold, dense air and warm, less dense air, and the energy input into the system decreases rapidly.

It says much for the original Bergen model of mid-latitude depressions that it was devised when meteorologists knew little about what was happening in the upper

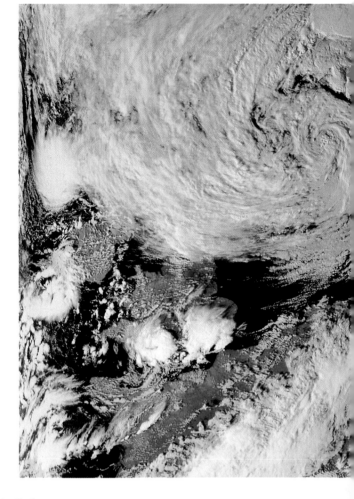

SEEN FROM SPACE *A swirl of cloud marks a mid-latitude depression over the North Sea. This particular depression brought the Great Storm that wreaked havoc in western Europe in October 1987.*

atmosphere and yet it remains a fundamental feature of mid-latitude weather charts to this day. Later research, using information gathered from, for example, satellite images, only confirmed the basic accuracy of the Norwegian scientists' findings.

GALES OF DESTRUCTION

With their complex structure of fronts and air masses, mid-latitude depressions are far from being symmetrical, and wind strength can vary hugely within them. Sometimes they bring destructive gales and storms, especially in the winter half of the year. Wind speeds can exceed 75 mph (120 km/h), and sometimes top 100 mph (160 km/h).

Severe westerly gales brought in by mid-latitude depressions are a familiar feature

WHEN THE WINDS ARE HIGH AND THE SEAS ARE ROUGH

High winds bring rough seas – that much is obvious. But the relationship is by no means straightforward. Much depends on water depth, the expanse of unbroken water, the length of time the wind has been blowing, and changes in wind speed and direction. For example, winds blowing over shallow water will generate steeper waves than over deeper water. The equation is further complicated by ocean swell. 'Swell' waves are ones that have travelled far from where they were generated. When the wind is calm they appear as smooth, regular, rolling waves, with little or no white water. But when a gale is raging, a heavy swell underlying large wind waves can result in very confused seas.

Such a situation built up during the 'Fastnet Disaster' of 1979. The Fastnet Race takes place off the south coasts of England and Ireland. In 1979 a rapidly deepening depression struck midway. Sudden changes in wind direction resulted in heavy, confused seas, the steepness of the

KEEPING A WEATHER EYE
Offshore oil rigs are vulnerable to the rough seas whipped up by high winds.

waves accentuated by the relative shallows of the Labadie Bank to the south of Ireland. Of the 303 starters, 23 yachts were abandoned; 15 participants were drowned, and 136 had to be rescued.

Commercial shipping can cope with most conditions on the high seas, but driving through heavy seas costs time and fuel. Thus nearly all shipping lines use ship-routeing services provided by meteorologists. Similarly, the offshore oil industry buys in detailed weather forecasts every day – sometimes several times a day when critical operations are underway – in order to plan work schedules efficiently.

of winters in western Europe and along the Pacific seaboard of North America (occasionally as far south as Los Angeles). They also occur in the South Island of New Zealand, across the southern halves of Chile and Argentina and occasionally around the southern coasts of South Africa and Australia. In the Atlantic states of the USA, the Maritime Provinces of Canada and northern Japan, the wake or rear of mid-latitude depressions brings gales swooping down from the north-east – as 'nor-easters'.

There have been a number of dramatic examples of mid-latitude gales and storms in recent decades. High winds and surging tides swept the Atlantic seaboard of the USA in January 1982, claiming some 270 victims. Equally dramatic was a series of Pacific storms that pounded California in January and February 1983. The combined assault of surf-driven sand and collapsing cliff-faces re-arranged parts of the coastline and buried stretches of the Pacific Coast Highway.

Among the most violent of all recent mid-latitude windstorms was the Great Storm of October 15-16, 1987, which struck northern Portugal, north-western Spain, northern France, southern England, Belgium and the Netherlands, resulting in unprecedented property damage and huge insurance claims. Another was the Burns' Day Storm of January 25, 1990, which swept the whole of the British Isles and neighbouring parts of mainland Europe, leaving almost 100 people dead in its wake.

As a Texan oil-man once said, while enduring his first winter in the North Sea in

GREAT STORM, GREAT HAVOC
The Great Storm of October 1987 was probably the most powerful to hit southern England in nearly 300 years.

the oil exploration boom of the mid-1970s: 'They told me you never had hurricanes here … They lied … 'cept you don't call 'em hurricanes – you just call 'em depressions.'

THE POWER OF A HURRICANE

In September 1988 a young woman was observed banging furiously at the door of her local registry office on the Caribbean island of Jamaica. When quizzed about what was worrying her, she replied that she wanted urgently to change the name of her young son which had been registered a few days earlier. She had called him Gilbert – the day before the island was devastated by Hurricane Gilbert. Hurricane Gilbert in 1988 and Hurricane Andrew which swept across southern Florida in August 1992 are two recent examples of these windstorms at their most extreme and violent.

Although the word 'hurricane' is used informally to describe any exceptionally powerful wind, to a meteorologist it has a more precise meaning. Technically, a hurricane is a revolving storm of tropical oceanic origin, with sustained winds in its circulation of at least 74 mph (119 km/h). Confusingly, hurricanes are called 'hurricanes' only in the Atlantic, Caribbean and north-east Pacific. In the north-west Pacific, including Chinese and Japanese waters, they are 'typhoons', and in the south-west Pacific and Indian oceans they are 'cyclones' (not to be confused with mid-latitude cyclones or depressions).

SWIRL AROUND THE EYE
Hurricane Andrew (below) devastated southern Florida in August 1992, then crossed the Gulf of Mexico to take a swipe at the Louisiana coastline. Hurricane Hugo (right) approaches the coast of South Carolina in September 1989.

VIEW FROM ABOVE *The crew of the space shuttle* Endeavor *took this photo (above) of Hurricane Iniki as it swept across Hawaii in 1992. A photo of Hurricane Elena (left) in 1985 shows how the clouds rise highest over the eye.*

A hurricane is the most destructive of the revolving storms encountered in the tropics. Warmth at the ocean surface provides an upward impetus, which creates an area of low pressure in the lowest layers of the atmosphere. The warmed air starts to spiral; at the centre of the spiral, the air pressure drops still further. The spiralling

MEASURING WIND THE BEAUFORT WAY

The Beaufort scale for classifying winds was originally devised in 1805 by the British naval officer Francis Beaufort. He based it on the effects of wind on a fully rigged sailing man-of-war. It was later adapted for land use. In 1874 the Beaufort scale was officially adopted by the International Meteorological Committee for use when telegraphing weather information across the globe.

Force	Average speed	Description	Observable effects
0	0 mph (0 km/h)	Calm	Smoke rises vertically.
1	2 mph (3 km/h)	Light airs	Smoke drifts in the wind.
2	5 mph (8 km/h)	Light breeze	Leaves rustle.
3	10 mph (16 km/h)	Gentle breeze	Leaves and small twigs move constantly. Small flags extended.
4	15 mph (24 km/h)	Moderate wind	Wind raises dust and loose paper.
5	21 mph (34 km/h)	Fresh wind	Small trees sway.
6	28 mph (45 km/h)	Strong wind	Large branches move. Whistling in phone wires. Difficult to use umbrellas.
7	35 mph (56 km/h)	Very strong wind	Whole trees in motion.
8	43 mph (69 km/h)	Gale	Twigs break off trees. Difficult to walk.
9	50 mph (80 km/h)	Severe gale	Chimney pots and slates removed.
10	59 mph (95 km/h)	Storm	Trees uprooted. Structural damage.
11	69 mph (111 km/h)	Severe storm	Widespread damage.
12	over 74 mph (119 km/h)	Hurricane	Widespread damage.

air climbs, and as it climbs it cools gradually. Having originated over the ocean, it is very moist, so that the cooling process results in rapid condensation in the form of banks of dense cloud and torrential downpours of rain. This in turn releases massive quantities

NAMING HURRICANES

The practice of giving hurricanes names dates from the Second World War. US Navy radio operators used it to follow storms from one day's weather chart to the next, especially when the chart may have contained several hurricanes and tropical storms. Crackly voice transmissions were often the only way of sending detailed weather information from one point to another. For instance, the class of '88, when Gilbert graduated, also included Alberto, Beryl, Chris, Debby, Ernesto, Florence, Helene, Isaac, Joan, and Keith.

of latent heat – heat energy released when a substance changes phase, as when water vapour changes into liquid water – which further fuel the storm's development. At the core of the spiralling air currents, the low-pressure centre is a small, relatively

calm area, often free of cloud, known as the 'eye' of the storm.

Because of their enormous potential for destruction, such storms are exhaustively categorised, analysed and investigated, so that the first signs of intensification can be picked up as soon as possible. They are classified as 'tropical depressions' until their winds reach 43 mph (69 km/h), 'tropical storms' when sustained winds reach between 43 and 73 mph (69 and 117 km/h), and 'hurricanes' when winds reach 74 mph (119 km/h) or more. A fully mature hurricane may measure up to 1000 miles (1600 km) across, although 250-300 miles (400-480 km) is more typical. The cloud banks may stretch upwards for 8 to 10 miles (13 to 16 km) above the ocean surface, and the eye may have a diameter of about 15-20 miles (24-32 km).

CLOUD COMMA *A satellite view of Hurricane Gilbert as it swirls across the Caribbean in September 1988, its clouds forming a comma-like signature.*

The visible signature of a hurricane viewed on a satellite picture is hard to mistake. The cloud system is much more symmetrical than in a mid-latitude depression, with 'arms' of cloud spiralling outwards, and a tiny dark circular eye at the centre of the brilliant white cloud mass.

THE RIGHT CONDITIONS
Hurricanes develop only over tropical oceans where the necessary supplies of moisture and warmth exist together. Few, if any, develop when the temperature at the sea's surface is below 26°C (about 79°F), so they are never seen in the Atlantic south of the Equator, or off the Pacific coast of South America, where cool ocean currents maintain water temperatures below that level. Nor are they found within about six degrees of latitude of the Equator, as there is not sufficient rotational force here to get the storm revolving.

In contrast to mid-latitude depressions, hurricanes drift slowly from east to west under the influence of the easterlies which prevail in the upper atmosphere of the tropics. They also tend to swerve right as they *continued on page 54*

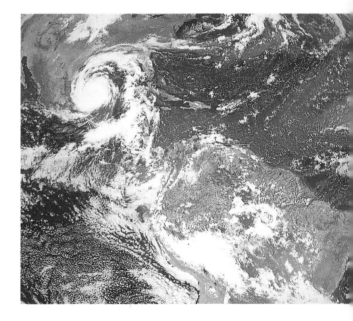

MEASURING THE WEATHER

More than 2000 years ago, the ancient Greeks took the first steps towards designing instruments that could measure the state and behaviour of the air. The ideas of scholars such as Philo of Byzantium (who proved that air expands when heated) and Hero of Alexandria (who demonstrated that air has weight) formed the basis of the modern thermometer, barometer and hygrometer – instruments for measuring the air's temperature, pressure and humidity.

After the Greeks, however, no significant advances took place until the the late 16th century when the Italian astronomer Galileo Galilei devised a kind of primitive thermometer, showing how air expands and contracts according to temperature. It consisted of a tube with a bulb at one end and a container with coloured water. He warmed

the bulb, and then placed the tube, bulb uppermost, in the container. As the air inside the tube cooled, it contracted and coloured water was drawn up the tube. Since the container was not sealed, however, changing air pressure affected the level of the fluid as well as changing temperature.

The first sealed thermometer dates from about 1640. It is sometimes credited to Ferdinand, Duke of Tuscany, although it was probably invented by a court scientist under his patronage. The court resided in Florence, so this first true thermometer is usually referred to as the 'Florentine thermometer'. It consisted of a sealed tube with a bulb at one end; inside it was alcohol distilled from wine. As the temperature rose, the alcohol expanded and rose up the tube; as the temperature cooled the alcohol level fell. A rudimentary scale was devised using the temperature of snow as its lower point and the blood temperature of animals as its upper point. Alcohol thermometers have the disadvantage, however, that alcohol boils at 78.5°C (173°F) – so they cannot be used in scientific experiments involving temperatures higher than this.

The familiar mercury-in-glass thermometer was devised by Florentine scientists a few years later, in 1657. Mercury is ideal for measuring how warm or cold it is because it expands and contracts rapidly with changes in temperature. It also remains in liquid form between its freezing point at –39°C (–38°F) and its boiling point at 357°C (674°F).

Galileo also played a part in the invention of the barometer. He had spent some time working on the efficiency of water pumps, and became aware that, however good the pumps were, it was impossible to raise water

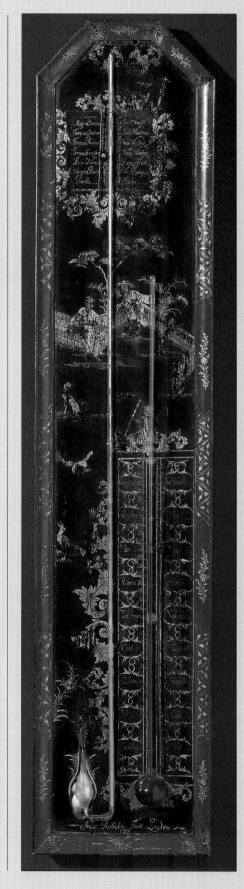

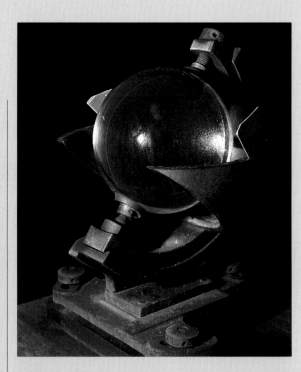

CAMPBELL-STOKES *The Sun's rays pass through a glass sphere and are focused onto a chemically treated card to record sunshine hours.*

more than 34 ft (10.5 m) above the original water level. Galileo never discovered exactly why these water pumps failed, but within two years of his death, one of his pupils had solved the problem. His name was Evangelista Torricelli, and the apparatus he devised to demonstrate that air exerted a downward pressure (which permitted water to be pumped to a certain level but no higher) was actually a prototype barometer. He filled a 4 ft (1.2 m) tube with mercury and inverted it in a container also filled with mercury. The mercury level in the tube fell, but not to the level of the mercury in the container. He concluded that air pressure was pushing down on the mercury in the open container and thereby keeping the level in the tube higher.

For a long time, the English-speaking world measured barometric pressure in 'inches of mercury'; Continental European countries used centimetres or millimetres. Early in the 20th century, however, scientists decided that a more precise unit of measurement was needed. Pressure is defined as force applied over a particular area, and so the 'millibar' was introduced to measure degrees of force applied over 1 m² (just under 11 sq ft). In recent years, the millibar has

been renamed the hectopascal, after the 17th-century French scientist Blaise Pascal, who was an important researcher into atmospheric pressure.

An apparently simple task for early weather enthusiasts was measuring rainfall. All they had to do was place a container in the open, then measure the depth of water in it at regular intervals. Unfortunately, a proportion of the rainwater evaporated when the Sun shone and the wind blew. Rain-gauges therefore evolved into double-sided cylinders to minimise evaporation, surmounted by a funnel with a large vertical lip to reduce splashing.

Nowadays, instruments called radiometers measure the intensity of radiation from the Sun, but for more than 100 years the usual means of monitoring sunshine has been to measure the duration each day that the Sun shone brightly. The standard instrument for this is the Campbell-Stokes sunshine recorder, invented by the Scottish amateur scientist John F. Campbell in 1853, and refined by the physicist Sir George Stokes in 1879. It works on the principle

seen when schoolchildren use magnifying glasses to make scorch marks in their desk tops by focusing the rays of the Sun into a point. Instead of the magnifying glass it has a solid glass sphere with a piece of card in place of the desk top. The Sun's heat burns a narrow trace along the length of card which has time marks every half an hour.

The earliest of all meteorological instruments told people the direction from which the wind was blowing. Wind vanes have been popular for centuries and remain the basis of modern methods of measuring wind direction. Wind speed posed more of a problem. Very rough approximations have been possible by describing the behaviour of trees, soil particles, and smoke, while mariners studied closely the height and amplitude of waves and the way blowing spray affected visibility. Early instruments tried to ascertain the force exerted by the wind using a broad metal flap fixed along one edge only. It was placed in an exposed location and left to swing in the breeze. In 1846, however, the English instrument-maker John Robinson invented a very different 'anemometer' involving an arrangement of hemispherical cups attached to a vertical shaft which rotates as the cups rotate. This forms the basis of many present-day anemometers.

CATCHING THE WIND *John Robinson's anemometer of 1846 was one of the first instruments that successfully measured wind speed.*

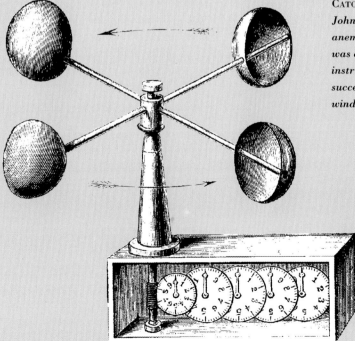

AFTER THE WIND, CHAOS
Many strange sights greeted
Jamaicans when they began to
clear up the mess in the wake
of Hurricane Gilbert. Aircraft
had been tossed into trees,
boats transported far inland
and dozens of cars swept out to
sea, never to be seen again.

cross the Atlantic and Pacific oceans – an effect of the Earth's rotational force – and thus wander out of the zone of upper easterlies. In the Northern Hemisphere, once they move north of the 20th parallel, the latitude

WEATHER MAN AND PIRATE

The earliest-known European description of a hurricane (or typhoon) was penned by the English buccaneer William Dampier (1652-1715). For many years, he roved the seas as a plundering freebooter, though he also found more legitimate employment as commander of the *Roebuck*, commissioned by the British Admiralty to explore the South Pacific and Indian oceans. He was also a keen weather watcher. His book *A New Voyage Round the World*, published in 1697, with descriptions of weather conditions at sea, remained a key mariners' manual for more than 100 years.

of Cuba's southern coast, they are liable to get caught up by the upper westerlies which hurry them away into middle latitudes. Lower ocean temperatures in subtropical and temperate latitudes will not support a

fully fledged hurricane, so the storms gradually change character as they move away from the tropics, losing some of their violence. Although hurricanes cause immense damage when they hit land, they rarely survive for long if their path takes them over land for a sustained period of time. Deprived of the moisture of the ocean, they again lose their violence.

The hurricane season lasts as long as the sea-surface temperatures reach more than 26°C (79°F). In the Atlantic and Caribbean the official season lasts from June 1 to November 30, although occasional rogue storms have happened outside these dates – for instance, Hurricane Allison which formed in the western Caribbean before the end of May in 1995. The season reaches its height between the beginning of September and the middle of October, and this is the period when the biggest and most destructive storms generally occur. None has been more intense than Hurricane Gilbert 1988, which at its peak produced sustained winds of 170-175 mph

(274-282 km/h) and maximum gusts of 200-205 mph (322-330 km/h).

In 'Typhoon Alley' – the name given to a stretch of the western Pacific bordered by the Philippines, Taiwan and southern Japan – the season continues throughout the year, although the frequency of typhoons is at its greatest between June and November. A few Pacific storms are even more violent than Hurricane Gilbert, with sustained winds approaching 200 mph (322 km/h).

The destruction caused by hurricanes, not only by winds but also by tidal floods and torrential rain, can be almost total, with serious loss of life. Furthermore, before

SURVIVING A TEXAS TWISTER

One experienced weather observer had his home destroyed by a tornado but survived to recount the events of that day in the journal *Weatherwise*. Roy Hall, a retired captain in the US army, lived in the small township of McKinney, north of Dallas, Texas, when the twister struck on May 3, 1948. His home had already been wrecked when he came face to face with the tornado itself:

'Sixty feet [18 m] south of our house something had billowed down from above, and stood fairly motionless, save a slow up-and-down pulsation. It presented a curved face, with the concave part toward me, with a bottom rim that was almost level, and was not moving either toward or away from our house. I was too dumbfounded for a second, even to try to fathom its nature, and then it burst on my rather befuddled brain with a paralysing shock. It was the lower end of the tornado funnel! I was looking at its inside, and we were, at the moment, within the tornado itself!

'The bottom of the rim was about 20 feet [6 m] off the ground, and had doubtless a few moments before it destroyed our house as it passed. The interior of the funnel was hollow; the rim itself appearing to be not over ten feet [3 m] in thickness, and, owing possibly to the light within the funnel, appeared perfectly opaque. Its inside was so slick that it resembled the interior of a glazed standpipe. The rim had another motion which I was, for a moment, too dazzled to grasp. Presently I did. The whole thing was rotating, shooting past from right to left with incredible velocity.

'I lay back on my left elbow . . . and looked up. It is possible that in that upward glance my stricken eyes beheld something few have ever seen before and lived to tell about. I was looking far up the interior of a great tornado funnel! It extended upward for over 1000 feet [300 m], and was swaying gently, and bending slowly

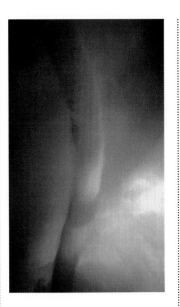

DECEPTIVE BEAUTY *The setting Sun shines through a 'twister' (above). Tornadoes spawned by Hurricane Hugo in 1989 caused great damage (below) in South Carolina.*

toward the south-east. Down at the bottom . . . the funnel was about 150 yards [137 m] across. Higher up it was larger, and seemed to be partly filled with a bright cloud, which shimmered like a fluorescent light. . . .

'Up there, too, where I could observe both the front and back of the funnel, the terrific whirling could be plainly seen. As the upper portion of the huge pipe swayed over, another phenomenon took place. It looked as if the whole column were composed of rings or layers, and when a higher ring moved on toward the south-east, the ring immediately below slipped over to get back under it. This rippling motion continued on down toward the lower tip.

'If there was any debris in the wall of the funnel it was whirling so fast I could not see it. And if there was a vacuum inside the funnel, as is

commonly believed, I was not aware of it. I do not recall having any difficulty in breathing, nor did I see any debris rushing up under the rim of the tornado, as there surely would have been had there been a vacuum. I am positive that the shell of the twister was not composed of wreckage, dirt or other debris. Air, it must have been, thrown out into a hollow tube by centrifugal force. . . .

'When the wave-like motion reached the lower tip, the far edge of the funnel was forced downward and jerked towards the south-east. This edge, in passing, touched the roof of my neighbour's house and flicked the building away like a flash of light. Where, an instant before, had stood a . . . home, now remained one small room with no roof. . . . When the funnel touched it, the building dissolved, the various parts shooting off . . . like sparks from an emery wheel.'

TWIN PILLARS OF DEVASTATION
*This pair of waterspouts was
photographed over Lake
Winnipeg in Canada.*

and can be seen in their entirety by a single observer, though not from a weather satellite.

A tornado is a very rapidly rotating funnel of cloud that develops from the base of a dense towering bank of cumulonimbus cloud. This is the kind of cloud, with extremely powerful updraughts and downdraughts of air, that is sometimes known as a thunderhead, producing heavy rains, thunderstorms or hailstorms. In its embryonic state, the funnel cloud extends downwards only a short distance from the parent cloud, and many such funnels develop no farther, dissipating after ten minutes or so. Occasionally, however, the funnel will grow bigger and bigger, the speed of rotation will increase, and eventually it will touch ground.

At first, the cloud consists of water droplets only, condensed from the moist atmosphere, but as soon as the tornado hits the ground, dust and debris will be swept up into the rotating column, giving it an almost black appearance. A tornado which travels out to sea becomes a waterspout, sucking up vast quantities of water, sometimes with seaweed, fish and other marine debris as well.

Despite their small size, tornadoes are extremely destructive. Indeed, a full-blooded tornado is arguably the most awesomely destructive atmospheric phenomenon that exists. Wind speeds are difficult to measure because most recording equipment is destroyed by the turbulence, but they probably exceed 300 mph (480 km/h). Damage to buildings, trees and crops is often total, although the track of damage is rarely more than a few hundred yards wide.

the age of scientific weather forecasting, hurricanes could often arrive almost unannounced, so that no one was able to take any kind of protective action. A typhoon that struck south-east China in October 1881 is believed to have claimed some 300 000 lives.

The behaviour of hurricanes is notoriously difficult to predict. At most, in the old days, coastal areas could be warned about the existence of a potentially destructive storm out to sea, even if it was still almost impossible to forecast where the landfall would happen. In the last quarter of the 20th

century, however, hurricane forecasting has become a good deal more reliable thanks to satellites, and sensible precautions can now be taken to preserve life, if not property, in threatened coastal areas. The record-breaking Gilbert caused immense damage in Jamaica, but only one life was lost.

TINY TWISTING TERRORS

The word 'tornado' comes from the Latin verb *tornare*, meaning to 'turn' or 'twist'. In North America, tornadoes are often colloquially known as 'twisters'. They are small

Most years bring a substantial number of severe tornadoes to the USA with much property damage and some loss of life. Although weather forecasters can predict the days on which these ferocious windstorms are likely to occur, they still do not know enough about them to say exactly when they will hit and where. They have been known to happen in all months of the year, but the USA has a distinct season which lasts from March to September. The peak months are May and June with almost 150 tornadoes on average in each. Weather watchers have observed that they are most likely to happen in the afternoon and early evening, and are least likely at night.

Most of what we do know about tornadoes comes from the United States, because that is where most of the scientific research has been carried out. It has also been a source of good photographs of severe tornadoes, and in recent times there have been some good examples of amateur video recordings. However, devastating tornadoes also happen regularly in parts of Canada,

Argentina, China, Australia and the Indian subcontinent. A swarm of tornadoes struck the Madaripur district in Bangladesh, for example, on April 2, 1977, killing almost 900 people and injuring more than 6000 – the heaviest-known toll of casualties.

Serious damage has also been caused from time to time in most European countries where minor tornadoes occur much more frequently than most people realise, although they are generally much less violent than their American or Asian counterparts. A particularly destructive European 'twister' capsized an Italian

RAISING DUST *The tornado below was snapped in Kansas in March 1990. When the tip of a tornado's funnel touches down, large quantities of soil, dust and debris are carried skywards (right).*

pleasure cruiser in the Gulf of Venice on September 11, 1970, and wrecked a nearby camping site. Forty-seven people in all lost their lives, some drowned on the capsizing yacht, some died on the camp site; hundreds were injured.

THE GRANDEUR OF THE SKIES

Blue sky and clouds, sunshine and shade, provide a daily pageant for those who care to cast their eyes upwards.

Clouds come in endless variety, some small and soft and white, some intricately patterned, others dark and ominous.

Skyscapes are an endless source of interest and wonder for the beholder – sometimes static, sometimes changing, the interplay of sunlight and shadow on the Earth beneath adding to the enjoyment. Even urban scenery, drab and depressing under grey skies, can take on a fresh lease of life when the clouds break and sunshine streams through, glinting on windows and puddles and granite building blocks.

The 19th-century English artists J.M.W. Turner and John Constable were notable students of the sky. Turner was an avid experimenter with skyscapes, using them to emphasise the drama of his pictures. A story – possibly apocryphal – is told of an elderly lady who commented to him: 'I NEVER see your skies in nature, Mr Turner,' to which he replied, 'Then God help you, Madam.' John Constable was more of a literalist in his rendering of skies and clouds. His work includes a remarkable series of views across London – many of which can be seen in the Victoria and Albert Museum – whose principal subject was clouds in their variety of forms. He painted them in the summer and autumn of 1821 and 1822.

CLOUDS ON THE TOPS *Even clear air contains water vapour. Most clouds – even these fair-weather cumulus (right) – consist of billions upon billions of water droplets condensed from the vapour. John Constable painted this view of Hampstead in London (opposite, below) in the early 1820s. It is one of a series of paintings where sky and clouds dominate the picture.*

Clouds form when invisible water vapour in the atmosphere condenses into visible water droplets. All air contains some water vapour, but a particular volume of warm air can hold more water vapour than the same volume of cool air. When a flow of air is forced to rise – over hills or mountains, or over a large mass of cold stagnant air, or when it becomes buoyant through contact with the warm ground or ocean beneath – it moves into a part of the atmosphere where the pressure is lower and so the air will expand. As it expands it cools, and as it cools it reaches the point where it is no longer able to hold on to all its moisture. Some of the water vapour condenses into droplets; some may also become ice crystals – in this way, clouds are formed.

CLASSIFYING CLOUDS

A countryman with years of experience of watching the weather would probably recognise two kinds of cloud – rain clouds and fair-weather clouds. Essentially, rain clouds are ones with strong vertical updraughts of air which encourage large water droplets or ice crystals, or both, to form. Eventually, these become heavy enough to fall through the bottom of the cloud as precipitation – rain, snow, hail and so on. Much depends on the temperature and humidity of the surrounding air, but as a broad general rule the shallower the cloud, the less chance there is for rain drops – or snowflakes or hailstones – to form and fall to the ground.

A countryman uses clouds to forecast the weather over the next few hours – and, if he

is skilled at the task, may be able to do so with a fair degree of accuracy. Meteorologists see clouds as part of the weather machine as a whole. In the first place, they classify them according to their shape or form, dividing them into two basic categories: layer or 'stratiform' clouds and heaped or 'cumuliform' clouds. Then they look at the level at which clouds form, assigning them to three loose categories: low, medium and high. Broadly speaking, low clouds are ones whose bases lie below 7500 ft (2300 m) above the ground; medium clouds form at altitudes of 7500 to 17 500 ft (2300 to 5330 m); high clouds float at heights of about 18 000 ft (5500 m) or more. Bringing these classifications together,

weather experts recognise ten basic cloud types, although the boundaries between them are often blurred and there may also be wide variations within each type.

COTTON WOOL AND CAULIFLOWERS

Low-level clouds include cumulus and cumulonimbus (both of which, as their names suggest, are cumuliform clouds), stratus (a layered cloud) and stratocumulus (a layered cloud, though with a few, very limited characteristics of heaped clouds).

Cumulus clouds are probably the easiest to recognise. Small undeveloped ones are often described as cotton-wool clouds; bigger ones may resemble cauliflower heads.

They form when the Sun-heated ground or warm ocean water heats the air above it, creating bubbles of rising air or 'thermals'. The air expands and cools as it rises, and its water vapour condenses to form clouds. These tend to grow upwards in mounds, domes or towers. Typically, the cloud base is

ANVIL IN THE SKIES *This view (below) of cumulonimbus clouds was taken from an aircraft above the Texas High Plains. In the foreground, a cumulus head is still growing upwards; in the background, an earlier cloud top has formed an 'anvil cloud'. A growing cumulus cloud (opposite) obscures the Sun, but rays shine through on either side. These are called 'crepuscular rays' – or 'Jacob's ladders'.*

between 2000 and 4000 ft (600 and 1200 m) above the ground. However, if the air is very moist – as over an ocean, for example – it will reach the point at which it can no longer hold its moisture sooner, and so the cloud base may be as low as 800 ft (240 m). If the air is very dry air, by contrast – as over a continental interior – the cloud base may be as high as 6000 or 7000 ft (1800 or 2100 m).

Cumulus clouds are commonly seen against a backdrop of blue sky; distant cumulus 'towers', especially towards sunset, can look like a far-off mountain range. The sunlit parts of the clouds are mostly brilliant white; their bases are relatively dark and nearly horizontal, marking the level of the atmosphere at which condensation occurs. If there is any precipitation, it is usually showery. Under certain conditions cumulus clouds may form themselves in files – 'cloud streets' – running approximately parallel to the wind direction.

When a cumulus cloud grows large enough, it becomes a cumulonimbus. This is the most dramatic sort of cloud, responsible for producing sudden fierce showers of rain or hail or snow, often with thunder and lightning as well – hence its popular name, thundercloud or thunderhead.

These huge shower clouds normally develop from smaller cumulus ones, but grow larger because of strong rising air currents and plenty of moisture in the atmosphere at a wide range of levels. As with a cumulus cloud, the base of a cumulonimbus cloud can lie anywhere between about 1000 and 6000 ft (300 and 1800 m). A fully developed example in the tropics may be as much as 8 miles (13 km) thick, with its base around 3000 ft (900 m) above the ground and its summits approaching 45 000 ft (13 700 m). The important difference between cumulonimbus and cumulus is that the top of the cloud is high enough in the atmosphere to

SKY DRAMA *Cumulonimbus and large cumulus clouds produce dramatic skyscapes. Their bases may be inky black (above and left) because of the thickness of cloud above, while the sunlit summits glisten snowy white (left).*

be made out of ice crystals rather than water droplets – these play a vital role in the formation of precipitation.

A large cumulonimbus will cover the sky completely for a time, bringing a downpour that lasts from half an hour to an hour. Then within five minutes of the end of the downpour, the active part of the cloud has already moved on. The rain has stopped completely and the sun is shining strongly.

These clouds appear as mountains or huge towers. At least a part of their upper portions are usually smooth, fibrous or formed into a series of narrow ridges. The top is almost flattened, spreading out in the form of an anvil or a vast plume. This is because the cloud has reached the level of the bottom of the stratosphere, where the air starts to become warmer with altitude rather than cooler. The process by which the air

cools and its water vapour condenses to form a cloud is arrested.

Under the base of cumulonimbus, which is often very dark, there may be trails of rain or snow – known as 'virga', from the Latin for twig or stripe – that evaporate before they reach the ground.

LOW-LYING CLOUD COVER

Stratus is grey, featureless and unchanging. It forms when air is cooled to the point at which its water vapour starts to condense close to the Earth's surface. It is a feature of coastal fringes with cold offshore currents, or when relatively warm or mild winds blow across a relatively cool sea. It is characteristic of the beaches of southern California bathed by the cold California Current, especially in spring and early summer. It is also a

CLOUDS IN SHEETS *The Sun peeps through a gap in an otherwise uniform sheet of stratus cloud (above). The crew of the space shuttle* Atlantis *took this view (above right) of a stratocumulus cloud sheet.*

regular visitor to the coastal strip of northern Chile and Peru and the Namibian coast, all washed by cold currents. North-easterly winds in spring and early summer bring persistent North Sea stratus to the east coast of England.

Stratus is also sometimes caused by the lifting of fog, and usually gives the impression of being a 'high fog' even when it has originated in some other way. When the Sun is seen through a layer stratus cloud, its

outline is clearly discernible. Stratus may last for days on end, but it typically forms and dissipates very rapidly. Stratus clouds have their base anywhere from the surface to 1500 or 2000 ft (460 or 610 m) above the ground, and may be no more than 50 ft (15 m) thick. They do not usually produce

HIGHEST CLOUDS OF ALL

Almost all the clouds we see are formed within the troposphere, the innermost layer of the Earth's atmosphere. But isolated cloud patches are observed at much greater heights. Because they are in the stratosphere, they have no impact on weather patterns lower down. These tenuous but sometimes brilliantly lit stratospheric clouds may take the form of mother-of-pearl (nacreous) clouds about 15 miles (24 km) up, or noctilucent (night-shining) clouds at an altitude of about 50 miles (80 km). It is not known for sure whether they consist of tiny ice crystals, dust particles or a combination.

precipitation; when it does occur it is in the form of minute particles such as drizzle.

Stratocumulus is essentially a layer cloud that does, however, develop upwards and downwards to some extent. It forms in various ways. If the ascending currents that produce cumulus or cumulonimbus slow

LUKE HOWARD — GODFATHER OF THE CLOUDS

The London apothecary Luke Howard (1772-1864) was a man of many parts. He was an active Quaker and wrote extensively on Biblical matters. He was also a prolific author on chemistry, botany, geology, meteorology and the natural sciences and philosophy in general. Among his many correspondents was the German poet Goethe. Excited by his friend's ideas, Goethe wrote poetry about clouds, using names Howard had invented for the various types of clouds.

Howard was most interested in meteorology and it is through his meteorological researches that he is known to us today. He was sometimes referred to as the 'Father of Meteorology', even the 'Godfather of the Clouds'. His legacy to the meteorological world was enormous. He kept daily weather records in London between 1806 and 1823, and when he retired to Ackworth, near Pontefract, in Yorkshire, in 1824, he kept regular records there, too. He wrote the first serious analysis of London's weather, *The Climate of London*, published in 1818. He also produced a substantial text book called *Seven Lectures on*

Meteorology, published in 1837. Howard first proposed his system for classifying cloud types in 1802, and it still forms the basis of cloud

classification. This is especially remarkable in that he had no real knowledge of the atmospheric physics that explains how clouds form and develop. His cloud categories are based on the system of botanical classification that was devised by the 18th-century Swedish botanist Linnaeus (Karl von Linne). Linnaeus classified all plants by genus (family) and species. In a similar way, Howard recognised three basic cloud types: cirrus, cumulus and stratus, which he described respectively as 'fibrous', 'heaped' and 'a continuous sheet'. He also suggested four hybrids: cirrocumulus, cirrostratus, cumulostratus and cumulocirrostratus. Nimbus – the rain cloud – was not one of his basic categories, but a modifying label for a species of cloud from which rain fell. After Howard's death, his system of

classification was extended and refined, so that virtually all possible variations of clouds can now be described. Thus, in addition to genera and species, we now use latinised words to describe special varieties. A huge thundercloud with a markedly anvil-shaped summit and developing funnel-cloud or tornado beneath, will be called cumulonimbus incus tuba – from the Latin words for 'anvil' and 'trumpet'. A medium-level cloud developing upwards into shapes like turrets or battlements, and with precipitation trails beneath, is called altocumulus castellanus virga – from the Latin for 'of a fortress' and 'twig'. A thin irregular layer of low cloud formed from the flattening out of cumulus clouds has the title stratocumulus perlucidus cumulogenitus – from the Latin for 'transparent' and 'born of cumulus'.

SKETCHING THE SKIES *Luke Howard (above) illustrated his cloud classification system with sketches. This one (right) shows small cumulus clouds overlain with patches of cirrostratus.*

---

down or stop, the upper parts of the mother cloud dissipate, while the lower parts spread horizontally, producing stratocumulus. It may also form from the lifting of stratus.

Stratocumulus often takes the form of broad rolls of grey cloud separated by streets of lighter cloud or narrow zones of blue sky. Many stratocumulus 'sheets' are rainless; even the thickest banks rarely produce anything more than a little intermittent rain or drizzle or snow. The cloud base may be anywhere between 1000 and 7000 ft (300 and

2100 m) above the ground, above which it merges into its medium-level counterpart, altocumulus. The cloud layer is typically around 1000 ft (300 m) deep.

SUPERCOOLERS

Medium-level clouds, which mostly form between 2 and 4 miles (3.2 and 6.4 km) above the Earth's surface, include altocumulus, altostratus and nimbostratus. They are mainly composed of water droplets, even though the temperature at that altitude is well below

freezing except in the tropics. This is because water droplets can survive in pure air as cold as –40°C (–40°F), thanks to the protecting influence of the drops' surface tension. Ice crystals and water droplets can exist together between –22°C (–8°F) and –40°C; between these temperatures drops and crystals form around nuclei of differing physical and chemical characteristics.

As water clouds, medium-level clouds are clearly set apart from their high-level counterparts which are primarily composed

FLOATING CASTLES *Cumulus clouds grow upwards from relatively small bases, as here (above) over the Comoros Islands in the Indian Ocean. Fair-weather altocumulus clouds have formed (right) from water droplets in a shallow layer of air some 2 miles (3.2 km) above the Earth's surface. Thicker cloud patches mark areas of gently rising air currents, while the small clear patches denote gently descending air currents.*

of ice crystals. Water-droplet clouds tend to have sharp outlines, while ice-crystal clouds are rather fibrous in appearance. Medium clouds are far enough above the ground for their shapes and patterns to be clearly visible from beneath, and towards sunrise and sunset they are often splendidly coloured as the sunlight plays on their undersides.

This is particularly true of altocumulus, whose many varieties provide some of the most beautiful and unusual of fair-weather clouds. They include clouds that resemble

continued on page 70

THE WEATHER WATCHERS

Scattered around the world are thousands of weather stations, staffed by people whose jobs are to gather and collate measurements, all made to the same standards and at exactly the same time in different parts of the globe. As we approach the 21st century, their work has been made easier by the automation of many of the routine observing tasks.

Some of these observing points are meteorological stations, which are usually found at commercial airports and military airfields, where weather observations are carried out every 30 or 60 minutes. This is because pilots and the air-traffic controllers who guide them need to know precisely the conditions in which the aircraft are taking off and landing. Clearly, wind and rain and visibility are vitally important. So is air pressure, because an aircraft's altimeter, which measures its height above the ground, is actually a special kind of barometer, and its zero setting is the barometric pressure observed at ground level. When the air pressure is changing rapidly, pilots have to adjust their altimeters accordingly.

At the other end of the spectrum are climatological stations, where a single daily observation is carried out. The job of the observers at these stations is essentially to

SUN POWER *A solar panel provides the power for an automatic weather station. The data may be transmitted to a central office, using computers and telephones.*

build up an archive of the climate at their particular location by making one daily reading, logging the maximum and minimum temperatures since the last observation, measuring the rainfall and sunshine and the speed and direction of the wind every 24 hours and keeping a diary noting the most notable features of each day's weather.

Such stations are often found in schools and colleges (especially agricultural colleges), at holiday resorts, police stations, post offices, coast guard stations, lighthouses, reservoirs, sewage works, on farms, and in managed forests. Many countries also have groups of amateur enthusiasts who keep their own observations, many of which are accepted as official weather records.

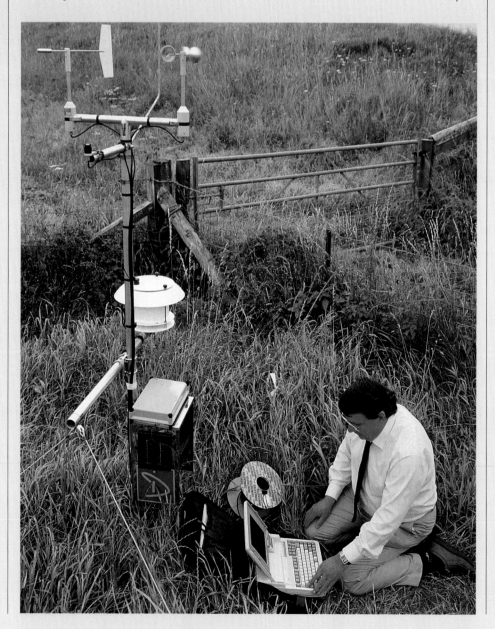

KEEPING A LOG *An observer downloads data from the logger (computer) of an automated weather station.*

A typical observing station is found on an open site, although this is not always possible, especially in urban areas, and it occupies a plot roughly 20 x 30 ft (6 x 9 m). No fixed object – a tree or building, for example – should be closer than twice its own height, but nor should the site be over-exposed, as on a cliff-top or the summit of a hill. A fully equipped station will record the

WEATHER IN THE WILDS
In the foreground (above) a Stevenson screen contains equipment to measure temperature and humidity. In the Canadian Arctic (right), a meteorologist defrosts his sunshine recorder by pouring alcohol on the glass sphere.

temperature and humidity of the air, the temperature on the surface of the ground and at varying depths in the soil, rainfall amount and duration, sunshine duration, and also wind speed and direction. The observer will also make additional notes, describing, for example, rain, snow, fog and thunder, the state of the ground (whether dry, damp, wet or frozen) and the depth and character of any snow-cover.

The thermometers measuring the air temperature are housed in a white box with louvred walls and a ventilated floor and

INSIDE THE SCREEN
Thermometers inside a Stevenson screen record maximum and minimum temperatures and humidity.

roof, known as a Stevenson screen. This box keeps the thermometers sheltered from the weather, screened from direct sunlight or from radiation reflected from the ground, and yet also allows free movement of air into and out of the interior. It was designed around 1868 by the Scottish engineer Thomas Stevenson, father of the author Robert Louis Stevenson.

Inside the Stevenson screen, along with the thermometers, there may also be a thermograph and a hygrograph. These are instruments designed to provide a continuous record of temperature and humidity through a specified period – usually a week – so that the timing of maximum and minimum temperatures and of any sudden changes can be ascertained. A similar device records the timing and level of rainfall.

SHAPES ABOVE US *Altocumulus clouds (left) are at their most striking when the rising or setting Sun illuminates their undersides. Smooth-edged, lens-shaped altocumulus lenticularis (above) forms over South Georgia in the South Atlantic. An isolated lenticular cloud has formed (opposite) over the Three Sisters range in Oregon, USA. Such cloud formations are sometimes mistaken for UFOs.*

the turrets of a castle, appropriately dubbed 'castellanus'; others that are roughly the shape of an almond or a lens, which are called 'lenticularis'; and clouds that gather in little groups of woolly tufts which are described as 'floccus'.

Altocumulus clouds sometimes form directly in clear air. They can also occur at different levels in the same patch of sky and are often associated with clouds of other types. Most altocumulus clouds have their base between 8000 and 16000 ft (2400 and 4900 m) above ground. They are normally white or light grey.

Altostratus is much thicker and greyer. It does not always produce precipitation, but often heralds rain or snow. It is frequently found, for example, in the sequence of clouds that gradually get lower and thicker as a warm front approaches. Altostratus very often covers the whole sky, and may in fact cover an area of several thousand square miles. If gaps and rifts appear, they are irregularly shaped and spaced.

Altostratus tends to spread vertically as well as horizontally, and within this spread the cloud particles are widely enough dispersed not to obscure the Sun – altostratus

is the sort of cloud through which a 'watery Sun' is seen. Rain, snow and even ice pellets are present in altostratus and sometimes fall as precipitation, though this may not actually reach the ground, making the base of the cloud indistinct. When precipitation does reach the ground it is usually very light and continuous.

Nimbostratus, the chief rain-producing cloud, is a layer cloud. It is essentially a thicker and lower version of altostratus, and although it is classed as a medium-level cloud, its base may be found anywhere from about 1000 ft (300 m) above the ground to 10 000 ft (3000 m). Grey coloured and often dark, nimbostratus is made diffuse by more or less continuously falling rain, sleet and snow. In most cases the precipitation reaches the ground, but not necessarily. Nimbostratus spreads widely both outwards and

DEGREES FAHRENHEIT AND DEGREES CELSIUS

Daniel Gabriel Fahrenheit was of German extraction, born in 1686 in the free Polish city of Danzig (now Gdansk), and he conducted most of his work as a physicist in the Netherlands. He probably produced the scale that bears his name following discussions with the Danish mathematician Olaf Romer around 1709. In its original form it had three fixed points: 0°, which he specified as the temperature of a mixture of ice, water and ammonium chloride; 32° which was the temperature of a mixture of ice and water; and 96°, the temperature of a healthy person's armpit. This scale rapidly gained popularity in northern Europe, and Fahrenheit was elected to the British Royal Society.

Anders Celsius was a Swedish physicist and astronomer who published a scientific paper in 1742 in which he described a thermometer with freezing point at 100° degrees and boiling point at 0°. This was not, in fact, the first 'centigrade' or 'centesimal' scale to be used in Europe. As a young scientist Celsius

DECEPTIVE FAME *Anders Celsius (1701-44) is famous for a temperature scale he did not, in fact, invent.*

would almost certainly have used thermometers devised by his compatriot, Palmburg. Palmburg's scale had 0° as the temperature of the coldest day of the year and 100° as the temperature of the hottest day. It was more in line with modern thermometers in having 0° as its

cold point and 100° as its hot one.

There is evidence that a French scientist, Jean-Pierre Christin, independently developed the present centigrade scale around 1740 or just after. This has the freezing and boiling points of water as its fixed points, as in Celsius's scale, but with 0° at freezing point and 100° at boiling point. However, the scale was officially named after Celsius, rather than Christin, in 1948.

Christin was, it seems, a modest man who also lived in the shadow of his much more famous countryman René-Antoine Ferchault de Réaumur. He had invented his own scale with freezing point at 0° and boiling point

at 80° in 1730. Christin found it difficult to publish his work and his much more celebrated compatriot is also believed to have discouraged competition. Réaumur's scale never became popular outside France, however, although to this day many French household thermometers are marked in degrees R as well as degrees C.

RISE AND FALL *The constriction just above a thermometer's bulb allows the mercury to rise, but prevents it from immediately returning into the bulb when the temperature falls.*

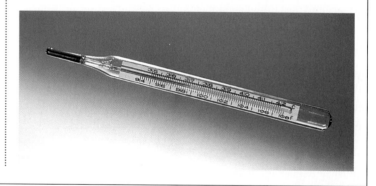

---

upwards through the atmosphere. These clouds are very dense and may be many thousands of feet thick, so that the Sun cannot be seen through them.

TOP-FLIGHT CLOUDS

High clouds, which include cirrus, cirrocumulus and cirrostratus, are ice-crystal clouds. They are nearly always fair-weather clouds, although certain types of cirrus and cirrostratus sometimes herald the approach of a depression or front, appearing several hundred miles in advance of the weather system.

MARES' TAILS *Tufts of cirrus cloud, consisting of tiny ice crystals, are sometimes called 'mares' tails'. These clouds form 5-6 miles (8-10 km) above the Earth's surface, and are normally associated with fine, settled weather.*

They are often so tenuous that the Sun shines through with little loss of power; the blue of the sky is diminished rather than obscured.

Cirrus comes from the Latin for 'thread' – a characteristic, in fact, of most ice-crystal clouds. It takes the form of delicate white filaments, white (or mostly white) patches or narrow bands. The clouds are fibrous in appearance and have a silky sheen. Sometimes, wind patterns at cloud level cause the trails to be slanted or curved or hooked in shape.

Cirrostratus appears as a whitish veil, usually fibrous but sometimes smooth, which may totally cover the sky. The Sun seen through this veil often appears with a halo. Sometimes cirrostratus cloud appears to be banded, with thinner veils of cloud between the bands. The edge of a veil of cirrostratus may be straight and clear-cut, but more often it is irregular and fringed with cirrus. It may occasionally be so thin and transparent that it is nearly indiscernible, especially through haze or at night. At such times, the existence of a halo may be the only revealing feature. When the Sun is high, cirrostratus never prevents objects from casting shadows.

Cirrocumulus is probably the rarest of all the main cloud types, and arguably the most beautiful of them. It consists of tiny delicate cloud particles which form close together, rather like the scales of a fish – hence its popular name, 'mackerel sky'.

RISING AIR *Many clouds develop when rising air currents result in large-scale condensation of water droplets. The upward thrust may be triggered in a number of ways. Here, above Jasper National Park, Alberta, an otherwise clear air mass is forced to rise over the Rocky Mountains.*

DRIZZLE, DOWNPOURS AND DELUGES

Nobody enjoys getting caught in a downpour, or finding his home or street flooded. But we do need rain to grow food, to provide drinking and bathing water, and to keep our gardens green. Rain nourishes the land and keeps us alive.

Of the various elements that make up the weather, rain is easily the most important. Our supply of water for drinking and bathing depends on rain. So does water for industrial and leisure activities and for raising crops and livestock. In areas where rainfall is not sufficient for crops to be grown or animals to be reared, water may be 'imported' by irrigation; for instance, it can be brought from wet mountainous areas to the dry plains – as long as the rains in the mountains do not fail.

Even in places where rain normally falls regularly, in Britain or Ireland, for example, or along the eastern seaboard of the USA, a dry summer brings problems. Springs and wells fail; reservoirs dry out. The usually green countryside turns brown, and the supply of water to every home – taken for granted for most of the time –

may be rationed. In lands where seasonal rains are the norm, such as India and China and the Sahel region of Africa, a delay or a false start to the rainy season will seriously affect the amount and quality of the food grown. A failure of the rains may lead to famine.

RAIN AT SEA *A cumulus cloud seen from the Seychelles produces a shower, which shows up as a diffuse greyish curtain beneath the cloud.*

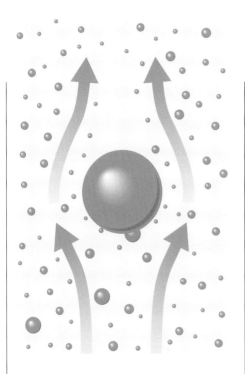

Much more rain than normal is also unwelcome, washing away crops, damaging property and causing disruption in urban areas. Flooded rivers may burst their banks, drowning livestock and making farmland unusable for months. In wealthy countries such events are rarely catastrophic, but in those where farmers can produce little more than they consume and where stocks of food for the population as a whole may be insufficient, the consequence will again be famine.

WHERE RAIN COMES FROM

Rain always falls from clouds, but not all clouds produce rain. Some banks of cloud may last for days on end without releasing a speck of drizzle, while others may cause a torrential downpour within a couple of hours of first appearing. Particular atmospheric conditions are needed for ordinary clouds to grow into rain-making clouds. These trigger the processes by which tiny cloud particles grow into drops big enough and heavy enough to fall to the ground.

Broadly speaking, ascending air within the cloud is what distinguishes a cloud that

FAIR WEATHER *These cumulus clouds near Flagstaff, Arizona, are of very limited vertical extent and well broken up. They are therefore unlikely to produce precipitation.*

EVER BIGGER *A large raindrop is heavy enough to fall through a gently rising air current. As it falls, it captures tiny cloud droplets on its forward side and grows bigger and bigger.*

produces rain from one that does not. All clouds are formed by rising air. Air cools as it rises, and cooler air holds less moisture than warm air. Eventually, some of the moisture condenses as minute water droplets to create clouds. These droplets, which are still much smaller than raindrops, grow on even tinier particles of dust, soot, salt and pollen – microscopic grains of matter called 'condensation nuclei'. If our atmosphere were totally pure, life on Earth would be very different – probably intolerable to humans – because there would be no clouds and therefore no rain or snow.

There are two principal ways by which these cloud particles grow into drizzle droplets and ultimately into raindrops that are heavy enough to fall to Earth. One, the

'coalescence process', involves minute droplets coalescing to form larger ones that eventually become full-sized raindrops. Since it can happen in clouds with no ice, it generates most of the rain that falls in the tropics.

In any particular cloud there are a range of droplet sizes, probably due to the different sizes and characteristics of the condensation nuclei. Where the rising air currents are particularly strong, as they are in cumulus or cumulonimbus clouds, the droplets are carried farther and farther upwards. The larger ones, however – and even these ones are minute, measuring up to $1/250$ in (0.1 mm) in diameter – are carried upwards more slowly than the smaller ones. This will result in collisions between water particles. Sometimes a larger droplet will fracture on collision into millions of tiny ones; sometimes, on the other hand, two drops will coalesce.

This process is more efficient the higher the cloud rises, and the stronger the updraughts are. When the bigger droplets finally reach the top of the cloud, they will

no longer be supported by the rising air current and will therefore fall back through the cloud, growing further as they continue to collide with smaller water particles. Eventually, they will fall out of the base of the cloud and reach the ground as rain. It is a somewhat laborious process, since thousands of individual collisions are needed to create even one full-sized raindrop.

RAIN FROM ICE CRYSTALS

The other way by which cloud particles develop into raindrops is known as the 'ice-crystal process' – or the 'Bergeron-Findeison process' after the Swedish and German meteorologists who first described its workings. It is characteristic of temperate and polar latitudes. Here, most clouds contain ice crystals as well as supercooled water droplets. It is the ice crystals that form the basis of raindrops.

At any given temperature, water droplets evaporate more easily than ice crystals. When supercooled water droplets and ice crystals exist together in a cloud, moisture evaporating from the water droplets condenses on the ice particles, causing them to

SKY HIGH These cirrus clouds over Great Sand Dunes National Monument, Colorado, are roughly 6 miles (10 km) above the ground.

ICE ACTION A large cumulus cloud starts life comprised mostly of water droplets with just a few ice crystals in its upper reaches. As time passes, ice crystals grow further by absorbing water vapour from adjacent cloud droplets. Eventually snowflakes are the main component of the cloud.

grow rapidly. The net effect of this process is that the ice crystals grow at the expense of the water droplets.

The larger ice crystals coalesce with smaller ice crystals to form snowflakes. These continue to grow until they become too heavy to be held up by the updraught, and they fall through the cloud. When the snowflake reaches the lower part of the cloud, where the temperature may be above freezing point, it begins to melt, and it is at this point that falling snow particles are most likely to stick together to form giant snowflakes. If, as it continues to fall, the snowflake passes through warmer air, it melts and falls to Earth as rain – if not, it falls as snow.

Drizzle, meanwhile, occurs when the rising air currents are sluggish, or even non-existent, and the rain-making processes become weak and inefficient. Water droplets take a long time to grow into full-sized raindrops. Limited upward movement in a

cloud means that the water droplets remain small but are able to fall through the cloud. In a cloud with negligible upward air movement, raindrops as small as $1/250$ in (0.1 mm) in diameter are just heavy enough to fall to the ground.

GIVING UPLIFT TO THE AIR

The rising air currents that create rain clouds are given their upward impetus in different ways. One, known as 'convection', happens when a cool air mass is warmed at the surface of the Earth, either because the ground is heated by bright sunshine (heating, in turn, the air above it) or when a polar air stream flows across a warm ocean. Pockets or bubbles of warm air become buoyant, developing into updraughts or

Ice crystals

Ice crystals only in the upper reaches

Water droplets

Ice crystals grow

Cloud mostly composed of ice crystals

thermals. The rising air cools and the moisture in it condenses to build large cumulus and eventually cumulonimbus clouds. These produce sudden heavy downpours and sometimes thunderstorms.

The rainstorms produced by convection tend to be short-lived, however. When heavy rain falls, the supply of warm air feeding the cloud is cut off. At the same time, the falling rain drags cool, moist air downwards from the interior of the cloud. As a result, the shower cloud dies quickly.

Convective clouds often form a patchwork over areas of land that have been warmed by the Sun, and result in a mixture of sunshine and showers. On other occasions, the convection is concentrated into a narrow but more-or-less continuous band, known as a squall line, which usually moves ahead of an advancing cold front.

'Orographic uplift' is the technical name given to the flow of air over a mountain range. Even a relatively small mountainous area such as Scotland or New Zealand's South Island is too large for an air stream to be diverted around it, so air is forced upwards, over the mountains. Water vapour in the air is condensed into clouds over a wide area above the mountains and for a considerable distance upwards into the atmosphere. Occasionally, the orographic effect acts alone, and rain falls over the mountain range and nowhere else, but more often it combines with other rain-producing mechanisms such as convection. It thus

RAIN AND MORE RAIN Moist air from the ocean forms an 'orographic cloud' which hugs the mountain tops. Rain falling from higher-level clouds becomes heavier as it falls through the orographic cloud.

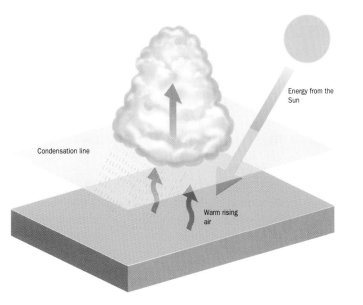

Condensation line

Energy from the Sun

Warm rising air

has the effect of increasing the amount of rainfall in mountainous regions, and this contribution can be huge. For example, at Caernarvon in north-west Wales the average annual rainfall is 40 in (1000 mm), while on the slopes of Mount Snowdon, just 10 miles (16 km) away the average annual figure is almost 170 in (over 4300 mm). On Snowdon, the effects of orographic lift operate in combination with all other major rain-making processes.

SUN AND RAIN Convection currents sometimes make a fair-weather cloud become a rain cloud. Strong sunshine warms the ground which warms the air above it. Warm air rises, creating a convection current and clouds are formed above the condensation level.

'Dynamic rain' is the scientific name given to the rain that falls in association with warm fronts, cold fronts and occluded fronts. These weather fronts mark the boundaries between huge masses of air of sharply differing characteristics, with the warmer air masses forced to rise above the colder ones, creating extensive banks of layered cloud, called altostratus and nimbostratus, extending over hundreds and sometimes thousands of miles. Where the air is being forced upwards continuously at an active boundary between air masses, the result is prolonged, steady rain over a wide area.

When an active front crosses a mountain range, the frontal and the orographic processes join forces, and together produce

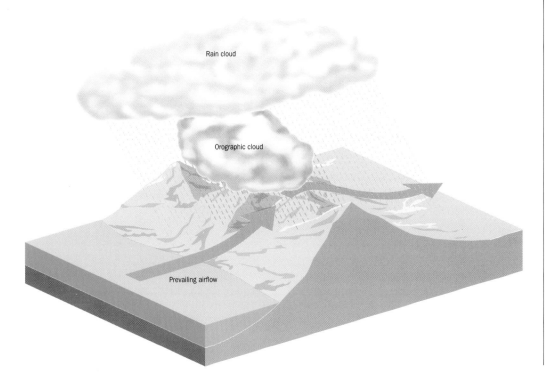

Rain cloud

Orographic cloud

Prevailing airflow

the heaviest falls of rain found in middle latitudes. Steady rain falls from the frontal cloud-mass through the orographic clouds, which cling to the windward slopes of the mountains. The falling raindrops coalesce with the orographic cloud particles, and so increase the intensity of the rain. In effect, the frontal cloud 'seeds' the orographic cloud and 'feeds' on the cloud droplets: the combined effect is therefore sometimes referred to as the 'seeder-feeder mechanism'. Long-lasting downpours occurring as a result of this combination are well known in mountainous areas across the world such as Scotland and Wales; British Columbia, Washington and Oregon; the Chilean Andes and the Southern Alps in New Zealand.

INESCAPABLE CLOUDS *Even on a fine, sunny morning in Wales, rain clouds cling to the slopes of Mount Snowdon. There is, on average, over four times as much rain near the summit of Snowdon than there is in the nearby town of Caernarvon.*

WHERE DOES IT RAIN?

Rain does not necessarily fall where humidity levels (levels of water vapour in the air) are persistently high. The lands bordering The Arabian Gulf and the Red Sea are among the most humid areas on Earth, but they receive very little rainfall. The pattern of air circulation caused by the rotation of the Earth means that warm air rising at the Equator sinks across subtropical latitudes where the Sahara, Arabian and other deserts are found, producing predominantly descending, dry, warm air in these regions. The same conditions occur along the coastal fringe of the Namib Desert. The rainy parts of the world are those where the various rain-making processes are most active, and the wettest of all are those where the different mechanisms join forces.

Regions where most rainfall is convective include the equatorial zone, affecting countries such as Brazil, the Democratic Republic of Congo (formerly Zaire), and Singapore. The limited rain that falls in deserts is usually convective, although the mountainous desert areas on the Arabian peninsula do receive some orographic rainfall. Summer rains in middle-latitude continental interiors, such as those of central North America and central Europe, are similarly convective; air masses of polar origin are warmed from beneath as they flow across sun-heated land.

Orographic rain is, of course, found in virtually all mountainous areas on the planet, but it is most prominent where the prevailing westerly winds of temperate latitudes meet a mountain barrier running north-south. Such areas include the Coastal and Cascade ranges of the western Rockies in Canada and the USA and the mountains of Norway and western Britain. Orographic

ARTIFICIAL RAIN-MAKING

In regions of the world with low or unreliable rainfall, people have for centuries tried to 'make' rain. The ancient Chinese fired cannons into clouds in an attempt to bring down the rain. More recently, especially in the USA, attempts have been made to 'seed' clouds – that is, to sow or sprinkle them with particles that will act as condensation nuclei, 'jump starting' the rain-making process.

The most suitable clouds to seed – fairly deep, extending above the level in the atmosphere at which the temperature drops below freezing point, and consisting solely of water droplets – are found in tropical regions. Such clouds are not big enough for the coalescence process to develop properly, nor do they have the freezing nuclei required for the ice-crystal process to get under way.

The best method would be to seed the clouds with ice crystals, but it is not feasible to carry enough water ice in an aircraft. The next best thing is to cool the air in the upper part of the

RAINMAKER *When the aircraft enters the cloud it will release a solution of silver iodide to trigger the rain-making process.*

cloud so that ice crystals will form by themselves. This can be done by releasing particles of dry ice (solid carbon dioxide) above the cloud. Other experiments have attempted to

deceive the water droplets into acting as though ice crystals were present by seeding the cloud with grains of silver iodide – a chemical with a structure similar to that of ice crystals.

It is difficult to establish how successful these methods are, because it is impossible to know how much rain would have fallen from the cloud if it had not been seeded.

years for 1 mile of water (or 45 years for 1 km of water) to fall upon that particular place.

The Hawaiian islands have the place on the planet where it rains more regularly than anywhere else. On the island of Kauai, the summit of Mount Wai'ale'ale records rain on an average of 335 days per year and the average annual rainfall amounts to 450 in (11 430 mm). The yearly rainfall average at sea level on Kauai is just under 20 in (500 mm), illustrating the effect of orographic rainfall on the mountain summit.

FLOODS AND DROUGHTS

Too much rain causes a flood; too little creates a drought. In their mildest forms, both flood and drought are no more than an inconvenience. Droughts may bring a temporary increase in the price of foodstuffs and domestic water supply may be rationed. After floods, cellars may need to be bailed out, and local transport systems may be disrupted. At their most extreme, floods and

rains also fall where monsoon winds meet high ground, such as the Western Ghats near the Indian west coast, the Khasi hills of Assam, the mountainous interiors of Sumatra, Java and Papua New Guinea, and the hills of north-eastern Queensland.

Dynamic rains fall where mid-latitude depressions and their associated fronts occur most frequently, especially where they make landfall after crossing vast tracts of warm ocean. These areas include much of western, central and northern Europe; the Pacific seaboard of North America from the Alaskan panhandle southwards to northern California; the southern half of Chile; Tasmania; and South Island in New Zealand.

The wettest place on Earth (for which regular rainfall records are available) is Cherrapunji on the southern flank of the Khasi hills in Assam. Here, the very heavy

seasonal convective rains of the Indian monsoon are made still heavier by the orographic effect. The funnelling of air currents up deeply incised valleys intensifies them still further. In the monsoon season of 1861, a colossal 884 in (22 453 mm) of rain was recorded in the six months from April to September. At that rate, and allowing for a dry season every year between October and March, it would only take just over 70

UNDER A CLOUD *Regular rainfall on Mount Wai'ale'ale, Hawaii, produces thick forests and teeming waterfalls. Rain falls more regularly here than anywhere else on Earth.*

droughts are probably more catastrophic than any other natural phenomena, bringing massive loss of life and the devastation of vast tracts of farming land.

PREDICTING A DISASTER

Since the 1970s, flood-warning schemes have been used in many Third World countries, as well as most wealthier ones, as a result of scientific and technical advances.

In the United Kingdom, most rivers are short, which means that floods develop in a very short time after heavy downpours. Such floods can be highly destructive to life and property in heavily populated river–drainage areas. To counter this problem, a network of rainfall radars was built during the 1980s and early 1990s, allowing predictions of rainfall over 15 minute periods. These predictions are fed into complex computer models that work out how the rivers and streams will respond to rain, and flood warnings are issued over public broadcast systems when required. Other early-warning schemes exist around the world. Indeed, there are now hundreds of men and women whose jobs are to monitor the weather in order to predict potential disasters. If a major rainstorm develops, or a hurricane appears on the horizon, they move into action, giving the earliest possible warning.

The effectiveness of a good warning scheme can be seen in the statistics – for example, those for deaths caused by hurricanes in the USA. Hurricane warnings have been issued routinely for many decades, improved by aircraft reconnaissance in the 1940s and 1950s, by the advent of satellite pictures from the

IMMINENT ARRIVAL *Men board up a restaurant in San Juan, Puerto Rico, to protect it against Hurricane Luis.*

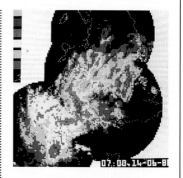

RAIN PATTERN *A radar display shows the intensity of a storm, ranging from dark blue for light rain to pale blue and white for very heavy rain.*

1960s and by the huge improvement in the accuracy of forecasts in the 1980s and 1990s. Before warnings were available, the Galveston hurricane of September 1900 drowned an estimated 10 000 people, and two hurricanes in 1893 were responsible for the loss of almost 4000 lives in Louisiana and South Carolina. By contrast, two of the worst hurricanes of recent decades, Hugo in September 1989 and Andrew in August 1992, resulted in five and twelve deaths respectively.

narrow canyon into the city. Within two hours 237 people had died and $164 million damage was done.

Similar floods can occur in any narrow valley after heavy or prolonged downpours. The Johnstown flood of May 30, 1889, was one such, made worse by the collapse of an old reservoir dam in the Conemaugh Valley above the town. Some 2100 residents of the small Pennsylvania town were drowned. Probably the worst British disaster of this type was the Lynmouth flood of August 15, 1952, when a raging torrent of water and rocks pounded through the north Devon resort, after a 10 in (250 mm) downpour over the hills of neighbouring Exmoor. Thirty-four people were killed.

By contrast, widespread and prolonged rain occurring over most or all of a large river drainage area causes a 'slow-active' flood, as water from the river's headwaters and tributaries gradually travels downstream to the main river artery. Such floods are often worst where two major arteries converge in a broad plain, especially where the river level is naturally higher than the land on either side, which is normally protected by dykes or levees.

Medium-sized rivers, such as the Thames and Severn in the UK, carry their floodwaters out to sea within five or six days, but a larger river system such as the Rhine can take up to two weeks to go through a flood cycle. This happened in January and February 1995. The Rhine flooded Cologne in Germany and other areas upstream, and millions of Dutch people had to wait for 12 days before the threat of catastrophic flooding in their country passed. The dykes held – but only just.

Major river systems such as the Mississippi-Missouri, the Nile and the Chang Jiang can be in flood for a whole season, especially if

---

Prolonged drought, meanwhile, perhaps lasting several years, hits lands bordering deserts, such as sub-Saharan Africa, worst, bringing extensive famine. In the Sahel – the region south of the Sahara stretching from Senegal to Sudan – the droughts of 1972 to 1975 and 1982 to 1985 each led to between a quarter and half a million deaths. The Indian drought and famine of 1965 to 1967, when the monsoon rains failed in two consecutive years, is thought to have resulted in the loss of 1.5 million lives in the subcontinent.

A flood happens when water invades a land area. It may be the result of torrential rain, either localised or covering a wide area, or it may be caused by a river bursting its banks or the sea breaching coastal defences. The flood may be sudden, short-lived and localised, as in a flash flood, or it may be gradual, protracted and widespread, as in the Mississippi floods of the spring and summer of 1993.

A true flash flood typically occurs in a desert area when a cloudburst above one part of a valley results in a wall of water and debris sweeping down the valley, destroying everything in its path. The flood arrives 'in a flash', often with no warning because no rain has fallen in the lower part of the valley. Destruction can be total and almost instantaneous. If a town or village lies in the lower part of the valley, hundreds of people may die, as happened in Rapid City, on the edge of the Black Hills in South Dakota, on June 9, 1972. No significant rain fell in the city, but a massive thunderstorm over the upper part of the Rapid Creek catchment area deposited 15 in (380 mm) of rain in five hours. A huge flood swept through a

DELAYED REACTION *Khartoum endured two months of flooding in 1988, following very heavy rains over the headwaters of the Blue Nile some months earlier.*

heavy rain recurs. The Khartoum flood of 1988 lasted for some two months, bringing great misery to a million inhabitants of the desert city. The River Nile burst its banks in the Sudanese capital where its major tributaries, the White Nile and the Blue Nile, converge. The flood followed exceptionally heavy spring rains over the headwaters of the Blue Nile in the Ethiopian mountains. Water levels in the White Nile, which rises in the mountains of central Africa, were around normal, but the convergence of the two streams was sufficient to trigger the flood.

Melting snow can add large quantities of meltwater to an already flooded river – for example the Rhine in 1926 and 1995, the Ohio in March 1913 and the Thames in March 1947 – turning an average flood into an historic one.

THREAT FROM THE SEA

Sea floods can be caused by a combination of naturally high (spring) tides, a storm surge and big waves. The storm surge results from high winds piling up water along a coastline, especially in a funnel-shaped sea area and especially where the sea is shallow. These high winds also create huge waves. The surge may be accentuated by a local rise in sea level caused by low air pressure – the strong winds are often associated with an area of exceptionally low pressure.

The flooding can be quite catastrophic where the coastal areas are extensive low-lying plains, perhaps reclaimed from the sea over many centuries and protected by hundreds of miles of sea defences. Areas at risk include those around the North Sea, the Gulf of Lyons in south-east France, the

DESERT FLOOD *The Kuiseb River, Namibia, in flood following a rare torrential downpour in the heart of the Kalahari Desert. For much of the time it is a dry watercourse, but in conditions like these water may flow for up to 100 miles (160 km) reaching the sea at Walvis Bay.*

Gulf of Gascony in south-west France, the northern Adriatic especially around Venice and, in the USA, Long Island Sound and Chesapeake Bay. Storm surges brought on by hurricanes or typhoons can lead to dramatic floods around the Gulf of Mexico coastline of the USA and Mexico, and above all at the top end of the Bay of Bengal, where Bangladesh and the adjacent parts of India are the most frequently flooded parts of the world.

Protection against such floods is not always as simple an issue as might at first appear. In economic terms, the decision whether or not to provide or maintain flood defences involves balancing the costs

of building and upkeep against the cost to the local and national economy of allowing floods to continue.

Clearly, for the Dutch, keeping the sea at bay is part of the national tradition. Maintaining the dykes that protect the thousands of square miles of land reclaimed from the North Sea in the Netherlands is something its government is bound to do for the foreseeable future. But many experts now think that some protection schemes are a false economy, especially along major rivers where the watercourse may have been artificially straightened out and channelled between built-up banks. Such measures simply increase the threat

THE BENEFITS OF AN UMBRELLA

When a few people first used umbrellas to protect themselves from the rain, they were subjected to ridicule. As sunshades, however, umbrella-like devices have a long history. In the East, the parasol has been used for centuries. In medieval times, similar inventions were used in Mediterranean countries, mainly by women, against the overpowering rays of the Sun. Indeed, the English word 'umbrella' is of Italian origin, meaning 'little shade'. By the 17th century, the parasol was

known among royal and aristocratic women in Britain, and it is possible that some found it a useful protection against sudden and unexpected summer downpours.

Among the first men to venture into the streets of London carrying umbrellas – of their own devising – were John 'Beau' Macdonald and Jonas Hanway, in 1778. They used their contraptions to shield their dandified costumes against the rain, and both were the subject of much ribaldry. Under this pressure Hanway soon gave up, but Macdonald persevered, much to the annoyance of coach-drivers, who considered his device a threat to their livelihood.

Yet the umbrella soon proved its worth to those who saw the two men sporting their shelters in a rainstorm, and despite the initial mockery, the idea caught on. Within five years, umbrellas were common

PORTABLE SHELTER *Jonas Hanway's novel way of keeping dry quickly caught on among Londoners.*

THE RAIN IT RAINETH EVERY DAY *By Victorian times, the umbrella had become an indispensable item for a day at an English seaside resort.*

in London, and by the end of the 18th century they were widely used throughout the kingdom.

From the 1790s onwards, many inventors took out patents on different versions of the umbrella, most of which were aimed at reducing its weight. Until then, the average umbrella weighed almost

11 lb (5 kg), and was difficult to keep erect for any length of time by any but the strongest. By the 1830s most of them were under 2 lb (roughly 1 kg), and in the early 1850s a man named Samuel Fox designed one with hollow steel tubes, combining strength with lightness. The unofficial historian of the umbrella, R.E. Jerome, writes that Fox's invention, called the 'Paragon', brought him some £300 000 in royalties, a substantial sum at that time. As Jerome notes: 'Presumably he put it aside for a rainy day!'

---

of flooding in lower parts of a river's course. This happens in Köln, where the natural flood plains of the river have been built on. Such schemes can cause more damaging floods than previously because the river has nowhere to expand into at times of flood.

Man-made protection may also create a sense of security, which encourages local government authorities to grant planning permission for houses and factories to be built in the flood plain. This in turn leads to a demand for better and more complete protection. In a number of countries, local planning regulations have been abandoned altogether, or are regularly ignored by speculators, but that does not stop the new residents in a flood-prone region from seeking as much protection as they can get.

THIRSTY TIMES

Drought is simply a shortage of water – for crops, animals and humans. The normal supplies of water affected by a drought may come directly from rainfall or from rivers or ground water by means of pumps and wells.

Deserts can be described as areas of permanent drought, but a shortage of water has its greatest impact in other areas – ones that normally receive adequate supplies. Even advanced economies may suffer. They are tailored to the extensive use of available water, so in these countries even a modest reduction in supply over a period of just a few months can have a noticeable impact on industry, agriculture and people's normal

COASTAL PROTECTION *Sea defences along the Namibian coast at Oranjemund protect diamond mines from the heavy Atlantic surf. This coastline is very exposed to the west and south-west and 5000 miles (8000 km) of open ocean can build up a 20 ft (6 m) high swell.*

way of living – which often includes the abundant use of, for example, washing machines and garden hoses.

A chronic shortage of rainfall leads to aridity, and this occurs whenever the natural loss of water by evaporation and transpiration (the process by which moisture moves from the soil through plants into the air) exceeds the natural supply of water to a region in the form of rain. In this situation, there is not enough moisture for most vegetation to survive, although some types of plant are particularly adapted to surviving in rainless climates. Some simply require very little moisture to continue growing, while others lie dormant between rare falls of rain. In some places, aridity is a normal part of life, happening on an annual or seasonal basis. Crops have to be planted so that important periods of their growth happen during the wetter seasons. Irrigation, too, is usually essential.

The effects of drought make themselves felt at different rates. Crops will suffer first (unless irrigation is available), but in due course the water level in the local well will also suffer. Equally, renewed rain will freshen up the face of the countryside almost immediately, but it may take 12 months or more to replenish the aquifers (water-bearing strata below the ground) which the wells tap into.

In some parts of the world, it is the failure or reduction of seasonal rains that causes drought. The impact of this is particularly serious in heavily populated areas, such as China and India, or in semidesert regions such as the Sahel, all of which depend heavily for their water supply on regular rainy seasons. The economies of countries as different as Zimbabwe, South Africa, Australia, Spain, Portugal and the USA have also suffered in recent years when seasonal rains failed over an extended period of time.

In the zone of regular travelling weather systems – the mid-latitude westerlies – rain usually occurs at frequent intervals, albeit in quite small amounts in some areas. But occasionally the sequence of systems is halted by a 'blocking anticyclone'. This is a large, slow-moving, high-pressure system that may dominate a sizable area for weeks on end. As its name suggests, it blocks the normal progress of rain-bearing depressions and fronts.

Descending air currents are a defining feature of anticyclones. As a result, rainclouds dissipate and precipitation is minimal. The drying-out process is accelerated by excessive sunshine and low humidity. When blocking patterns recur during a succession of seasons, a serious drought will ensue, as occurred during 1975 and 1976 over a large tract of northern, central and western Europe, including the British Isles.

DRYING UP *At Haweswater Reservoir, north-west England, normally submerged roads and walls were exposed during the 1995-6 drought.*

SNOWSTORMS AND ICE FLOES

Snow crystals viewed through a microscope are among the most beautiful things in nature. Moreover, no two crystals are the same. Put several trillion of them together and you get a blizzard that can disrupt the lives of millions of people.

Few people who grew up in countries where snow is a relatively infrequent visitor forget the childhood sensation of waking up on a snowy morning. A strong white light filters through the curtains, even though the sky is grey. The usual traffic noises from the road outside are muffled or absent. The whoops and shrieks of playing children penetrate the unnatural silence. Drawing the curtains, the familiar views are transformed by a uniform mantle of white, and the heart leaps at the thought of a journey to school through a winter wonderland. Adulthood, of course, brings the realities of transport dislocation, heating bills and rheumatic joints, but some grown-ups keep a corner of their hearts where excitement at the sight of freshly fallen snow continues to thrive.

In some parts of the world, such as the Arctic, Antarctic and high mountain areas, snow and ice form the natural environment.

In the Arctic, its importance in the lives of the Inuit (Eskimo) people is illustrated by the large number of words – more than 40 – they have for different kinds of snow. Over large parts of the northern continents – across Canada and the northern parts of the USA, in Scandinavia and northern Russia and across Siberia, Mongolia and northern China – snow is a regular seasonal visitor. To people here, the excitement felt at the sight of snow by the citizens of more temperate climes would seem decidedly odd. In countries where it falls frequently and regularly, it is usually coped with adequately, though rarely welcomed, except where a winter-sports industry has developed.

In some parts of the world, by contrast, snow is so rare that it comes to many people as a surprise, even when successfully forecast. Downtown Los Angeles came to a halt on January 15, 1932, when almost 1 in (2.5 cm) of wet snow accumulated on the sidewalks. Residents of Miami remember the 'Great Snow of '77' when a trifling amount of slush collected on the ground for an hour or so. Snow fell heavily on the Saudi Arabian capital of Riyadh on January 2, 1973, for the first time in 30 years. The inhabitants stared

SNOW TRACERY
A snowstorm rages in Minneapolis, USA, piling up in drifts and bringing the transport system to a halt.

ONE-TIME WONDERS: SNOWFLAKES

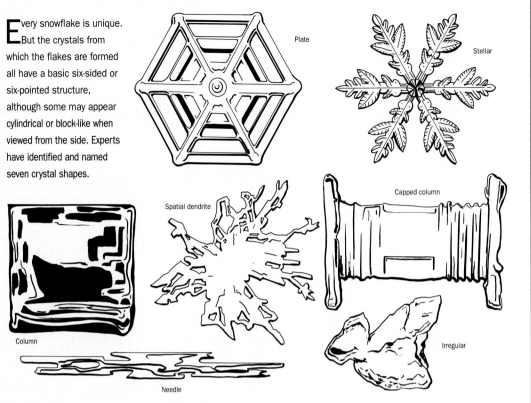

Every snowflake is unique. But the crystals from which the flakes are formed all have a basic six-sided or six-pointed structure, although some may appear cylindrical or block-like when viewed from the side. Experts have identified and named seven crystal shapes.

Plate

Stellar

Spatial dendrite

Capped column

Column

Irregular

Needle

wide-eyed and open-mouthed at something many had never seen before, and were unlikely to see again.

WHAT CAUSES SNOW?

Snow forms in a similar fashion to rain. Ice crystals grow in clouds, especially where there are rising air currents, until the snowflakes are large and heavy enough to fall through the cloud. If their entire journey is through air colder than about –15°C (5°F), the ice crystals contain a negligible amount of water and rarely stick together. Under these conditions, the snow falls as a fine dust known as 'spicules' – from the Latin *spica*, 'point'. But a journey through air with a temperature close to 0°C (32°F) may result in a partial melting of the crystals, which then bond together easily to form large snowflakes. Under special conditions, especially when there is no air movement, giant snowflakes up to 4 in (10 cm) across may form.

Precipitation in these temperatures does not necessarily fall as snow, however. It can take any of a variety of forms, especially if, on its journey from cloud to ground, it passes through contrasting layers of air where the temperature is alternately above freezing and below freezing. This happens, for example, when cold polar or continental air meets warmer air from tropical regions. Such conditions occur from time to time in north-west Europe, including the British Isles; in New England and the mid-Atlantic states of America; in the Pacific north-west of the U.S. and British Columbia, Canada, and in northern Japan.

In these circumstances, weather forecasters have a problem predicting what will fall from the skies. Having decided that some sort of precipitation is likely in the first place, they have to choose between rain, drizzle, sleet, snow, freezing rain and freezing drizzle. (Confusingly, sleet is defined in Britain as a mixture of rain and snow, or a fall of partly melted snow, whereas in the USA it is the name given to frozen raindrops, those that have fallen through cold air near the ground and refrozen.) There are also some more exotic forms of solid precipitation that appear from time to time, including ice pellets, soft hail, snow grains and ice needles.

Much depends on whether the temperature of the air is changing. This may cause snow to turn to rain, or rain to snow, or both to fall together – sleet, by the British definition. The falling precipitation may itself change the temperature of the air between the cloud and the ground. The melting process absorbs latent heat, so if

AT HOME *Inuits camp on the ice off the coast of western Greenland in early summer, in order to reach stocks of fish found in the open sea.*

HOT AND COLD *In Natal, South Africa, the Drakensberg mountains, which tower over the warm, dry interior, are snow-covered most winters.*

snow falling heavily is melting as it travels downwards, latent heat is removed from the surrounding air and as a result the temperature drops. If the precipitation is heavy enough and lasts long enough, and especially when the wind is light or non-existent, so much latent heat may be absorbed that the air temperature falls close to 0°C (32°F), allowing the snowflakes to penetrate all the way to the ground.

WHERE DOES IT SNOW?

On a bitterly cold day, people sometimes observe: 'It's too cold to snow.' Strictly speaking this is not true, for snow falls frequently in both the Arctic and the Antarctic even when the temperature falls below –50°C (–58°F). It is, however, true that the colder the air is, the less moisture it can hold. Since moisture is the raw material of snowflakes, intensely cold air temperatures will yield comparatively little snow at any one time. The snow of the Arctic and Antarctic falls little and often.

The heaviest snowfalls occur in regions where the air temperature is frequently between –5° and 0°C (23° and 32°F) – warm enough for the air to contain a reasonable amount of moisture, cold enough for snowflakes to survive all the way to the ground. Given the right air temperature and moisture content, snow can fall in all latitudes, including parts of the higher slopes of Mount Kenya, located almost exactly on the Equator. These are permanently snow-covered from 15 000 ft (4500 m) up to the summit at 17 058 ft (5199 m).

At sea level, snow is rare within the tropics although it has occasionally been seen on the Tropic of Cancer in southern China and on the Tropic of Capricorn near São Paulo

SPANISH SIERRA *The Sierra Nevada in Spain receives heavy snowfalls despite its close proximity to the Costa del Sol.*

in Brazil. The air temperature in such regions is, generally speaking, too high. In the subtropics it falls occasionally on the coasts, though it rarely settles. In hilly or plateau areas inland, however, where the higher altitude means that the air is less dense and therefore colder than it is at sea level, large amounts of snow are deposited from time to time.

For example, snow falls in most winters around the northern coasts of the Mediterranean, but is rare in Algiers or Tel Aviv on its southern and eastern shores. A short way inland, by contrast, the foothills of the Atlas Mountains in Algeria and Morocco have severe snowstorms from time to time. Jerusalem, just 30 miles (50 km) from the

coast but 2500 ft (750 m) above sea level, is blanketed in snow once every two or three years on average. One memorable storm in 1920 dumped over 3 ft (1 m) of snow in the region around Jerusalem with drifts 10 ft (3 m) high. Similarly, the Spanish interior has some snow in most winters and heavy falls in a few. The northern slopes of the Sierra Nevada, just 20 miles (32 km) as the crow flies from the Costa del Sol, are the site of Europe's fastest-growing ski resorts.

In South Africa it hardly ever snows at sea level, but mountains within sight of the

SNOW AND SAND *In Morocco a
northerly airflow straight
from the Arctic Circle deposits
heavy falls of snow over the
Atlas Mountains during winter.*

when moisture levels rise because the air is warmer than in the depths of winter.

The lowlands of western and central Europe and the Pacific fringe of the USA and Canada are often too warm for snow, even in midwinter. But when the prevailing south-westerly winds blowing in off the ocean give way to north-westerlies coming from the Arctic or north-easterlies from the cold continental interior, the temperature drops close to freezing or just below. In these conditions, snow falls readily, and when the weather patterns are just right a dramatic snowstorm will result. Seattle's worst recorded snowstorm was one of these. It deposited level snow – as opposed to drifts – 24 in (61 cm) high on January 6, 1880, most of which melted within two days. Then a further storm struck on January 9, paralysing the region's embryonic transport system. The main transcontinental railway into Portland, Oregon, was blocked for weeks.

One of the United Kingdom's worst recorded snowstorms struck on January 18-19,

coastline are sometimes capped with white. A cold southerly blast from the Antarctic, forced to rise over the mountains of the interior, cools further, and its abundant moisture (picked up over the Southern Ocean) condenses as snow clouds, bringing snow to the Karoo in Cape Province and to the High Veld in Transvaal and Orange Free State. However, except over the highest mountains, it always melts within a few days.

SNOWFALLS IN TEMPERATE LANDS

Temperate latitudes have huge variations in how often and how heavily snow falls. Again, the general rule holds that the largest quantities fall where there is a copious supply of moisture and where temperatures are not exceptionally low.

SNOW OVER EUROPE *Intensely
cold air from northern Russia
flows westwards; warm moist
Atlantic air flows eastwards.
Where the airstreams meet, an
active front develops. The warm
air is forced upwards; moisture
condenses, falling as snow.*

The continental interiors of Asia and North America, for example, are cold enough for snow to fall frequently between October and April, but the air contains only small amounts of water vapour so the snowfalls are often very light. Some of the heavier falls occur in autumn and spring

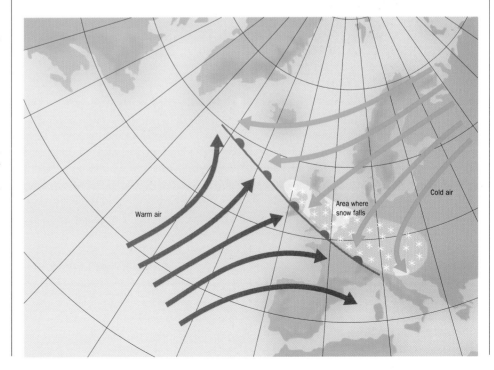

Warm air

Area where snow falls

Cold air

THE DANGERS OF ICE STORMS

Freezing rain, or 'glaze', falls more frequently in Continental Europe than over the British Isles, and is a common visitor to large parts of the USA from the eastern seaboard to the Pacific north-west. It happens when a large mass of warm air over-rides a stagnant mass of dense, cold air at the Earth's surface. Rain from the warm air falls through the cold layer, keeping its liquid state thanks to the surface tension of the

GLAZED *This road surface may look wet, but in fact it is covered by a sheet of clear ice.*

raindrops. It freezes on impact with any solid object, coating roads, paths, trees and power lines with a thick varnish of clear and potentially lethal 'black' ice.

The worst ice storm in American history struck a wide swathe from Texas to Virginia between January 28 and February 1, 1951. Tennessee was worst hit. Everything was coated with 3-4 in (7.5-10 cm) of clear ice, which in Nashville was not completely cleared from the streets until ten days after. Twenty-five people died in accidents on the ice, and more than 500 others were badly injured.

An earlier storm, which paralysed much of New England in November 1921, was described by the American meteorologist Charles F. Brooks: 'At night it began to rain steadily and ice as steadily to form. Morning saw an inch-thick [2.5 cm] armour of ice over everything out-of-doors, and still it rained and froze, while the north-east wind increased to a gale . . . A wild and terrible night followed. Electric lights were extinguished, and cities and towns lay in blackness, trolley cars ceased running, telegraph and telephone service was gone,

streets were impassable to vehicles, some of them to pedestrians . . .'

Britain's worst recorded ice storm struck on January 27-29, 1940. It affected a band stretching from Sussex, Hampshire and Dorset as far north as Montgomeryshire and Shropshire. The former President of the Royal Meteorological Society Charles Cave wrote: 'The formation of ice began at 4 pm on the 27th. By next morning everything was covered with ice, the depth on the thermometer screen being nearly half an inch [13 mm]. It was almost impossible to walk, paths and roads were covered with a smooth coating, and on the

FROZEN BEAUTY *Glazed ice weighs heavily on pine twigs in Yosemite National Park.*

grass the ice was more irregular but it was almost as difficult to walk on. The vicar of a neighbouring parish told me that he went to church on his hands and knees. It went on raining more or less all day on the 28th, and many windows became so stuck by the ice that they could not be opened . . . Telephone wires 1.5 mm [$6/100$ in] in diameter were encased with ice 30 mm [more than 1 in] in diameter, and twigs were covered with ice in the same proportion.'

1881, when a combination of high winds and prolonged snow caused widespread disruption – indeed there was no transport between London and Oxford for four days. Worst hit were counties bordering the English Channel. A second storm on January 21 left 3-4 ft (90-120 cm) of snow on the Isle of Wight, with drifts 15 ft (4.6 m) high. Much more recently, a severe storm struck western Britain on February 5-6, 1996, dumping 12-24 in (30-61 cm) of level snow on south-west Scotland, north-west England and parts of Wales, with consequent traffic chaos and failure of the electricity supply.

Arguably the most astonishing snowfall for a low-lying location anywhere in the world happened at Holne Chase on the lower slopes of Dartmoor, midway between Exeter and Plymouth in south-west England. The date was February 16, 1929, and snow fell heavily and continuously for 15 hours, accompanied by no wind, allowing the snow to accumulate without drifting. When the storm finally stopped, snow lay 6 ft (1.8 m) deep.

SNOW HAVOC

The places in the world where snow causes the most regular and widespread disruption to life in a modern industrial society are probably the eastern seaboard of North America and the region around the Great Lakes. These are the snowiest parts of the world, with a dense population and sophisticated transport network.

North America's Atlantic coast encourages depressions to develop, feeding off the contrasting air masses emanating from the subtropical Atlantic Ocean and the interior of North America. Many of these depressions track north-eastwards along the coast as they intensify. When temperatures are low enough, the precipitation caused by them falls as snow over enormous areas. The so-called 'Blizzard of the Century' of early March 1993 deposited large amounts of snow all the way from Alabama and Georgia in the south to the Maritime

Provinces of Canada in the north, blanketing a zone 1500 miles (2400 km) long and 500 miles (800 km) wide.

A huge blizzard in January 1996 – having dubbed the 1993 storm the worst of the century, the American media did not know what to call this one – affected a slightly smaller area, but dumped record-breaking quantities of snow on the big north-eastern cities. Boston recorded 18 in (46 cm), New York 20 in (51 cm), Baltimore 22 in (56 cm), Washington DC 25 in (64 cm) and Philadelphia 31 in (79 cm). In the Allegheny Mountains, Pocahontas County in West Virginia recorded 4 ft (1.2 m) of level snow at the end of the storm.

In New England the winter of 1995-6 as a whole broke many records. Boston recorded a total snowfall over the season approaching 9 ft (2.7 m), the first time in its history that the city has passed above the 100 in (8 ft 4 in/2.5 m) threshold.

The Great Lakes exert their own special influence on the winter weather of the surrounding region. Bitterly cold westerly,

SNOWFLAKES GALORE

The German astronomer Johannes Kepler was the first scientist to describe ice crystals accurately. As early as 1611, he noted that virtually all such crystals have a hexagonal (six-sided) structure, although no two ice crystals are ever the same. More than two centuries later, in 1858, the English meteorologist James Glaisher wrote a paper describing more than 100 different forms of snow. The 20th-century American amateur scientist Wilson A. Bentley spent a lifetime photographing ice crystals through a microscope. His book *Snow Crystals*, containing more than 2000 of his best photographs, was published in 1931.

north-westerly and northerly winds from the interior of the continent do not normally contain enough moisture for a disruptive snowstorm. But the waters of the Great Lakes are extensive enough to inject substantial amounts of water vapour into these icy winds. The results are known as

SNOW CHAOS *On December 9-10, 1995, 3 ft (1 m) of snow fell on Buffalo, the snowiest big city in the USA and one of the snowiest in the world, thanks to the 'Lake Effect'.*

'Lake Effect' snows on the southern and eastern shores of the lakes. Some districts average total falls of 12-15 ft (3.7-4.6 m) over the whole of the season. A similar effect around the shores of the Gulf of St Lawrence results in seasonal totals of 8-10 ft (2.4-3 m).

Buffalo, at the western extremity of New York State, is the snowiest major city in North America, receiving 'Lake Effect' snows from Lake Erie in a westerly wind and from Lake Ontario in a northerly wind. In January 1977, snow fell in the city on every day of the month, totalling 5 ft 8 in (1.7 m), of which almost half fell in a blizzard on the 30th and 31st.

Without the 'Lake Effect', dry continental winds deposit less snow in the frigid interior of North America – the High Plains of the USA and the Prairie Provinces of Canada. Here, despite the prolonged cold of a typical winter, seasonal totals are usually a comparatively modest 2-4 ft (61-120 cm). Even so, conditions are still right to feed several blizzards during an average winter, when dry, powdery snow, high winds and intense cold combine to create some of the most dangerous winter conditions known to mankind. The British meteorologist Sir George Simpson described a typical blizzard experienced during the British Antarctic Expedition in 1911:

'In a true blizzard the wind is accompanied by clouds of driven snow. The snow is in the form of exceedingly fine grains which penetrate through the smallest chink or hole in a house or tent. The whole air appears to be full of drift, so that it is impossible to see any great distance, and when it is at its worst even a tent cannot be seen for more than a few yards. Not only does the drift make it difficult to see, but anyone exposed to it seems to become bewildered and to lose all power of thinking clearly. For these reasons it is sheer folly to attempt to travel in a blizzard even when the temperature is relatively high and the wind at one's back.'

MOUNTAIN SNOWS

On the Equator, only the highest mountains are snow-capped. Mount Kilimanjaro in Tanzania is an example at latitude 3°S. It has glaciers extending from just below the summit to 15 000 ft (4500 m) above sea level.

Mountain ranges in temperate latitudes often receive enormous quantities of snow, thanks to the upward impetus as airstreams flow over the mountains. The additional upward push – 'orographic uplift' – increases the amount of water vapour that condenses from the atmosphere in the form of clouds. This is why the high Alps, for example, are snow-covered throughout the year. European ski enthusiasts can find glacier skiing there in July and August, while at lower levels snow is usually so reliable that hundreds of thousands of visitors hit the ski-slopes every winter from mid-December until late April.

The west-facing slopes of the various ranges of the Rocky Mountains – the Coastal Range, the Cascades and the Sierra Nevada (Spanish for 'snowy range') – have even higher snowfalls than the Alps. Total falls on the Sierra Nevada in eastern California amount to more than 40 ft (12 m) each winter. In the USA as a whole the biggest monthly total on record was over 32 ft (10 m) at Tamarack, California, in January 1911. The highest seasonal total ever recorded was almost 94 ft (28.7 m) at Paradise Ranger

ALPINE EFFECT *The French Alps are snow-covered all year on their higher slopes. The lower slopes support a busy skiing season in winter.*

Station on Mount Rainier, Washington, in the winter of 1971-2.

In South America, the southern Andes offer the only physical barrier to the westerly

---

HOW WET IS SNOW?

As a rule, 10 in (25 cm) of snow yields the same amount of water as 1 in (2.5 cm) of rain. There is, however, considerable variation from one fall to another, depending on the water content of the snow. Very dry, powdery snow falling at very low temperatures may give a ratio of thirty to one – 30 in (76 cm) of snow yielding the same amount of water as 1 in (2.5 cm) of rain. Soft, wet snow falling at a temperature fractionally above 0°C (32°F) compacts readily as it reaches the ground, as little as 4 in (10 cm) of snow producing a rainfall equivalent of 1 in (2.5 cm).

---

winds – the so-called Roaring Forties or Brave West Winds – that throughout the year blast their way around the Southern Hemisphere's oceanic middle latitudes. The slopes of the southern Andes above

roughly 2700 ft (800 m) are constantly snow-covered, and glaciers reach sea level in the fiords carved into the coastline south of the 45th parallel in Patagonia.

WHEN THE SEAS FREEZE

Snow is a special sort of ice. We are fortunate that most 'solid' precipitation is so light and full of air that it causes no damage as it actually falls. At ground level – both on land and at sea – ice presents itself in a more solid form.

Ice forms in different ways in fresh water and salt water. Fresh water reaches its greatest density (mass per volume unit), and therefore its heaviest, just above freezing point, at 4°C (39.2°F). The effect of this is to prevent much circulation between the different layers of freshwater lakes such as the Great Lakes. The densest waters naturally stay along the bottom, so that the temperature there is always around 4°C. In summer, the warm surface waters stay on the surface since they are above 4°C. In winter, they may cool to below 4°C, which again means that they are less dense, or lighter, than the water below. So when the temperature of the

SALT WATER *At Red Island Harbour, Newfoundland, pancake-like pieces of ice form over shallow water during the first severe spell of winter.*

air above any body of fresh water remains below the freezing point for a long period, the ice forms first on the surface, where the freezing air meets a stable layer of water around freezing point. The surface ice may then spread and thicken gradually. This is as true of a rainwater tub in a garden as it is of Loch Lomond or Lake Superior.

Salt water, by contrast, is densest below freezing point, at around –2°C (28°F), the exact temperature depending on the degree of salinity (saltiness). So, however cold it is in the air above, the waters of the deep oceans do not readily freeze. The cooled surface water is denser than the slightly warmer water beneath, and is therefore constantly sinking and being replaced by water from the immense depths below. Any

FRESH WATER *A stream freezes first near the banks, where the water moves relatively slowly. Ice then extends slowly towards the middle of the stream.*

extensive ice found above deep water has usually been driven there by wind or ocean currents, or a combination of the two.

In shallow water, on the other hand, the same sinking water will spread the cooling

process through the whole body of water relatively quickly, and freezing will follow. At the point of freezing, the salt and other minerals are precipitated out, making the water below the ice even saltier – the ice itself is practically free of impurities. The more salty the water, the lower the temperature at which it freezes, slowing down the freezing process.

The first signs of freezing in the sea are 'frazil crystals', small separate particles of ice. These soon concentrate into 'sludge', which makes the surface layer of the sea thick and soupy to a depth of about 1 ft (30 cm). In the next stage, solid ice forms, in sheets, pancakes or floes of various shapes and sizes. 'Pancake ice' consists of individual, roughly circular pieces of ice, frequently 3-4 ft (1-1.2 m) across. An 'ice floe' can be almost any size or shape and often consists of an agglomeration of old pancakes. As the weeks go by, these separate ice elements merge into pack ice, blocking seaways and closing harbours.

THUNDER, LIGHTNING AND HAIL

Thunderstorms are massive powerhouses of energy that assault at least four of our senses – with blinding lightning flashes, deafening peals of thunder, soaking rain and even the sulphurous smell of a nearby lightning strike.

Thunder has been explained in many ways over the ages. 'God is moving his furniture about', some children are still told at their mother's knee, when cowering, uncomprehending, at the awesome violence of an overhead thunderstorm. In times past, pagan gods were invoked to explain the power and fury of a full-blooded thunderstorm. In Norse mythology, Thor, usually depicted wielding a hammer, was the god of thunder – Thursday was named after him. Even today economic losses resulting from thunderstorms are regarded as 'acts of God' in some countries. As we approach the 21st century, meteorologists still do not know every detail of what happens in a thundercloud, but they believe that they know most of it, and it is very complex.

The cumulonimbus is king of the clouds. It is the giant towering thundercloud that, in the right conditions, boils furiously through the whole depth of the troposphere, sometimes penetrating into the lower stratosphere some 50 000 ft (16 000 m) or more above the surface of the Earth. As well as thunder and lightning, these clouds bring torrential downpours,

STORM FURY *Torrential rain can be seen during a thunderstorm off the Namibian coast at sunset. The storm will probably have vanished within hours.*

STORM IN THE MAKING
Cumulonimbus clouds, fed by
powerful updraughts, penetrate
a layer of cirrostratus (ice
crystal) cloud.

explosive hailstorms, savage squalls of wind and, on occasion, tornadoes. All this comes out of thin air – literally – thanks to the interaction of warmth from the Sun and invisible water vapour in the atmosphere.

The harnessing of electricity for use in factory and home is a relatively recent development, but electricity was known to the ancient Greeks. *Electrum* is the Latin for 'amber', and comes from the Greek *elektron*. As long ago as the 6th century BC, ancient philosophers knew that amber, when rubbed

gently, would attract small pieces of cloth and other debris. They failed, however, to make the link between this form of 'static' electricity and the drama of the thunderstorm.

It was not until the 18th century that scientists proved beyond reasonable doubt that lightning was a manifestation of electricity. The pioneer was the American Benjamin Franklin, who performed a famous series of experiments in which he flew a kite beneath a thundercloud. Contrary to popular belief, he did not succeed in attracting a lightning stroke to his kite – he would have been unlikely to survive such an experience – but he did collect enough electrical charge down the rain-soaked line to make a spark between his hand and a metal key attached to the rope.

The Earth and its atmosphere are always electrically charged. The atoms from which all matter is made contain both positively charged particles, called protons, and negatively charged particles, called electrons. Atoms have the same number of each. However, like charges repel each other, and opposites attract, and high temperatures and high voltages provide enough energy for electrons, which are situated in the outer layers of an atom, to escape to another atom. A deficit of electrons in one material will give it a positive charge, and a surplus in another will give it a negative charge. If two bodies have different charges, a movement of charged particles, a current, will seek to flow between the bodies in order to neutralise them.

The Earth's electrical field is normally quite stable. There is a positive charge in the ionosphere – a layer in the atmosphere between about 35 and 250 miles (60 and 400 km) above the Earth's surface, where radiation from the Sun interacts with tiny air particles to produce an electrical charge – and a negative charge at the surface itself. In fine weather, this negative charge gradually leaks away from the ground, dissipating itself in the air. Water is a good conductor of electricity and so water vapour in the lower atmosphere increases the rate at which the electricity leaks away.

Thunderstorms are important because they effectively 'revitalise' the electrical field. Left to itself, the normal, comparatively gentle current flowing between earth and air would result in all the electricity at the Earth's surface leaking away. We now know that the lightning discharges that occur during thunderstorms restore the negative charge at the surface, and they do so on a large scale. At any one moment, there are approximately 1800 thunderstorms in progress scattered around the planet. The British climatologist C.E.P. Brooks calculated that approximately 44 000 thunderstorms take place on the Earth during the course of each day, and an average of 100 lightning discharges per second.

Thunderclouds have vertically moving currents of air called updraughts and downdraughts. In a vigorous storm, updraughts

FORKED LIGHTNING *A time-lapse photograph of a storm over Arizona captures several electrical discharges from cloud to ground.*

can reach a speed of more than 70 mph (113 km/h), although speeds of 20 to 30 mph (32 to 48 km/h) are more typical. Such powerful currents easily carry sizable raindrops from the bottom of the cloud to the top, where the temperature may be as low as –50°C (–58°F). By this time the raindrop will have frozen into a small hailstone.

The hailstone may remain in the cloud for some time, depending on the strength and staying power of the updraught. It is

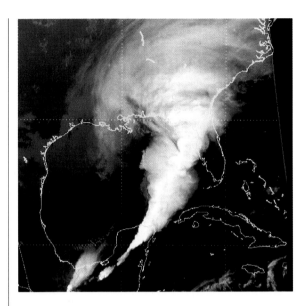

SATELLITE VIEW *A trail of cloud from Florida to the Yucatan Peninsula marks an active cold front that produces a series of violent thunderstorms.*

believed that collisions between small hailstones and tiny ice crystals create an electrical charge. The charge on the hailstones is negative, while that on the ice crystals is positive.

The positively charged, tiny ice crystals move to the top of the cloud, and the negatively charged, larger hail pellets gather in the lower half. The result is a separation of the electrical charge within a cumulonimbus cloud – negative at the bottom and positive at the top. The surface of the Earth and objects on it such as trees and buildings also carry an electrical charge. When a sufficient difference has built up, electricity is discharged, both between the cloud and the ground and within the cloud. More rarely, a discharge may also occur between two adjacent clouds. All these electrical discharges are what we know as lightning.

An electrical discharge occurring between cloud and ground carries a negative charge, known as the 'negative leader', that searches for the quickest route from cloud to ground, and will be attracted by tall objects such as trees or buildings extending above the ground. Because opposite charges attract each other, the negative leader induces a positive charge in the ground (or tree or building), which streaks back to the cloud. This is called the 'return stroke', and it is this that we see as the lightning flash. Sometimes, there is too great an electrical charge in a cloud for a single stroke to release, and several discharges occur along the same channel, resulting in a brilliantly flickering lightning stroke that may last two seconds or more.

Lightning tries several paths before finding one that conducts it to the earth, which gives it its 'forked' appearance. All lightning is 'forked' lightning, but if the discharge has happened inside a dense cloud mass, or at a great distance, all you may see is a diffuse reflection of the lightning stroke on the water droplets of the cloud or on other clouds nearby. This is generally termed 'sheet lightning'. Sheet lightning is visible from a great distance at night, perhaps reflected on high-level ice-crystal clouds.

WHERE THUNDER COMES FROM

A bolt of lightning carries a massive electrical current. It is estimated that a typical flash carries between 10 000 and 50 000 amps, producing around 100 megawatts of power per yard (metre). This in turns heats the air along the lightning stroke to a temperature of 30 000°C (54 000°F) or more.

This enormous, almost instantaneous heating prompts an explosive expansion of the air surrounding the lightning channel, which is heard as thunder. Thunder, of course, travels at the speed of sound, which is slower than the speed of light. We therefore see the lightning before we hear the thunder. Knowing this, we can calculate how near the lightning stroke was. A count of 15 seconds between the flash and the thunder means that the discharge occurred roughly 3 miles (5 km) away, but we also have to remember that the flash may have

---

LIGHTNING STRIKES TWICE

It is not true that lightning never strikes twice – especially as tall buildings have lightning conductors designed to attract lightning and conduct it safely to earth. The Eiffel Tower, for instance, gets struck at least 20 times every year.

Some communities seem to be particularly prone. On July 25, 1670, lightning struck and badly damaged the 93 ft (28 m) steeple of the Church of St Mary the Virgin at Steeple Ashton in Wiltshire, England. The villagers set to work repairing their steeple and had almost finished when, on October 15, lightning struck again. The new steeple collapsed, killing two workmen. Some 300 years later, on June 26, 1973, Steeple Ashton suffered another hit. Lightning struck a hay barn and, a few yards away from the barn, the impact hurled an appropriately named 84-year-old, Mr Bolt, across his kitchen.

Many people have been struck by lightning and survived, including international golf star Lee Trevino. He was slightly injured at the Butler National Golf Course at Oak Brook, Illinois, on June 27, 1975. Only one person has survived seven lightning strikes. Park Ranger Roy Sullivan, from Virginia in the USA, was nicknamed 'the human lightning conductor'. He was first struck in 1942 when his big toe was burnt and the toenail lost. His eyebrows were singed in 1969, his shoulder badly burnt in 1970, his hair set on fire in 1972 and again in 1973, his leg damaged in 1976, and he suffered chest and stomach burns in 1977.

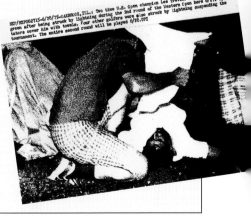

UNLUCKY STRIKE *Golfer Lee Trevino collapses after being struck by lightning.*

happened more than a mile (1.6 km) above the Earth's surface.

If the lightning strike was very close, an observer will see the lightning and hear thunder almost simultaneously. In these circumstances, the deafening initial thunder crash will probably continue to reverberate for several seconds. This is because the sound from the distant part of the lightning channel takes longer to reach us than the sound from the lower end of the channel.

CLOUDBURSTS AND SQUALL LINES

The worst thunderstorms are brought by a large number of individual thunderclouds, which meteorologists refer to as 'storm cells'. Each of these cells has a life of roughly one to two hours. Thunderstorms that last many hours are constantly generating new storm cells. A thundercloud's life cycle can be described in three stages – the developing stage, the fully developed stage and the dissipating stage. During the developing stage, the growing cumulonimbus cloud consists almost entirely of upward-moving air currents. As the cloud grows, it may appear very black because of the density of water droplets, but there is no precipitation yet since the updraughts prevent any raindrops from falling. Nor is there any thunder and lightning as the

SQUALL LINE The curved line of dark storm cloud marks the convergence of two contrasting airflows above Sundance, Wyoming.

contrasting electrical charges have not built up.

During its mature stage, the storm cell produces lightning and thunder, and the amount of rain and hail it holds grows so large it can no longer be supported in its entirety by the updraughts. Warm air is still feeding into the cloud at the forward edge of the storm. But underneath the middle and rear portions of the cloud, the falling raindrops and hailstones drag cold air downwards from the interior of the cloud, setting off a downdraught. Once the downdraught is established, the rain and hail fall to the ground in a rush, while powerful gusts of cold air spread out horizontally once they reach the ground. At this point, the storm starts to dissipate.

These developments explain the familiar sequence of events that someone on the ground observes while the mature thunderstorm passes over. As the storm approaches, both temperature and humidity are high and no rain falls, even though it may be growing almost as black as night. A warm wind (supplying the updraught) blows in towards the storm from the region of fine weather ahead of it. Lightning can probably be seen or thunder heard from some distance away. The warm wind stops blowing; everything becomes still for a few minutes, and then one or two large raindrops splatter onto the ground. It is the very largest raindrops that fall first through the faltering updraught. All of a sudden there is a powerful squall of wind, sometimes gusting over

UP AND DOWN Air currents in a thundercloud first flow upwards, then both upwards and downwards, finally downwards.

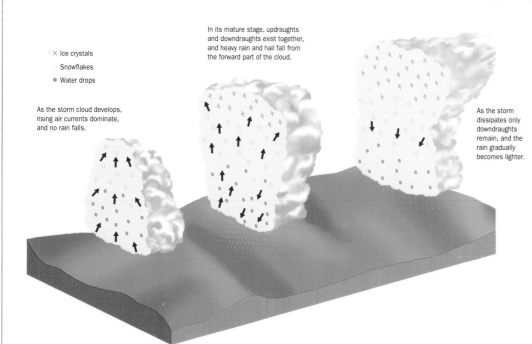

× Ice crystals
○ Snowflakes
● Water drops

As the storm cloud develops, rising air currents dominate, and no rain falls.

In its mature stage, updraughts and downdraughts exist together, and heavy rain and hail fall from the forward part of the cloud.

As the storm dissipates only downdraughts remain, and the rain gradually becomes lighter.

70 mph (113 km/h), roaring through the trees and carrying dust and debris with it. This is immediately followed by a steadier, cold wind blowing from the opposite direction. The temperature drops almost instantaneously, in extreme cases from 35°C to 15°C (95°F to 60°F). A wall of black cloud passes overhead and the approaching sky appears a rather lighter shade of grey. A few more moments pass before the rain begins in earnest. Once it has started, though, it comes down in torrents. It is at this point that the lightning is most likely to strike overhead. This is also where any hail will fall. Often the heaviest rain falls at the peak of the electrical activity. Thereafter, the rain gradually eases off, while the lightning and thunder move slowly away.

Eventually, the cold downdraught spreads out beyond the forward edge of the storm,

THUNDER AND SQUALLS *A squall line forms ahead of a moving thundercloud where warm air flowing into the cloud meets cold air flowing from its base.*

cutting off the warm air flowing in. This switches off the storm's main source of energy, and it begins to die. There are now only descending air currents in the cloud. The electrical activity ceases, and the rain gradually diminishes in intensity until the cloud's water supply is exhausted. In due course, the cloud will gradually disintegrate.

When thunderclouds are ranged in a line along an advancing front, this is known as a squall-line storm; when they are grouped in clusters, as a multicell storm. During a squall-line storm, new storm cells form on the forward edge of old ones. The cold air flowing out from the old cell undercuts the mass of warm, humid air ahead of the storm, providing sufficient upward impetus to set off new updraughts. If there is still a big enough supply of warm air ahead of the storm cluster, these updraughts will strengthen and a new thundercloud is born. In multicell storms, new cells form behind existing storm clouds. Clusters of storm cells explain why, when

observed from the ground, there may be a succession of drenching downpours separated by periods of rather gentler rain.

ICE FROM THE SKIES

Raindrops carried by powerful updraughts high into sub-zero (0°C/32°F) parts of a thundercloud freeze solid, becoming small hailstones. As it goes higher, the updraught runs out of steam, allowing the new hail pellets to fall. Alternatively, they may fall out of the side of the updraught. The hailstones now descend to the ground or get picked up again by the updraught. This cycle of falling and then being picked up again is sometimes repeated several times, the hailstones growing larger each time.

As the thundercloud reaches maturity, a point is reached where the millions of hailstones still held aloft become too heavy to stay there. Because of their weight they descend rapidly, and within a matter of minutes, usually, the cumulonimbus cloud ejects most of its icy contents. For someone observing the storm from the ground the effect is spectacular. The storm breaks suddenly, a deluge of hailstones clattering to Earth. They reduce visibility and, even though the air temperature minutes before may have been as high as 32°C (90°F) or more, they quickly cover the ground with

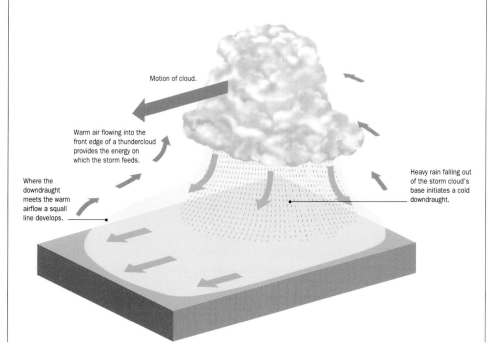

Motion of cloud.

Warm air flowing into the front edge of a thundercloud provides the energy on which the storm feeds.

Where the downdraught meets the warm airflow a squall line develops.

Heavy rain falling out of the storm cloud's base initiates a cold downdraught.

RAINING FISH AND FROGS

Thunderclouds have been known to deposit some strange objects along with their rain and hail. These have included showers of grass, hay, nuts, shellfish and even small pieces of coal.

The strong updraughts associated with cumulonimbus clouds, along with the waterspouts and tornadoes that occasionally accompany the most violent storms, are responsible. They carry all sorts of debris high into the cloud before finally releasing it as a downdraught develops. For example, a small tornado passing over a lake will not only suck water into its circulation, but also weed, reeds, frogs and fish.

The Tornado and Storm Research Organisation (TORRO), a privately funded group based in the United Kingdom, has studied and catalogued such events – so most of the best descriptions come from Britain. One of the earliest references found by TORRO came from the *Athenaeum* magazine. It described a fall of small fish and frogs in the English city of Derby early in July 1841. In March 1859, in a letter to the *Evening Mail*, the vicar of Aberdare in South Wales described a shower of small fish.

TORRO also noted a fall of grass and hay in Poole, southern England, on August 9, 1977, and one of tiny frogs at Canet-Plage, near Perpignan in southern France, on the 28th of the same month. Maggots fell on Acapulco, Mexico, during a storm in October 1968. Odder still were the events of January 3, 1978, when a vigorous cold front swept eastwards across England. As the front reached East Anglia a marked squall line developed with several small tornadoes. A flock of pink-footed geese from the fringes of The Wash, on the east coast of England, were startled into the air by the squalls and most likely were caught up in a mini-tornado or two, for they were all killed. Subsequently, 136 dead geese fell from the sky along a track 28 miles (45 km) long, running from west-north-west to east-south-east across Norfolk.

Several authenticated falls of coal were reported from the Bournemouth-Poole district on the English south coast during violent storms on June 5, 1983. It is believed that a small tornado may have picked up coal debris from a merchant's yard. On the same day, a crab fell among large hail farther along the coast at Brighton.

MENAGERIE *Umbrellas offer no protection in the downpour depicted by the 19th-century artist George Cruikshank.*

---

ice. Most hailstorms last less than ten minutes, and the area worst hit is relatively small. Weather forecasters talk about a 'hail streak' because damage from a typical hailstorm affects a long, narrow zone – elongated because of the movement of the storm.

On rare occasions, several hailstones fuse together into a huge chunk of ice. The largest authenticated stone weighed 27 oz (758 g) and was almost 8 in (20 cm) in diameter. This monster fell at Coffeyville in Kansas, on September 3, 1970. Before that, stones almost as large fell in Dubuque, Iowa, on June 16, 1882, and in Potter, Nebraska, on July 6, 1928.

Huge stones have also been reported in South Africa. One storm was described in the *Mafeking Mail* in December 1915: 'In the vicinity of Hildavale [in the far north of Cape Province] there followed a hailstorm of exceptional violence. For nearly five minutes great isolated chunks of ice fell. We have the authority of Mr Durand for stating that four of these chunks together turned the scale at four pounds [1.8 kg]

and the measurements of one were, width four inches [10 cm], depth four inches, and length four and a half inches [more than 11 cm]. Into ploughed land the bigger penetrated to a depth of two to three inches [5 to 7.5 cm], and it would be better to imagine than experience a bombardment with such missiles had it been accompanied by a heavy wind. As it was, Mr Durand's losses in livestock were considerable. Of one flock of sheep fourteen were killed outright and sixteen died later; thirty or forty, though very badly bruised and bleeding, are recovering.'

More recently, in November 1984, three separate hailstorms in different parts of

RARE GIANTS *These hailstones were collected after a storm at Lanseria, Transvaal, South Africa, in February 1992.*

Transvaal caused some $50 million worth of damage to property, livestock, and crops. Sydney was hit by a particularly savage storm in December 1946, when giant hail smashed windows and damaged vehicles. More than 300 people were treated for injuries caused by the hailstones themselves or by flying glass broken by them. Unfortunately, no

reliable measurements of the biggest stones are available. A similar storm in and around Sydney caused more than $50 million-worth of damage on October 3, 1986.

The hailstorm that caused greater loss of human life than any other on record happened in the township of Moradabad, Uttar Pradesh, India, on April 30, 1888 – in all, 250 people were killed. The most costly

---

THUNDER CAPITAL

The city of Bogor (formerly Buitenzorg) on the Indonesian island of Java is famous for two things – its splendid botanical gardens which were laid out in 1817 by Dutch settlers, and its almost daily thunderstorms. Bogor is believed to be the most thundery place on the planet, with storms recorded on an average of 322 days per year. Thunder and lightning are most frequent during the afternoon and early evening.

---

was a storm that struck Munich in Germany on July 12, 1984, when insurance losses amounted to more than $1 billion. There were hundreds of injuries as a result of the storm, but no lives were lost.

In the United Kingdom, one of the most damaging storms struck Essex, Hertfordshire and Bedfordshire on the afternoon of Midsummer Day – June 24 – in 1897. It ruined some of the celebrations marking Queen Victoria's Diamond Jubilee. Poultry and gamebirds were wiped out in their thousands. Some livestock were seriously injured and had to be put down, and several people suffered bad cuts and bruises. The biggest stone was picked up at Writtle, near Chelmsford, in Essex, and measured 4 in (10 cm) across.

WHERE THUNDERSTORMS HAPPEN

There are few places on Earth that never experience thunder and lightning. Thunderstorms will happen wherever there is enough moisture in the atmosphere, provided there is a trigger to set off upward-moving currents of air. That uplift may come in the form of convection from surface heating by the Sun, from a cold

airstream flowing over a warm ocean, at fronts between contrasting air masses (especially when a cold front is advancing) and where air flows over mountain ranges. It follows that thunder is most frequent where two or more of these triggers occur together and where the atmosphere is moistest – for instance, over the mountainous tropical islands of Indonesia. It is practically unknown over the Arctic and Antarctic icecaps, where there is little to encourage the development of convection currents.

As well as Indonesia, other hot and humid tropical regions with frequent thunderstorms include Central America and the northern half of South America, especially the Amazon Basin; Central and West Africa; much of the plateau of southern Africa and Madagascar; the Malay peninsula, and northern Queensland in Australia.

In these equatorial regions, thunder strikes most frequently during the afternoon and evening – that is, immediately after the hottest part of the day – on land. At sea it happens most often at night, when the sea retains heat while the air cools down. The warm water heats the cooler air above, creating updraughts. The great deserts of the tropics – the Sahara, the Arabian desert and central Australia – have only about five days of storms per year. Deserts bordering cold ocean currents, where the air is very dry and there is little convection, such as the Atacama Desert of northern Chile and southern Peru and the Namib Desert of south-western Africa, are virtually thunder-free.

In temperate latitudes, the number of thunderstorms closely

follows the seasonal variations in temperature – most thunderstorms happen on hot summer afternoons and evenings. This is particularly true of continental interiors, but also of countries with a relatively maritime climate such as the United Kingdom. The Alps of central Europe have a yearly average of 40 to 60 days with thunder; the English Midlands have around 20; Florida has around 90, and the eastern flanks of the Rocky Mountains in Colorado and New Mexico have about 75. By contrast, the cold, mid-latitude oceans, where there is little to create an updraught, have thunderstorms on fewer than five days annually.

WATERLOGGED *On the Indonesian island of Java thunderstorms occur on over 300 days each year.*

SWELTERING HEAT AND PERISHING COLD

Early humans thrived on the East African plateau, where the temperature is usually between 10° and 25°C (50° and 77°F).

Today, people survive in the most extreme environments, as hot as 58°C (136°F) and as cold as –89°C (–128°F).

A l'Aziziyah, lying in the baking Gefara plain of north-western Libya, some 22 miles (35 km) south of the capital Tripoli, is one of the hottest places on Earth. Writing in the 19th century, the French traveller H. Schirmer described the region and its climate of extremes:

'Suddenly, after hardly any twilight, the sun rises into the clear sky. In this dry atmosphere its rays are already scorching in the early morning, and under the influence of the reflection from rock and sand the layer of air next to the ground is heated rapidly. There is no active evaporation to moderate the rising temperature. After 9 o'clock the heat is intense but goes on increasing till 3 or 4 in the afternoon, when the quivering mirage is sometimes seen. It cools slowly towards evening, and the sun, just before it sets, suffuses the cloudless sky with a glow of colour. In the transparent night the rocks and sand lose their heat almost as rapidly as they acquired it. We shiver with cold and it is no uncommon thing in winter to find water on the surface of the ground frozen in the morning.'

SAHARAN SUN *The sun blazes in a cloudless sky, humidity levels are very low, and the moderating effect of the distant ocean hardly ever intervenes.*

In 1922 a group of scientists, working in Al'Aziziyah under the auspices of the National Geographic Society of the United States, reported one of the highest air temperatures ever recorded. The date was September 13, and the reading on the thermometer was a truly sizzling 58°C (136.4°F). In fact, some controversy surrounds this figure. It is still not recognised by the Libyan authorities and was contested, at the time it was reported, by the eminent German climatologist G. Helmann. It is certainly not in line with other extreme temperatures recorded in Libya. The nearby site of Castel Benito at Idris, near Tripoli, has a relatively modest September record of 49.4°C (121°F) – although the weather station at Castel Benito was not opened until 1924, two years after the reported 58°C (136.40°F) at Al'Aziziyah.

On the other hand, the geography of Al'Aziziyah may favour abnormally high readings under certain circumstances. It lies to the north of a marked escarpment, or steep cliff face, 2000 ft (600 m) high. As hot south-westerly winds from the Saharan interior descend the escarpment, they are warmed by compression (since the air pressure is higher at the foot of the slope than it is at the top of it). In this way, the already hot air of the desert could reach an extremely high temperature by the time it gets to Al'Aziziyah.

HOW HOT IS HOT?

Temperature plays a large role in our lives. We are bombarded with television and radio forecasts, newspaper weather reports, and digital displays found in banks, malls, airports and holiday resorts. These keep us abreast of the latest temperature fluctuations and any changes predicted for the next few days. We all want to know how hot or cold it is and what the weather will be like tomorrow. We are far less interested in such conditions as wind speeds and humidity levels, for example, unless these reach exceptional and newsworthy proportions. Curiously, despite their fascination with temperature, human beings themselves are remarkably poor thermometers. In a recent survey, a group of people were taken outside and asked to guess the temperature. Only 42 per cent of respondents were within 3°C

HOW HOT IT WAS

Gordon Manley, an English geography professor who lived from 1902 to 1980, spent much of his professional life collecting old weather records – not just thermometer and barometer readings, but also accounts of the weather from personal diaries, parish records, farm accounts and so on. This enabled him to construct a continuous series of monthly temperature readings for central England stretching from as far back as 1659 to the present day.

(5°F) of the actual temperature; 64 per cent were within 5°C (9°F). Some 5 per cent were more than 10°C (18°F) awry.

One reason for these levels of inaccuracy is that we actually feel heat and cold by the extent to which we gain or lose energy from

TAKING THE TEMPERATURE
A digital display records a temperature of 31°C (88°F) on a summer afternoon in Rio de Janeiro.

the air around us. Several factors, apart from the air temperature, influence this. They include the humidity level (which, confusingly, depends to a certain extent on the temperature, because warm air can hold more moisture than cold air), the wind speed and the strength and directness of sunshine. Thus our bodies tell us that it is 'hotter' when a high temperature is accompanied by high humidity, strong sunshine and no wind. Conversely, we feel colder when a low temperature is accompanied by high humidity, no sunshine and a strong wind.

Variations in humidity are particularly important – even in moderate heat, when the air temperature is between 20° and 30°C (68-86°F) – and they have a direct impact on our lives. When the weather is both hot and humid, the air feels sultry, or oppressive. Our reactions slow down; we feel lazy, and our work efficiency drops. This is particularly true of physical outdoor labor, but applies also to people working in factories,

offices and shops without air conditioning. Furthermore, high humidity levels bring warm, sticky nights, which in turn may result in poor or disturbed sleep, increased tiredness and loss of efficiency at work.

Moderately dry air, by contrast, is stimulating, leading to high work efficiency. With dry air, temperatures also normally drop briskly after dark. We get a better night's sleep, and are more likely to feel fully refreshed and raring to go the following morning. When the air becomes very dry, however, the effects are less beneficial. People become irritable, often because they are slightly dehydrated without realising it.

In great heat, with temperatures in excess of about 35°C (95°F), the effects of high or low humidity are more dramatic. Whether the air is dry or humid, outdoor physical labour in these temperatures is at best

SUN SCREEN *The Tuareg nomads of the Sahara Desert wear loose-fitting clothing that covers most of the body to protect the skin from the Sun.*

extremely uncomfortable, and at worst downright dangerous. Excessive humidity means that our systems have to work very hard at producing sweat to cool our bodies and keep the internal temperature stable. People perspire freely and keep physical exertion to a minimum. They seek shade,

drink water, and attempt to create air movement by using fans. People living where the climate is hot and humid most of the year, such as the coastal plains around the Arabian Gulf, have learned to wear loose, light-coloured clothing, which reflects heat and allows cooling breezes to circulate around the body. In extreme cases, heat stroke can occur when the body is no longer able to control its temperature, which rises to 40°C (104°F) and beyond. This may lead to death.

Exceptionally high temperatures allied to exceptionally low humidity are also dangerous. Again, people perspire rapidly to cope with the high temperature, though they are less aware of it because the perspiration quickly evaporates. Unless they maintain body fluid levels and body salts by frequent drinks enriched with the right minerals, they soon become dehydrated and disorientated. Heat exhaustion – a different condition from heat stroke, but also

caused by dehydration – follows, bringing dizziness; it may lead to collapse. Alcoholic drinks are not a good idea in either kind of heat. Alcohol in the bloodstream absorbs water from the cells in the body and the body becomes less efficient at cooling itself through perspiration, accelerating the onset of either heat exhaustion or heat stroke.

Meteorologists often combine information about both temperature and humidity in an attempt to give the public a better idea of expected levels of discomfort in their weather forecasts. Such information may be given in the form of a 'temperature-humidity index' or THI, sometimes more simply called a 'comfort index'. Some forecasters in the USA and the UK use the more user-friendly name of 'humisery rating'.

IN THE SHADE AND IN THE SUN

In June each year, tennis fans around the world tune in to the Wimbledon tennis championships in south-west London. Every year we are treated to pictures of a thermometer on Centre Court, usually located by the side of the heavy roller or the umpire's chair. It may be registering a 'temperature' of anything up to 47°C (116°F).

This is a splendid illustration of why official temperatures are all recorded in the shade – preferably in a suitable thermometer shelter, which screens the instruments from reflected radiation from the ground and walls. The extraordinary Centre Court temperature of 47°C was recorded in the summer of 1976 when the actual shade temperature

TURNING UP THE HEAT *In July 1995, the Centre Court thermometer, exposed to the sun, registered 42°C (107.6°F).*

was around 35°C (95°F), itself probably the highest temperature ever measured in London during Wimbledon fortnight.

There is, in fact, no such thing as 'the temperature in the sun'. If a thermometer is exposed to direct sunlight it will just absorb energy from the Sun and the mercury will register the temperature of the glass out of which the instrument is made. It will not measure the temperature of the air. And if the thermometer is ostensibly in the shade but is resting against an object – such as the heavy roller – which is in the sun, the thermometer will register the temperature of that object.

RAW AIR, KEEN AIR

At low temperatures the air holds comparatively little moisture, so the effect on the body of increasing or decreasing humidity is much smaller than in hot weather. Even so, we do detect some differences. For instance, we describe cold, damp air as 'raw' and cold dry air as 'keen'. A raw wind is the more unpleasant of the two, because it makes the clothing and any exposed parts of the body damp and we expend more energy trying to counteract these effects – in other words, it is harder to keep warm. Very dry air at low temperatures leads to dry, cracked skin, chapped lips and sore eyes.

Most very low temperatures are recorded when there is little or no air movement. This happens on calm, clear nights, especially in winter when the nights are longest and heat loss into the atmosphere from the Earth's surface results in a layer of cold air developing immediately above the ground. In these cold but still conditions, suitably clothed human beings cope very well with all but the most extreme temperatures. In effect, we develop our own microclimate, warmed by

body heat, within our clothing – with the help of the hair on our heads and beards and moustaches. Fur and feathers serve the same function for mammals and birds.

ACID RAIN, ACID SNOW

Most of us have heard of 'acid rain', caused by raindrops absorbing chemical pollutants from the atmosphere. If there is acid rain, there must also be acid snow. Between 1977 and 1979, several expeditions visited the mountains of Morocco and the Canary Islands to measure the acidity of snowfall. The results showed small but significant levels of acidity in the Atlas Mountains of Morocco, and surprisingly high acidity levels on the slopes of Mount Teide on Tenerife.

But as soon as the air begins to move, this microclimate starts to break down as the wind penetrates our clothes. This ability of a strong, cold wind to cool warm-blooded creatures is known as the 'wind-chill effect' and it is generally referred to in weather

forecasts as the 'wind-chill factor'. The wind-chill factor is calculated as a combination of wind speed and air temperature, and the information is available in tables from which the wind-chill 'equivalent' temperature can be read off. In some countries the 'real' temperature and the 'equivalent' one are given together in weather forecasts during cold, windy weather. In other countries this is regarded as misleading and forecasters prefer to give the 'real' temperature value adding that there is 'a large additional chill factor'.

HOT SPOTS

The highest temperatures in the world are recorded, not on the Equator, but in places such as Al'Aziziyah – that is, in the wide expanses of desert within the tropics in both hemispheres, where the weather is almost totally dry and the ground material absorbs heat from the Sun in a very efficient way. These include the Sahara, Arabia, Arizona, Namibia, Australia and a number of much smaller pockets of desert.

It is difficult to authenticate the very highest reported temperatures like the one at Al'Aziziyah, because they usually occur in sparsely populated areas where confirmation from neighbouring weather stations is not possible. In populated sites, the surroundings may cause problems, exerting undue influence on the temperature reading. In particular, expanses of asphalt, which heats up strongly in the sun, adjacent to a thermometer screen in urban areas or at airports may be sufficient to lift the temperature several degrees above the true air temperature.

For that reason, the rooftop reading of 60°C (140°F) made in August 1953 in the small settlement of Delta, in the far northwest corner of Mexico, is not recognised as authentic. Delta lies on the edge of the Desierto de Altar, a desolate region of sand desert spreading out between the northern end of the Gulf of California and the border with Arizona. The figure of 58°C

MATCHING PAIR *The Canadian dog-team driver emulates his canine companion by wearing a thick, fur-lined, one-piece suit to keep out the cold.*

(136.4°F), recorded in August 1933 at the nearby town of San Luis Río Colorado, is quoted by the Mexican meteorological service, but that, too, came from a rooftop site and is not accepted by international authorities. Just 20 miles (32 km) over the US border at Yuma in Arizona, the all-time high is a more modest 50.6°C (123°F).

Death Valley in California is the United States' hottest, driest place, where a well-authenticated temperature of 56.7°C (134°F) was reported in July 1913. In Australia's copper belt in northern Queensland, the temperature hit 53.1°C (127.5°F) at Cloncurry in January 1889 – another well-authenticated reading. Portugal holds the European record: 50.5°C (122.9°F) at Los Riodades. In Argentina, experts have reported 48.9°C (120°F) at Rivadavia; in Iran, 53.5°C (128.3°F) at Ahwaz. In complete contrast, the highest-recorded temperature in Antarctica is 13.9°C (57°F) at Hope Bay.

The British record stands at 37.1°C (98.8°F), reported on August 3, 1990, at Cheltenham in Gloucestershire. A few older reference books quote some higher figures,

including 37.8°C (100°F) at the Royal Observatory, Greenwich, in August 1911; 38.2°C (100.5°F) at Tonbridge in Kent in July 1868, and 38.4°C (101°F) at Alton in Hampshire in July 1881. However, recent research into factors such as the siting of the thermometer shelters and compatibility with reports from nearby stations, has shown that these old extremes were reported under nonstandard conditions, so they have been discarded. Nevertheless, it seems possible that, sooner or later, the elusive 37.8°C (100°F) mark could be exceeded somewhere in England.

LIFE IN THE DESERT *In the Namib Desert, isolated trees and scrub survive the arid environment against the odds.*

The most consistently hot place on our planet is probably Dalul which lies in northern Ethiopia, near the border with Eritrea. Dalul is located 258 ft (78 m) below sea level in the Danakil Depression, a lonely, arid region mostly populated by sheep and goat-herding nomads. An American chemical prospecting company maintained a weather station at Dalul between October 1960 and November 1966. During that period, the average daily maximum temperature was 41°C (106°F), more than 2°C (3.6°F) higher than any other site in the world for which records are available. The average daily minimum was 28.3°C (83°F), roughly 1°C (1.8°F) higher than at any other known location. The temperature reached or exceeded the 38°C (100°F) mark on an average of 290 days a year, although no single day exceeded 49°C (120°F) during the period when the observations were made. The coolest day registered a maximum temperature of 31.7°C (89°F), and the coolest night produced a minimum of 20.6°C (69°F).

IN THE FREEZER

The lowest temperatures on our planet are found in Antarctica. In the Northern Hemisphere, the North Pole is surrounded by the Arctic Ocean and temperatures are a little less extreme; the coldest spots are found thousands of miles away in the continental interiors of Siberia and Canada.

THE HOTTEST PLACE ON EARTH
In the Danakil Depression, northern Ethiopia, the mean daily maximum temperature is 41°C (106°F).

Vostok is a Russian scientific base some 11 500 ft (3500 m) above sea level on the South Polar Plateau, the heart of Antarctica. Here, the temperature fell to –89.2°C (–138.6°F) on July 21, 1983 – the lowest temperature recorded on Earth. Also in Antarctica, Plateau Station is the most consistently cold place for which we have records, with a mean annual temperature of –56.6°C (–70°F). At the US Amundsen-Scott base on the South Pole itself, the equivalent figure is –49°C (–56.2°F).

In Russia, the Siberian tin and gold-mining settlement of Verchojansk lies some 75 miles (120 km) north of the Arctic Circle on the Yana River. It is surrounded by mountains, rising to more than 7500 ft (2300 m) above sea level, which trap the freezing Arctic air. Here, a reading of –67.7°C (–90°F) was recorded in January 1885 and again in February 1892; the same temperature was recorded in February 1933 at Oymyakon, a small town 390 miles (630 km) away to the south-east. In February 1964, Oymyakon broke the Northern Hemisphere's record with a minimum of –71.1°C (–96°F). These represent the lowest temperatures known to have occurred in permanently inhabited locations – although Vostok is manned by scientists, it is not technically regarded as being permanently inhabited.

Canada's Yukon Territory is a spectacular wilderness of forests, plateaus and high mountain ranges gouged through with river valleys. One of these is the Klondike river valley, famous for its gold rush in the late 1890s. North of the Klondike, the Yukon stretches as far as the Arctic Circle

COLD SPOT *Charlotte Pass in the Australian Alps, New South Wales, set a new Australian low record of –23°C (–9.4°F) in June 1994.*

CLOTHES AND COMFORT

We wear clothes not only for adornment and modesty, but also to keep us warm in cold weather, to keep us dry when it is raining, and to ward off strong sunshine. In cold weather, the main purpose of clothing is to prevent loss of body heat to the air around, which is especially difficult when the wind blows strongly. The right clothing in these conditions is less a matter of thickness and weight than insulation by air spaces within the material.

The insulating capacity of our clothes is roughly proportional to the amount of dead air between our bodies and the outermost layer. This dead air includes the spaces within the various layers of cloth as well as the air between the layers. Thus close-woven and close-fitting garments are not very efficient at keeping the cold out, whereas many layers of thick, open-weave material are much more effective.

A strong wind decreases the insulation provided by our clothes by penetrating the various layers and disturbing the dead air within the cloth, and also by pressing the clothes against the body, thus squeezing out the dead air existing between the layers of clothing. In extreme conditions, the wind-chill effect can be minimised by wearing a wind-proof outer garment with drawstrings at the wrists, ankles and neck, and properly designed coverings for feet, hands and head.

A novel method of defining the wind-chill effect was made by physiologists and meteorologists working together in the late 1940s. They invented the 'clo' – a clothing unit defined as the

SUMMER SUITS *Scientists at the South Pole in the Antarctic 'summer' wear masks and insulating clothing to protect them against the cold.*

amount of insulation required to maintain comfort for a person of standard metabolic rate in an indoor environment where the temperature is 21°C (70°F) and the humidity 50 per cent or below. Very roughly, one clo amounts to two layers of thin clothing.

This idea could be adapted for forecasts. A weathercaster could say: 'The afternoon temperature will be zero, but there will be a large chill-factor thanks to the 20-25 mph [32-40 km/h] east wind; in other words it will be a six-layer day.'

and well beyond into a region of flat tundra with permanently frozen ground. Here, the settlement of Snag recorded North America's lowest-ever temperature: –63°C (–81.4°F) on February 3, 1947.

Prospect Creek in neighbouring Alaska holds the US record –62.1°C (–79.8°F) reported in January 1971. For the remaining US states, south of the 49th parallel, the lowest-recorded temperature is –56.5°C

(–69.7°F) at Rogers Pass in the Rocky Mountains in Montana, in January 1954.

In European Russia, Ust'Shchugor has logged –55°C (–67°F). In Australia, Charlotte Pass in the Australian Alps, New South Wales, dipped to –23°C (–9.4°F) on June 29, 1994. The South American record appears to be –32.8°C (–27°F) at Colonia Sarmiento, on Tierra del Fuego.

The British record stands at –27.2°C (–17°F) at Braemar in the Scottish Highlands, in February 1895. This figure was equalled at the same station in January 1982, and again at Altnaharra in the north-western Highlands in December 1995. As with the high temperature records, some older British textbooks refer to long discredited readings; thus the oft-quoted figure of –30.5°C (–23°F) at Blackadder in the Scottish Borders is not recognised as authentic.

DEEP FREEZE *With a mean annual temperature of –56.6°C (–70°F), Plateau Station in the Antarctic is the most consistently cold place on Earth.*

LIGHTS IN THE SKY

The interplay of sunlight, water droplets, ice crystals and dust particles is responsible for much of the colour we see in the sky, as well as a host of extraordinary optical phenomena, from rainbows and halos to coronas and glories.

The beauty of the rainbow has long impressed humans. The transparent ribbons of exquisite colour, forming a perfect arc across the sky, often against a backdrop of dark cloud, seem a fitting symbol of hope, of order returning after the storm.

For the ancient Norsemen of Scandinavia, the rainbow was a bridge linking the worlds of men and gods. In ancient India it was associated with the warlike sky god Indra; he fought with and killed the dragon Vrta who had been responsible for holding back the rain-bringing monsoon. In the Bible it has a special place as the sign of an agreement or covenant between God and man after Noah's Flood: 'And God said: "This is the sign of the covenant which I make between me and you [Noah] and every living creature that is with you, for all future generations: I set my bow in the cloud, and it shall be a sign of the

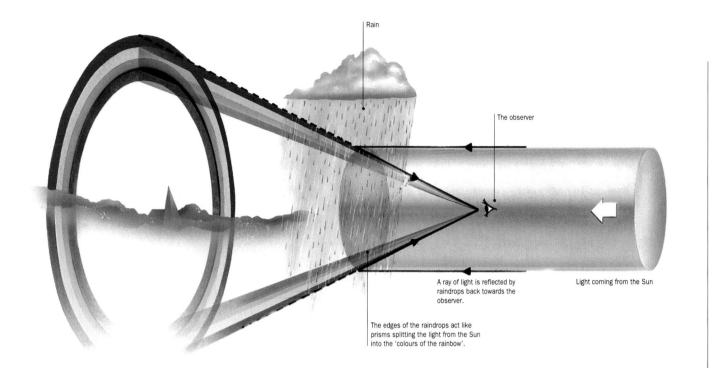

Rain

The observer

A ray of light is reflected by raindrops back towards the observer.

Light coming from the Sun

The edges of the raindrops act like prisms splitting the light from the Sun into the 'colours of the rainbow'.

covenant between me and the earth. When I bring clouds over the earth and the bow is seen in the clouds, I will remember my covenant which is between me and you and every living creature of all flesh; and the waters shall never again become a flood to destroy all flesh".'

The skywatcher has an ever-changing canvas of colour and beauty to enjoy. 'Lights in the sky' – known as photometeors, from the Greek *phos*, 'light', and *meteoros*, 'high in the air' – provide some of the most curious of all meteorological phenomena. The rainbow is the best known, but there is a range of others, including halos, coronas and glories (coloured rings around a shadow). Other 'lights' are of electrical or magnetic origin, including the aurora –

ARC OF LIGHT *A magnificent double rainbow arches over the Masai Mara in Kenya. The field in the foreground is brilliantly lit by the setting Sun.*

they are technically classified as 'electro-meteors'. The sky itself, meanwhile, is a paintbox of rich hues – not just the range of blues of a cloud-free sky or the common reds, pinks and golds of sunsets and sunrises, but also occasionally greens and purples. Very rarely – once in a blue moon – we may even be lucky enough to see the Sun or the Moon take on a bluish or greenish glow.

BENDING LIGHT

The way rays of sunlight change direction as they meet water and ice particles, and break up into their constituent colours, explains most of the optical phenomena we see in the sky. Sunlight actually comprises all the colours of the spectrum from red, through yellow, green and blue, to violet. Under normal conditions, these colours combine to create white light. Light rays travel in straight lines through air of consistent density, but when they are 'bent' by water or ice the colours separate. This 'bending' falls into three main categories: reflection, refraction and diffraction.

Reflection is the simplest to understand. It happens when rays of light bounce back off the surface of another substance, such as water or ice. The angle at which the light strikes the surface is equal to the angle at

RAINBOW COLOURS *Beams of sunlight are refracted as they pass through raindrops, breaking up into the colours of the spectrum.*

which it is reflected. This can be easily seen by shining a narrow-beamed flashlight at a mirror in a darkened room. Light can be reflected in this way on the inner surface of raindrops as well as the outer surface.

Refraction happens when a ray of light changes direction as it passes from one substance into another with a different density. It occurs, for instance, when sunlight passes from air into a water drop, or vice versa. It is most easily demonstrated by partly submerging a knife at an angle in a glass of water: viewed from the side, the knife appears to bend at the surface of the water.

Diffraction is harder to understand. It happens when a ray of light bends slightly as it passes an object in its path, so that small amounts of light invade the edges of the shadow created by the object. If you make a pinhole in a piece of card and hold it up to a strong light, the central bright patch should be surrounded by several very narrow alternating rings of light and dark. These are caused by diffraction.

Early weather observers knew that rainbows happen when the Sun shines on falling rain, but they did not know why. The first serious attempt to explain rainbows was made in 1637 by the French philosopher and mathematician René Descartes, who understood the key principle that light is refracted as it passes from air to water. He conducted an experiment with an enormous artificial raindrop – a spherical flask of water – and showed that a typical ray of light is refracted upon entering the water drop, then reflected once or twice inside the drop, and then refracted again as it leaves. Light leaves the raindrop in all directions, but because of the complex geometry caused by the combination of refraction and reflection, much is concentrated at an angle of 41° to 42° from the direction of the light entering the drop.

Most of the rainbows that we see result from a single, internal reflection within the drops of rain; these are known as primary rainbows. Sometimes we see a second, fainter bow, known as a secondary rainbow, some distance outside the primary bow. This secondary rainbow is caused by two internal reflections, so the colours are in reverse order. In this case, the concentration of light rays leaving the raindrop is at an angle of 51° from the rays entering it.

The primary rainbow is actually part of a full circle, but we normally see only the part of the circle above the horizon – it shines most brightly against a backdrop of dark clouds. However, if we look carefully at the horizon, we can usually see the bow extending faintly for a short distance across the distant countryside. The centre of the

LOW BOW *Given a combination of heavy rain, bright sunshine and a dark background below your point of observation, bows may be seen even when the Sun is high in the sky.*

circle is a point exactly opposite the Sun, known technically as the 'antisolar point'.

If two imaginary lines are drawn, one between the observer and the 'rim' of the circle (the rainbow itself), the other between the observer and the antisolar point, the angle between them – known as the 'angular radius' – is roughly 42°. A primary and a secondary rainbow being concentric circles, they have the same centre or antisolar point, and the secondary rainbow has an angular radius of 51°. These circles may occasionally be seen in all their glory from aircraft. Incomplete rainbows are seen when rain is falling or when the sun is shining over an insufficiently large area.

Rainbows are always the same size; their angular radii are always the same at either 42° or 51°, and they are always found opposite the main source of light. This is equally true of artificially generated rainbows such as the ones that form behind spray from a garden sprinkler. It means that a primary rainbow will never occur when the Sun is more than 42° above the horizon, simply because the entire circle surrounding the antisolar point will be below the horizon. Thus, in the tropics the time when rainbows can be seen is confined to a relatively short period in the morning and evening. In polar regions, by contrast, rainbows can be seen even at midday in summer – but only if it is warm enough for rain to fall rather than snow. The lower the Sun is in the sky, the higher the rainbow appears to be. On the rare

MAKE YOUR OWN RAINBOW
This is a simple task on a sunny day. You do not even need irrigation machinery as here. A simple hosepipe with your finger over the end will provide the necessary cascade of 'raindrops'.

occasions when the setting Sun shines brightly enough to create a bow, the antisolar point lies on the opposite horizon, and the primary and secondary rainbows describe semicircles with their highest points respectively 42° and 51° above the horizon.

Additional fainter bows appear from time to time on the inside of a primary rainbow and immediately adjacent to it. These bows are called 'supernumeraries' and are a result of diffraction. A faintly coloured rainbow may also sometimes occur opposite the Moon. But as moonlight is considerably

weaker than sunlight, these nocturnal bows are harder to see and much less spectacular than the ones that are created by sunlight.

Although Descartes understood the basic principles of reflection and refraction, he could not explain why rainbows are coloured as they are. More than 25 years after his experiment with the artificial raindrop in 1637, the Englishman Sir Isaac Newton provided the answer. He showed

BLUE SKY, BLUE SUNS, BLUE MOONS

Why is the sky blue? The answer involves the theory of scattering. Fundamental to this is the notion that rays of light travel as waves, and the wavelength of each colour of the spectrum is slightly different: blue light has a relatively short wavelength and red a relatively long one. Also,

light waves can be knocked off course – scattered – by particles in the atmosphere. The colour of the scattered light rays will predominate in the eye of the observer.

The Earth's atmosphere comprises lots of particles of different sizes. These include dust particles, which

are relatively large, and air molecules, which are very tiny. Blue light's short wavelength means that the small air molecules are enough to scatter it in all directions, leaving the yellow and red part of the spectrum, with longer wavelengths, virtually untouched. When the air is clear and pure, therefore, the sky will appear a deep blue. By contrast, when there are many impurities in the air, all colours are scattered, and recombine into white in the eye of the observer.

'Once in a blue moon' blue moons occur, as do blue suns; green suns and moons have also been seen. The most famous examples happened in the wake of the the eruption of Krakatoa in 1883, when they were

PRAIRIE SUNSET Haze particles have scattered all the blue light, letting the yellow and red parts of the spectrum dominate.

seen in many parts of the world for some time after.

Another example was observed in 1950 in North America and Europe. The cause was a forest fire in Alberta, Canada, on the eastern slopes of the Rockies. The fire produced a huge pall of smoke swept by strong upper winds across southern Canada, the USA and over the Atlantic towards Europe. In Saskatchewan and Ontario, and in US cities such as Detroit and Buffalo, the smoke was thick enough to blot out the Sun, but along the eastern seaboard the smoke thinned out and a blue Sun was observed in places. Three days later, a blue Sun was seen in Britain, Scandinavia, Germany, France and Italy. It was later shown that the soot particles in the cloud of smoke were of the correct dimensions to disperse the red and orange parts of the spectrum completely, leaving just blue, green and some yellow.

LIGHT THROUGH ICE *The colours of the rainbow may also be seen when the weather is fine. In fact, these phenomena have nothing to do with rainbows. They are the result of refraction of sunlight by ice crystals high in the atmosphere.*

that white light can be broken down into the colours of the spectrum and that each of these colours is refracted at a slightly different angle when passing from one substance to another. In rainbows the colours appear brightest when raindrops are moderately large – around $1/100$ in (0.25 mm). With smaller droplets, the red and orange colours become weak. With tiny particles of water such as those in fog, a white bow

THE SUN'S GREEN FLASH

Watch the Sun set over water and, as its red rim vanishes over the horizon, you may glimpse a green flash. This is because green light bends farther when refracted than red. For a second or two, light on all other wavebands is blocked by the horizon (red), absorbed by the atmosphere (orange and yellow) or scattered by air molecules (blue and violet). Only green light reaches the observer. The green flash can, in fact, be seen at sunrise and sunset wherever the air is clear and the horizon is sharply defined.

(known as a 'fog-bow' or 'Ulloa's bow') is occasionally seen. Very large droplets of $1/50$ in (0.5 mm) or more will produce rainbows dominated by red and orange.

Because each coloured arc is the result of sunlight falling on raindrops between the observer and the apparent position of the bow, it follows that different observers will be seeing the rainbow via different raindrops. In other words, each rainbow is personal to its observer, and it will always remain at the same apparent distance, even when the observer is travelling. Thus 'somewhere over the rainbow' must remain unattainable, as will the mythical 'pot of gold at the end of the rainbow'.

CIRCLE OF LIGHT *A complete 22° halo surrounds the Sun, with a reflection in the ice-strewn Antarctic beneath.*

Wispy, high-level cirrus and cirrostratus clouds often herald a warm front bringing rain. Look up at the Sun on a day when they cover the sky and it may well be framed by a luminous halo. This may be white, or if it is particularly well developed, gently coloured in hues of red, yellow and green.

Rainbows happen when sunshine falls on raindrops; halos occur when sunshine falls on ice crystals. Most halos form when the Sun shines through a layer of ice-crystal cloud – that is, either cirrus or cirrostratus – some 4 to 7 miles (6 to 12 km) above the Earth's surface. Because of these clouds' association with warm fronts, halos have traditionally been seen as a sign of rain.

HALOS IN THE SKY

Ice crystals, although basically hexagonal in structure, come in many shapes and sizes and may point in many different directions in the same cloud. The predominant shapes include columns (sometimes called 'pencil crystals' because they look like the shaft of a stubby pencil), plates and cones, but there are other, more complex types. On rare occasions, crystals may also cluster together in exotic shapes. There is therefore a wide range of surfaces at different angles to reflect and refract rays of light. This results in an equally wide range of halo phenomena, some quite common, others very rare.

If the clouds consist of a variety of ice crystals, all shaped differently and pointing in different directions, the common 22° halo is the most likely type to be seen. This appears as a luminous ring centred on either the Sun or the Moon and is a result of light being refracted 22° as it passes through the ice crystals in the cloud. In Britain such halos may be seen somewhere in the country on about 100 days each year, and at any one place on 30 or 40 days annually. In higher latitudes they occur even more frequently.

If ice-crystal clouds consist chiefly of one shape of crystal, with the majority of them

POLAR LIGHTS: THE AURORA

Among the most breathtaking sights Earth has to offer are the dramatic, unearthly displays of mobile, coloured lights, known as the northern lights or aurora borealis in the Northern Hemisphere, and the southern lights or aurora australis in the Southern Hemisphere. They are most often seen in polar latitudes, but occasionally penetrate as far as the 40th parallel, the latitude of northern Patagonia in the Southern Hemisphere and of southern Italy and Philadelphia in the Northern.

These stunning effects are electromagnetic in origin. They are the result of electrically charged particles emitted by the Sun interacting with the Earth's magnetic field, causing a patterned electrical discharge. This interaction takes place high in the atmosphere, usually between 100 and 300 miles (156 and 500 km) above the Earth's surface. They may be faint and almost monochrome, but occasionally there are brilliant, awe-inspiring, multi-coloured displays, with pulsating bands of luminescence, bundles of short rays, billowing curtains of colour and streamers of light shooting across the sky. Once seen, the astounding beauty of an aurora will remain in the memory for ever.

SHIMMERS OF COLOUR *The northern lights are most often seen in a belt – the Polar Light Girdle – across northern Europe, Canada and Alaska.*

facing in one direction, there is a chance of seeing much rarer arcs in the sky. An example is the 46° halo, which is usually fainter than the 22° one. It is normally white, and is rarely complete. It occurs when sunlight passes through clouds in which the ice crystals are aligned with their faces at right angles to each other.

Sometimes a bright white circle forms, passing through the Sun and running parallel to the horizon. This is known as a 'parhelic circle' (from the Greek *para*, 'beside', and *helios*, 'sun'), and it happens when the Sun's rays are reflected off plate-shaped ice crystals. If a parhelic circle crosses a 22° halo, mock suns may form, one on either side of the real Sun. Also known as 'sun dogs' or 'parhelia', these appear as very bright patches, sometimes coloured red and yellow, lying just outside the halo. At night,

mock moons, too, may occur, but they are a good deal less frequent than their daytime counterparts.

Brightly coloured 'circumzenithal arcs', shaded yellow, red and sometimes blue, are among the most spectacular of the sky's optical phenomena. They are part of a circle of light refracted 90° through the edges of vertically aligned crystals, and are normally brightest when in contact with the upper part of a 22° halo. Occasionally, they may be seen glowing brightly without any other

THE FULL WORKS *This display, photographed in Antarctica, includes a 22° halo, mock suns, a parhelic circle and a Sun pillar.*

halo effects. They look rather like rainbows and can puzzle observers, who wonder how it is that they are seeing a rainbow in the wrong part of the sky without a drop of rain in sight.

Sun pillars occur quite often around sunset and sunrise (both before and after) when ice-crystal clouds are in evidence. They are vertical bands of light extending through the Sun itself and sometimes stretching a considerable distance above the horizon. Caused by the reflection of sunlight from ice crystals, they are normally tinted with the same reds, crimsons, golds and yellows of a sunset or sunrise.

RINGS AROUND THE MOON

Sometimes a tight ring of light, usually coloured, forms around the Sun or Moon. Known as a corona, its colours are usually most striking when seen around the Moon. A rim of violet on the inside gives way to red on the outside, and quite often the sequence of colours is repeated up to three times. Coronas appear when the light of the Sun or Moon filters through relatively thin water-droplet clouds such as altocumulus or stratocumulus. They are caused by the diffraction of light passing through a layer of tiny droplets. The more uniform the size of the droplets, the clearer the colours.

LIGHT DIFFRACTED *Coronas are the result of diffraction of the Sun's rays by tiny water droplets in medium-level clouds such as altocumulus.*

For several years after the eruption of Krakatoa in Indonesia in 1883, observers worldwide noticed a special type of corona. It usually had a reddish tinge and, unlike ordinary coronas, did not actually touch the outer edge of the Sun and Moon. This type of corona, known as a Bishop's Ring, happens when light is diffracted through a layer of volcanic dust in the upper atmosphere. More recently, it was seen for about two years after the eruption in 1992 of Mount Pinatubo in the Philippines. It has nothing to do with ecclesiastic bishops, except in the most tenuous of

LIGHT ROUND MY SHADOW *British mountaineer Rebecca Stevens, on the Eiger summit in Switzerland, waves at her own shadow on the mist below. The shadow is surrounded by rings of light – a glory.*

ways – the first ever detailed account of this phenomenon was given by a clergyman, the Reverend Sereno Bishop, at Honolulu in Hawaii in September 1883.

THE GLORY OF A SHADOW

Hillwalkers and climbers in mountainous areas, standing with their backs to the Sun, with layers of cloud stretching out for miles and miles below them, may notice a strange effect around the shadows of their heads. Each shadow is surrounded by rings of coloured light. This is a 'glory', a sequence of coloured rings sometimes seen around a shadow as it is projected onto a cloud consisting of small water droplets. It is a result of diffraction and may also be seen against a background of fog or, very rarely, dew.

When the backdrop of cloud or fog is very close, the observer's shadow may loom menacingly. The rings of light surrounding it make it all the more frightening. This sort of glory is known as the 'Brocken Spectre', named after the Brocken, the highest peak in the Harz Mountains in Germany, where it has been regularly seen over the centuries.

These days a glory is most commonly seen by air travellers. Anyone in a plane flying above a layer of cloud, looking down through the porthole on the opposite side of the plane from the Sun, will almost certainly see the shadow of the aircraft on the cloud below surrounded by coloured rings of light.

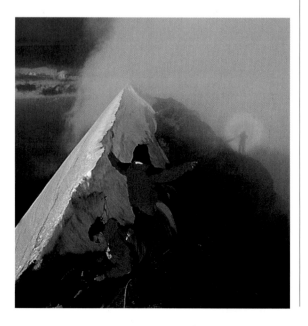

3

WORLD CLIMATES

SUMMER BLOOMS *Rose bay shrubs flower during the Arctic summer in north Canada.*

CLIMATE HAS BEEN DESCRIBED AS THE AVERAGE OF ALL THE WEATHER WE EXPERIENCE. WEATHER MAY VARY FROM DAY TO DAY, BUT THE CLIMATE OF A PLACE WHERE PEOPLE LIVE IS A CONSTANT THROUGHOUT THEIR LIVES. ITS CHARACTERISTICS DETERMINE WHAT CROPS WILL GROW, WHAT ANIMALS THRIVE, WHAT SORTS OF HOUSES PEOPLE BUILD AND WHAT SORTS OF CLOTHES THEY WEAR DURING THE VARIOUS SEASONS. CLIMATES VARY GRADUALLY ACROSS THE CONTINENTS AND THERE ARE FEW SHARP BOUNDARIES. EVEN SO, THREE BROAD ZONES CAN BE IDENTIFIED: TROPICAL, TEMPERATE AND POLAR. THESE ZONES CAN IN TURN BE SUBDIVIDED ACCORDING TO THE VARYING INFLUENCES OF LAND AND SEA, AND THE EFFECT ON THEM OF HEIGHT ABOVE SEA LEVEL.

RAINY SEASON *Floods during India's south-west monsoon.*

THE TORRID ZONE

Between the Tropics of Cancer and Capricorn lies a wide range of environments. Contrasting landscapes and vegetation owe much to contrasts in climate – from the torrential downpours of the equatorial belt to the aridity of tropical deserts.

As regular as clockwork the rain comes pouring down. Typically, days start fine and sunny after early mist banks have disappeared, but later clouds build up. It gets steadily hotter and stickier; by early afternoon it can be almost intolerably muggy. Thunderclouds form; on bad days sweat pours from the skin and any movement seems an effort. Then at almost the same time every day, the rain descends – dense, pelting rain in huge drops, driving people off the streets and fields, capable sometimes of bringing a car to a halt even with its windshield wipers going full tilt. Often there is the added excitement of thunder and lightning before the storm blows over. These daily downpours of the equatorial rainy season occur so regularly that people frequently organise their lives around them, agreeing, for example, to meet 'after the rain'.

MIST RISING *After heavy afternoon rains, trees and ground retain much moisture, leading to mist or fog that evening, which disperses the next morning.*

Tropical climates encompass immense contrasts. Prevailing over a broad band – the so-called Torrid Zone – either side of the Equator, they range from the wettest parts of the world, the equatorial rain forests, to the driest, the hot deserts. Between the two are vast tracts of tropical grassland (or savannah) where early man thrived. Around the Indian Ocean and the western Pacific are regions where the general patterns of a tropical climate are modified by the seasonal rhythms of the monsoon.

The tropics owe their name to their theoretical outer limits, the tropics of Cancer and Capricorn, corresponding to latitudes 23°30' N and S. The word comes from the Greek *tropikos*, 'of turning', and the two tropics are turning points. The Tropic of Cancer is the most northerly latitude at which the midday Sun shines directly overhead; the Tropic of Capricorn is the most southerly. Every year the Sun oscillates – from the point of view of the observer on Earth – between the two. It reaches the Tropic of Cancer at the Northern Hemisphere's summer solstice, June 21/22, then turns south again, reaching the Tropic of Capricorn six months later at the Southern Hemisphere's summer solstice, December

APRIL IN TANZANIA *A grey curtain between cloud and ground marks the approach of a late rainy season cloudburst.*

21/22. At the equinoxes, March 20/21 and September 22/23, it is shining directly overhead at the Equator at noon.

The prevailing winds across much of the tropics are the north-east trades in the Northern Hemisphere and the south-east trades in the Southern Hemisphere. Where

HEAT WITHOUT EXTREMES

The equatorial rain forest is a region of consistently high temperature and high humidity, but extremes of temperature are not normally found here. For instance, at Dar-es-Salaam in Tanzania the temperature has never exceeded 36.1°C (97°F) in 50 years of records, while the all-time high at Freetown in Sierre Leone is 36.7°C (98°F). These figures compare with the record for England – hardly a climate of extremes – of 37.1°C (98.8°F).

these converge, Sun-heated rising air is given added impetus. Rainfall is heavy and thunderstorms frequent in this belt, known as the inter-tropical convergence zone. If the Earth were upright in relation to the Sun and entirely covered with sea, the inter-tropical convergence zone would correspond with

the Equator. In fact, it moves considerably from season to season, partly following the oscillation of the Sun between the Tropics of Cancer and Capricorn, partly influenced by temperature contrasts between oceans and continents. It oscillates most widely in the Indian Ocean where it plays a major part in the flow of monsoons.

HOT AND HUMID

Rainy seasons are just about the only noticeable seasons in much of the tropics. In the band lying roughly within 12° of latitude north and south of the Equator, known as the Equatorial Zone, even these scarcely stand out. All months are essentially hot and rainy, though some are a little bit more so than others. This zone includes most of the Amazon Basin together with the Pacific coastal fringe of Ecuador and Colombia; the Congo Basin and the coastal strip of West Africa from Liberia to Gabon; the coastlands of Tanzania and Kenya; Sri Lanka, Malaysia and Indonesia. Dense rain forests cover much of the zone. Another of its characteristics is that there is very little variation in the hours of daylight through the year. Since the belt where the north-east and south-east trades converge is never far away, winds tend to be light and variable.

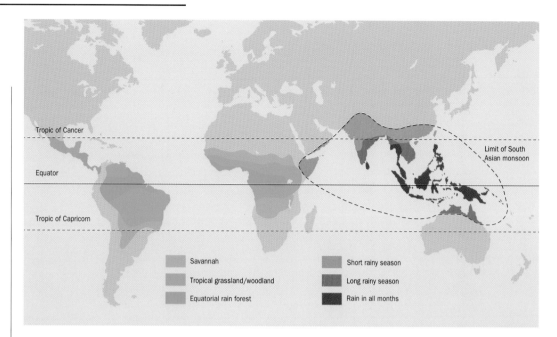

Savannah	Short rainy season
Tropical grassland/woodland	Long rainy season
Equatorial rain forest	Rain in all months

Tropic of Cancer
Equator
Tropic of Capricorn
Limit of South Asian monsoon

THE TORRID ZONE *Roughly bounded by the Tropics of Cancer and Capricorn, the world's equatorial and tropical climates are mostly hot and rainy. Monsoon climates have exaggerated wet and dry seasons.*

The combination of heat and humidity makes the equatorial climate uncomfortable and enervating, and it has long been regarded as unhealthy. Bacteria thrive; wounds become easily infected, and human resistance to illness is weakened. Materials also deteriorate more rapidly than in cooler parts of the world – metals corrode, clothing and furnishings rot, and foodstuffs go mouldy. European settlers in these regions soon discovered that they had to spend a lot of time taking care of their homes and food supplies if they were to stay fit and healthy.

Singapore, lying 1° of latitude north of the Equator, has a typical equatorial climate. Through the year temperatures are very high and very consistent. In January the highest average daytime temperature is 30.2°C (86.4°F); in May it is just 1.3°C (2.3°F) higher at 31.5°C (88.7°F). Humidity is high, and again consistently so, and there is frequent cloud-cover. Both of these help to lessen variations between day and night-time temperatures. Night-time temperatures rarely drop below 23°C (73.4°F) in January and February or 24.1°C (75.4°F) in June. Consistency within a narrow band of temperatures is very much a hallmark of

this climate. In 40 years of records in Singapore, it never got hotter than 36°C (97°F) or colder than 19°C (66°F).

This consistency is particularly true of coasts and islands, such as Singapore, where the stabilising influence of the ocean is at its greatest. But it is also true to a large extent of places inland. Kisangani (formerly Stanleyville) is a river port in the Democratic Republic of Congo (formerly Zaire), located on the site of a trading post set up by the 19th-

---

MONSOONS AND SAHARA SAND

The countries of West Africa experience a semimonsoonal climate, although not the huge contrast between the wet and dry seasons typical of India. The dry north-easterly wind that blows between November and March has been dubbed the harmattan and it provides relief from the high humidity and drenching rains which occur from April to October, but it often deposits copious quantities of dust picked up from the Sahara.

---

century British explorer, Sir Henry Morton Stanley. It lies some 940 miles (1500 km) from the Congo's mouth, 1320 ft (400 m) above sea level. Here, mean maximum temperatures are 31°C (88°F) in the warmest month and 29°C (84°F) in the coolest. Mean minimum temperatures are 21°C (70°F) in the warmest month and 19°C (66°F) in the coolest.

The heaviest rains in the Equatorial Zone come around and shortly after the

time when the input of heat from the Sun is greatest, the hot rising air generating thick rain clouds. Thus the rains follow the Sun in its march between the Tropics of Cancer and Capricorn. This means that the wettest months in the zone close to the Equator are around and just after the equinoxes, between March and May and September and November.

The intervening months can hardly be called dry, however. They are best described as marginally less wet. At Singapore, the annual rainfall is 95 in (2413 mm). Of that total, 6⁷/₁₀ in (170 mm) comes in July, which is the least wet month, and 10¹/₅ in (259 mm) comes in November, which is the wettest. At Kisangani the year's total averages 67 in (1701 mm). January is the least wet month with 2³/₁₀ in (58 mm); October is the wettest with 8¹/₂ in (216 mm).

SEASONAL VARIETY

Seasons become more marked as you travel north or south from the Equator towards either of the two tropics. The twin rainy seasons gradually merge into one, occurring around and just after the summer solstice. At the other end of the yearly cycle, the winter solstice brings a noticeable dry season. At this time of the year temperatures, too, are markedly lower. The rise in temperature towards the summer solstice is usually cut short by the arrival of the rains.

More seasonal rainfall cannot sustain the luxuriant forests of the Equatorial Zone. These give way to grasslands and scattered woodlands. Seasonal crops such as rice, millet, sorghum and maize are cultivated, the success of each harvest depending on the prompt arrival of the rainy season at crucial stages in the plants' growth.

Climates in this zone are more pleasant than in the equatorial region. Even in the Caribbean where humidity levels are high throughout the year, the trade winds provide natural air conditioning that provides some relief from the heat. Continental interiors can get suffocatingly hot for several weeks before the summer rains, but during the

GRASS AND WOOD *Mixed grass and woodlands mark the zones with only seasonal rains on either side of the equatorial belt – as in Brazil's Mato Grosso.*

'winter' months temperatures are comfortable. Where the heat is moderated by altitude such as the plateau lands of southern and eastern Africa and southern Brazil, the range in temperature is almost ideal, rarely rising above 30°C (86°F). The zone as a whole includes most of Brazil south of the Amazon Basin together with Paraguay and northern Argentina; the north coast of South America, the Caribbean, most of Central America and much of Texas; Madagascar and much of Africa south of the equatorial belt.

Each region within the zone has its own variations. In most places, the summer solstice brings the most unsettled weather. The inter-tropical convergence zone is nearby, bringing storm clouds and rain.

Where the trade winds blow from a continental interior, the rest of the year is mostly dry. However, on the western margins of Africa and South America, and in Central America and the Caribbean, the trade winds blow onshore, often bringing showers and thunderstorms. As a result these regions have some rain in all months.

Temperatures are consistently highest on islands and on coastal lowlands. Freetown in Sierra Leone, on the West African coast, is a good example. No matter which month it is, mean maximum temperatures range between 28° and 31°C (82° and 88°F). Similarly, mean minimum temperatures range only between 22° and 25°C (72° and 77°F). An island example is Kingston in

Jamaica, where a similar pattern exists: mean maximum temperatures range just 3°C (6°F) during the year between 29° and 32°C (84° and 90°F).

Temperatures vary more noticeably with the seasons in continental interiors. June and July are the coolest months in Harare in Zimbabwe, which lies 4800 ft (1460 m) above sea level. In these months the average daily maximum temperature is 21°C (70°F). Nights get positively chilly in July at 7°C (45°F). October is the hottest month of the year with an average daily maximum temperature of 29°C (84°F). Then the summer rains break and daytime temperatures slip back to 26°C (79°F) from November through to April. Night-time temperatures

STAPLE CROP *Women transplant rice plants in India's rainy season. From June to September the south-west monsoon brings heavy rains.*

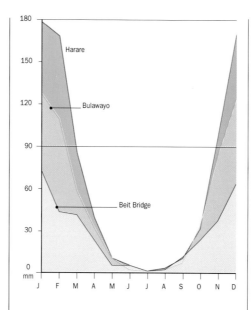

in January are reasonably low for the latitude at 16°C (61°F).

Seasonal rainfall varies most strongly along the West African coast, with the bulk of the year's rain falling in a well-defined

rainy season. The annual total at Freetown is 135 in (3429 mm). Of this, 88 per cent falls in the five months from June to October. During this rainy season, some rain falls on an average of 126 days out of 153. The wettest months are July and August, both with 35 in (889 mm). February's normal rainfall, by contrast, is just 1/10 in (2.5 mm).

Farther from the Equator, the seasonal rains become less reliable. In Zimbabwe, Harare lies 18° south of the Equator. Its annual rainfall is 33 in (838 mm). Bulawayo, also in Zimbabwe, lies 20° south of the Equator. The total here is only 23 in (584 mm). At Beit Bridge, 22° south of the Equator, the total is just 13 in (330 mm). Thus the savannah merges imperceptibly into desert.

The eastern margins of the continent are more blessed, with damp air blowing in off the Indian Ocean bringing some rain even during the dry season. Sofala on the Mozambique coast, lies just 250 miles (400 km) from Harare. Here, the annual rainfall is 60 in (1524 mm), of which just over 63 per cent falls in a four-month rainy season. The remaining 22 in (559 mm) falls during the drier part of the year.

WHEN THE MONSOON COMES

In Africa and South America land extends either side of the Equator, while the Atlantic and Pacific Oceans also straddle both hemispheres. As a result, there are few major contrasts in these tropical zones between the climates in each hemisphere. But between longitudes

CHERRAPUNJI: THE WETTEST PLACE ON EARTH

India, Hawaii and Colombia vie with one another for the rainiest place on Earth. The problem is that records have been kept for different periods at the three locations, so it is impossible to make comparisons that are scientifically valid. The rainfall pedigree of the Indian hill-station Cherrapunji, however, is beyond reproach. There is no doubt that the highest monthly and yearly falls ever recorded were measured here. Cherrapunji lies in the Khasi hills in the state of Meghalaya (formerly part of Assam), just over 4300 ft (1300 m) above sea level. These hills rise sharply from the Bengal plain to the south, and rain-bearing southerly winds are funnelled along several valleys which converge on the small sandstone plateau where Cherrapunji is sited. Regular weather records have been kept here since 1851.

The average annual rainfall is 432 in (10 972 mm) but, thanks to the monsoon, this shows marked contrasts across the year, peaking in June. The wettest year of all was 1861, with 905 in (22 987 mm), of which 366 in (9296 mm) fell in July. The wettest 12-month period was from August 1860 to July 1861, which produced the extraordinary total of 1041 4/5 in (26 462 mm). This huge figure is easier to appreciate if it is converted into 86 ft 9 1/2 in (26.4 m).

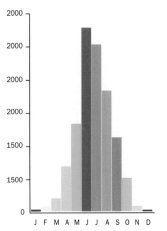

RECORD HOLDER *Perched on a small plateau (far left) above the steep slopes of the Khasi Hills, Cherrapunji holds the world record for the highest monthly and annual rainfalls. Mean monthly figures (above) range from just 1/2 in (13 mm) in December to a colossal 108 3/5 in (2758 mm) in June.*

40°E and 120°E, the picture is very different. Here, the huge Asiatic landmass sits north of the Equator while the broad expanses of the Indian Ocean lie to the south.

This juxtaposition of ocean and continent has a massive impact on the climate of the region. During the Northern Hemisphere's winter, most of Asia becomes intensely cold. Dense chilled air stagnates over the continental interior, forming a huge high-pressure system. Meanwhile, hot air rises over the warm waters of the Indian Ocean, creating an area of low pressure between the Equator and the Tropic of Capricorn. Air flows out of the continental 'high' into the oceanic 'low', and this is known as the north-easterly monsoon.

During the Northern Hemisphere's summer, the low pressure over the Indian Ocean moves north of the Equator, following the Sun's annual oscillation between the two tropics. At the same time, the heat of the Sun over the Asiatic landmass causes the pressure to drop there, too. These low-pressure systems join forces over the northern part of the Indian subcontinent. Relatively high pressure over the southern Indian Ocean, meanwhile, extends northwards towards the Equator. As a result, air now flows in the opposite direction, from the Indian Ocean into south Asia, and this is known as the south-westerly monsoon.

The north-easterly monsoon, which is of continental origin, is cool and dry; the south-westerly monsoon, of oceanic origin, is warm and exceptionally moist. The climate of this region therefore shows the most extreme contrast between winter drought and summer rains. The greatest heat occurs before the monsoon rains arrive and this creates a third recognisable season in India. Thus there is a cool dry season from December to February, the time of the north-easterly monsoon. A hot dry season follows, from March until late May or June, which corresponds to the build-up for the south-westerly monsoon. This arrives in June and lasts until November, the wet season.

The whole nation awaits the arrival of the rains – for relief from the furnace-like heat, the drought and the dust. Moreover, the year's harvest depends on regular, timely, but not excessive quantities of water. Meteorologists accordingly track the arrival

STREETS AWASH *Heavy monsoon rains bring floods to the heart of downtown Taipei, capital of Taiwan.*

RAIN CLOUDS OVER DARWIN
In northern Australia, it is the north-west monsoon that brings the rains, from November to March.

of the south-westerly monsoon and give regular bulletins on its progress. It appears first in the far south-west of India, then moves in fits and starts up the coast towards Bombay. After that it swings inland.

The rainfall statistics for Bombay illustrate the tremendous seasonal contrasts. The annual total is 71 in (1803 mm), of which none falls between mid-November and mid-May. The rains usually arrive around June 6. June has an average monthly fall of 19 in (483 mm). This increases in July to 24 in (610 mm), after which the figure drops again to 15 in (381 mm) in August and 10 in (254 mm) in September.

Temperature contrasts are less marked because Bombay's climate is strongly modified by its coastal location. Afternoon temperatures range only between 28° and 33°C (82° and 91°F) throughout the year. By contrast, New Delhi in the interior reveals a much more striking picture. In the first place, the cool season is noticeably cool. Maximum afternoon temperatures in January average 21°C (70°F); the lowest overnight temperatures are typically round about 7°C (45°F). Some days are decidedly cold, and slight frost has even been known to form around daybreak.

The weather becomes steadily hotter from mid-February onwards and by mid-April daytime temperatures are regularly breaking the 38°C (100°F) mark. May and early June is the hottest period, with mean maximum temperatures around 41°C (106°F). Then come the rains. Daily maximum temperatures slip back to 34° or 35°C (93° or 95°F) and stay there until mid-October.

The geography of south Asia is complex, resulting in many local variations on the general theme. Some stretches of coastline face the east, providing shelter from the very moist south-westerly monsoon. Small amounts of moisture may also be squeezed out of the normally dry north-easterly monsoon in these areas. Furthermore, the transition months of May and November may bring tropical cyclones. The result is completely different rainfall patterns from those of Bombay and New Delhi. The city of Madras, on the east coast of India, for example, receives most of its rain in October and November from tropical disturbances travelling across the coastline from the Bay of Bengal. The same is true of Vietnam and the Philippines where typhoons

are regular visitors especially between July and December.

In the Southern Hemisphere, northern and north-eastern Australia have monsoon climates. At Darwin, in the Northern Territory, the annual total rainfall is 59 in (1499 mm) of which 86 per cent falls between November and March. At Cairns in northern Queensland the total is 89 in (2261 mm) of which 79 per cent comes between December and April.

DESERT CLIMES

Deserts are not caused by low rainfall alone. Rain is rare in the lands alongside the Nile, Tigris and Euphrates, but these are fertile, intensively cultivated regions because the rivers provide the necessary moisture. Even

RED SANDS, BLUE SKY *Large parts of the Sahara Desert receive less than 5 in (127 mm) of rain each year.*

where rainfall is low and there is no great river to irrigate the soil, crops can be cultivated so long as the rain that does come falls reliably and regularly during the growing season. Conversely, no worthwhile agriculture can be undertaken where rain falls relatively abundantly but in sporadic and unpredictable heavy downpours. Extensive deserts form only where low rainfall is matched by low humidity, high temperatures and high levels of sunshine. Here, little or nothing will grow except along water courses and in isolated oases.

If one excludes Antarctica, which is technically a desert because it receives less than 5 in (127 mm) of precipitation a year, the world's most extensive desert is the Sahara, covering some 3.5 million sq miles (9.1 million km²) in North Africa. Others are the Arabian desert, with offshoots extending into Iraq and Iran and even as far as Pakistan and northwest India; the desert interior of Australia; the Namib (or Kalahari) Desert of southern Africa; the Atacama Desert of northern Chile and southern Peru; and the arid lands of north-western Mexico, southern California, Arizona and New Mexico.

All of these rainless zones lie around the outer fringes of the tropics where the trade winds blow out of dry continental interiors. Subtropical high-pressure belts lie over them or immediately to their north in the Northern Hemisphere or to their south in the Southern Hemisphere. Air heated at the Equator has risen, cooled, dropped its moisture as rain and now subsides in these belts – also known as the horse latitudes – as very dry air. Because the air is subsiding it creates high pressure and being compressed as it sinks, it is also warm. So the subtropical regions are dry, hot and sunny.

Because of their distance from the Equator, temperature varies considerably from season to season. Even winters are warm, but summers are very hot. At the same time, the clear skies that bring oven-like heat by day also allow rapid cooling during the hours of darkness. Nights are often surprisingly chilly during the winter half of the year. Frost has been recorded quite regularly as far south as 15°N in the Sahara, and at Tamanrasset in southern Algeria – lying 4600 ft (1400 m) above sea level – the temperature has been known to fall to −7°C (19°F). In the southern Sahara, by contrast, temperatures exceed 38°C (100°F) in all months of the year.

Elsewhere, cold ocean currents yield more tolerable climates along some desert coastlines. In California, Chile and Peru, Namibia and southern Morocco, persistent maritime breezes blow onshore, cooling things to a pleasant temperature, although mist and low cloud hang around for long periods. Nowhere is this more clearly seen than at Port Nolloth on the Atlantic coast of South Africa, just south of the border with Namibia. Here, the mean maximum temperature of the warmest month, February, is just 19°C (66°F), thanks to the chill Benguela Current. Only occasionally does the hot Berg wind blow from the desert interior lifting the temperature as high as 43°C (109°F).

From time to time, summer rains fall on the fringes of these deserts on their Equator side, so that the desert merges imperceptibly into savannah. At Tombouctou (Timbuktu) in Mali, for example, the annual rainfall is 9 in (229 mm), with 3 in (76 mm) falling in both July and August. The other fringes, facing towards the poles, merge into subtropical climates, often with scattered winter rains. Thus San Diego in southern California has an annual rainfall of 10 1/2 in (267 mm), with about 2 in (51 mm) each month from December to March. Even in the heart of the Sahara showers occasionally fall. By contrast, parts of the Atacama Desert in northern Chile are believed to have experienced no significant rainfall for some four centuries until a sudden downpour occurred in 1971. The longest authenticated rainless period lasted from October 1903 to December 1917, a total of 171 months, at Arica on the Chile-Peru border.

THE TEMPERATE ZONE

The notion of four seasons is most appropriate to temperate latitudes. It is most true where oceanic influences are greatest; in continental interiors, spring and autumn are merely brief transitions between long cold winters and long hot summers.

Most people in the world now live in the Temperate Zone – very roughly the bands of the globe between the Tropic of Cancer and the Arctic Circle in the Northern Hemisphere and the tropic of Capricorn and the Antarctic Circle in the Southern Hemisphere. It includes some of the most fertile places on Earth and, over the last 3000 years, has given rise to many of the world's great civilisations – from imperial China to ancient Greece and Rome to the Gothic glories of medieval Christendom. Even today, most of the

world's chief industrial regions lie within the Temperate Zone, from Japan to Europe, South Korea to the principal industrial areas of the United States.

The Temperate Zone encompasses many climates, with enormous variations among them. All, however, share clear-cut winter and summer seasons. For the rest, latitude is a vital influence, dividing temperate climates

into two broad categories. Warm temperate climates lie roughly between latitudes 30° and 45° N and S, including in the Northern Hemisphere the Mediterranean Basin and the bulk of the USA from the latitude of New Orleans in the south to that of Minneapolis in the north. In the Southern Hemisphere,

ROLLING WHEAT FIELDS *With hot sunny summers and mild showery winters, Andalucia in southern Spain has a typically Mediterranean climate.*

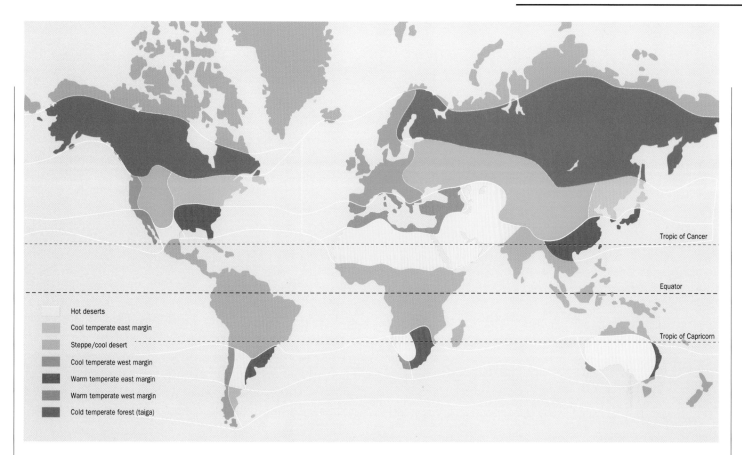

Hot deserts
Cool temperate east margin
Steppe/cool desert
Cool temperate west margin
Warm temperate east margin
Warm temperate west margin
Cold temperate forest (taiga)

Tropic of Cancer

Equator

Tropic of Capricorn

SUB-TROPICAL AND TEMPERATE
Encircling the world in both
hemispheres roughly between
the Tropics and the Polar
Circles, are a patchwork of
contrasting climates,
ranging from hot deserts to
cold forests.

they include much of Argentina, southern South Africa, southern Australia and most of New Zealand. Cool temperate climates include most of Canada, Alaska and northern Europe.

Within these two categories come further refinements. The dominant winds of the Temperate Zone are the mid-latitude westerlies. On the western margins of continents, in places such as Britain, the prevailing winds blow in, laden with moisture, from the ocean. In places like New York, on the east margin of North America, dry west winds from the continental interior alternate with moist north-easterlies from the ocean. Over the interiors, meanwhile, summer heating induces relatively low pressure; winter cooling encourages high pressure. The result is a climate with hot showery summers and freezing cold but dry winters.

Both warm and cold temperate zones can thus be subdivided into west-margin, continental and east-margin climates. All these categories are well represented in the Northern Hemisphere, where the picture is complicated by subcategories created by the geographical detail of each continent. The Southern Hemisphere has relatively little land in the temperate latitudes, so that the various climate regions are small or non-existent.

WHERE THE VINE AND OLIVE GROW

California and central Chile have classic Mediterranean climates – technically, west-margin warm temperate climates. Paradoxically, they are better examples than the Mediterranean itself. The Mediterranean region is the largest portion of the Earth falling within this category, but it abounds in quirks where the complexities of its geography have created a minutely detailed patchwork of subclimates. Other areas enjoying a Mediterranean climate are the eastern part of South Africa's Cape Province and the coastal fringe of Australia from Perth to Adelaide. Another such region lies at the heart of Eurasia, including the Black Sea, the lowlands of Georgia and Azerbaijan and the Caspian Sea coast of Iran.

These include some supremely fertile regions, the home, especially in Europe, of the vine and the olive. The mid-latitude westerlies bring warm, changeable winters with frequent showers. Summers are hot and sunny, thanks to the yearly oscillation of the Sun between the Tropics of Cancer and Capricorn. As it swings north in the Northern Hemisphere's summer, it shifts whole wind and pressure belts northwards, including the subtropical high-pressure belt where air heated at the Equator subsides once more. This high-pressure zone controls the Mediterranean summer, bringing clear skies and brilliant sunshine. As the Sun swings south in the Southern Hemisphere's summer, it triggers a similar process south of the Equator. Conditions are ideal for grain crops in winter and fruit in summer. Reliable warmth and sunshine encourage tourist industries.

Although exact temperatures vary considerably, depending on how close a region is to the sea, the classic Mediterranean climate has a mild winter, warm spring, hot summer and very warm autumn. Most winters bring some frost except in a few coastal areas, and occasional severe frosts occur inland. At Madrid the mercury dropped to –12°C (10°F) in January 1987. At Sagres on

GRAPES AND OLIVES *The vine grows prolifically wherever there is a Mediterranean climate – as in South Africa's Cape Province (above). The olive thrives best in the hotter, drier parts of the Mediterranean Basin, such as Andalucia (left).*

the south-western tip of Portugal, by contrast, frost has never been recorded.

Coastal fringes have the benefit during the hotter months of refreshing sea breezes – cool breezes drawn in off the ocean as the air over the land heats and rises. These are so reliable and important to the general well-being that in some places they have names – such as the Fremantle Doctor which provides regular relief from summer heat in and around Perth in Western Australia.

Cold ocean currents also serve to temper the summer heat where they flow along a coastline. This happens along the west-facing shores of Portugal and northern Morocco and California's Pacific fringe. In California, Eureka – lying on the Pacific coast, some 250 miles (400 km) north of San Francisco – is an extreme example. The cold California Current hugs the shoreline closely here. Thanks to cool air blowing off it, mean maximum temperatures hardly deviate from 16°C (61°F) between June and October, then they slip back gently to 12°C (54°F) in January and February. In San Francisco the cooling effect is less marked. Here, mean maximum temperatures rise as high as 23°C (73°F) in September, sinking to 13°C (55°F) in January. Away from the coast, Fresno, in the San Joaquim Valley of central California, has much more baking summers. The range here is from 38°C (100°F) in July down to 13°C (55°F) in January.

Mediterranean climates have rains in winter, drought in summer. Towards the Equator, the winter rains slowly diminish and the summer drought grows longer – the climate gradually becomes more arid and merges almost imperceptibly into that of the desert. In higher latitudes, the summer drought gradually becomes shorter and less reliable until the climate blends into the all-year rains of a cool temperate west-margin climate. Lisbon in

MEDITERRANEAN DOWN UNDER
Australia's Mediterranean zone is limited to the south-facing coasts of Western and South Australia. Perth shares its climate with Lisbon, Barcelona and Rome, rather than its Scottish namesake.

Portugal has a typical Mediterranean rainfall pattern, with an annual total of 30 in (762 mm). Of this 22 in (559 mm) falls in the winter half of the year, and just 8 in (203 mm) in the summer half of the year. A true drought usually prevails in Lisbon between mid-June and early September.

TEMPERATE DESERTS

To the south, Mediterranean climates merge with hot deserts; to the east, they merge with the mid-latitude deserts of continental interiors. These form – for example, in Utah and Nevada in the United States – where the winter westerlies gradually dry out. Low-pressure areas in summer bring occasional summer storms, but these fail to make up for scantier, less reliable winter rains.

Apart from Utah and Nevada, other examples of mid-latitude deserts are those of the central Asian republics of Kazakhstan, Uzbekistan and Turkmenistan and the Gobi Desert in north-western China and Mongolia. The only significant example in the Southern Hemisphere lies in parts of central and western Argentina. The main difference between these mid-latitude deserts

and hot deserts such as the Sahara is the cold – sometimes intensely cold – winters of the mid-latitude ones. There is less of a contrast in summer temperatures, though mid-latitude deserts never quite reach the sizzling levels of the hot ones.

SUDDEN DROP

The biggest change in temperature in one day is believed to have occurred at Browning, Montana, in the USA. On January 16, 1916, the temperature fell 55°C (100°F) during the day. Sudden rises of temperature are rarer than sudden drops, but dramatic jumps of temperature do occur at the onset of a warm Chinook or Föhn wind. At Havre, also in Montana, such a jump of 18°C (32°F) took place in just three minutes on one occasion.

The central Asian desert is the world's largest warm temperate desert. Near its heart is Samarkand, once famed as a key staging post on the Silk Road from China to Europe. Here, mean maximum temperatures are 34°C (93°F) in July, just 3°C (37°F)

DESERT BLOOMS *Poppies flower in the arid plains of Kazakhstan. Brief thundery rains fall in most springs, followed by a profusion of flowers as plants take advantage of the moisture.*

average maximum temperature in January is 26°C (79°F). Similar climates prevail in the south-eastern states of the USA; Uruguay and north-eastern Argentina; the south-east corner of South Africa; central China and southern Japan; Victoria and New South Wales and the North Island of New Zealand.

Rainfall is abundant, especially in summer. Winter westerlies, blowing from cold continental heartlands, have lost much of their moisture but interact with the moist air over the adjacent oceans. The result is that depressions often form near the coastline; these are responsible for the bulk of the winter's precipitation. In summer, however, subtropical high-pressure systems over the ocean draw in moist easterly winds.

In the USA, China, Japan and New South Wales, tropical cyclones make their contribution to the rains, especially in late summer and autumn. They also threaten widespread disruption if a major storm makes landfall. Further disruption comes in winter when sudden onslaughts of polar air may cause dramatic fluctuations in temperature. These

in January. Winter temperatures regularly fall to −15°C (5°F) at night. Annual rainfall amounts to 13 in (330 mm) with a slight peak in spring.

WARM IN THE EAST

Sydney in Australia has a climate typical of eastern continental margins in warm temperate latitudes. Winters are mild or warm – in Sydney the average maximum temperature in July is 16°C (61°F). Summers are hot, though rarely excessively so – in Sydney, the

BAY WATCHERS *The warm and often sunny climate of the New South Wales coastline encourages a 'beach culture' as seen here near Sydney.*

SMOKE AND SMOG: URBAN CLIMATES

Smoke pollution has long been a hazard. The Roman writers Horace and Seneca both complained about smoke and smells in imperial Rome, but it was not until the growth of medieval cities with their densely packed populations and growing concentrations of industry that pollution began to make a marked impact on urban climates.

In the Middle Ages and for many centuries after them, there were comparatively few big cities, but most of these had a wide variety of industries, especially in the production of iron and lime – lime was used in building materials. Initially, wood was burnt, but from about 1250 coal-burning began, and with it came the urban smoke plumes that would be associated with cities until the middle of the 20th century.

During the Industrial Revolution of the late 18th and 19th centuries, people flocked from the countryside to the towns and cities of western Europe and North America. By the end of the 19th century many countries had more than 50 per cent of their populations living in urban areas compared with less than 10 per cent at the beginning of the century. This rapid urbanisation produced vast new industrial conurbations. Chimneys belched out fumes; rivers were polluted. There was incessant noise and huge palls of smoke hung over industrial districts from the Ruhr in western Germany to cities such as Pittsburgh in the United States.

Large cities changed the climate of their regions. With their masses of buildings, they were warmer, wetter, less snowy and more windy than the surrounding countryside. The climate was further changed by air pollution, making the cities foggier, cloudier and markedly less sunny than other areas. Under some conditions, the influence of smoke pollution can be dramatic. When a winter anticyclone covers a district, heat energy escapes from the ground to outer space, resulting in a layer of cold air in the lowest few hundred feet of the atmosphere, with a much warmer layer of air above it – a so-called 'temperature inversion'. In these

BLACK COUNTRY *The 19th-century French artist Constantin Meunier painted this impression of the pollution-ridden English Midlands.*

circumstances, the city air becomes stagnant. There is no wind to disperse the pollution, and as the temperature gradually drops moisture condenses onto the soot particles to form an impenetrable smoke-based fog – 'smog'. Such a smog may last several days – until the anticyclone shifts – and the growing concentration of pollutants soon becomes a serious health hazard. London was notorious for its foggy climate, especially in the 19th and early 20th centuries. Its most famous smog occurred as recently as 1952 when over four days in early December some 7000 people are believed to have died as a result of the high pollution levels. Within a few years London had a Clean Air Act. Smokeless zones quickly followed, and within 20 years winter sunshine in central London had more than doubled. The industrial areas of Germany, Belgium, the Netherlands, Luxembourg, northern France and northern Italy were all similarly affected. Pittsburgh was probably the smokiest city in the USA during the early part of the 20th century, while large urban areas in the former Soviet Bloc countries did not see any drop in air pollution until the early 1990s.

---

damage crops and bring such disruption to people's daily lives that some have been given names: the 'pampero' of Argentina, the 'norther' of the US Gulf States and the 'southerly burster' of Australia. In summer, furnace-like winds, laden with dust, occasionally burst through from inland deserts to the coastal fringes. These include the 'brickfielder' in New South Wales and the 'zonda' in Argentina.

COOL, MOIST AND TEMPERATE

Rainfall in all months, mild winters, cool summers and protracted transition seasons in spring and autumn . . . the British climate is typical of west-margin cool temperate climates. It has been said that extreme examples of this climate have six months of spring followed by six months of autumn. It is an exaggeration, but indicates nonetheless the contrast with places where the difference between winter and summer is much more marked. This cool moist climate is found in the British Isles and adjacent parts of the European mainland, including southern Scandinavia; in Oregon, Washington state, British Columbia and the Alaskan panhandle; in southern Chile; and in Tasmania and the South Island of New Zealand.

The prevailing moisture-laden westerly winds blowing in off the ocean are a key influence. The oceans themselves respond to the westerly airflow with west-to-east ocean currents which keep these areas relatively warm for their latitude in winter. However, though the climate is essentially equable, it can also bring more extreme conditions. The mid-latitude westerlies are very variable and can break down completely as 'blocking' anticyclones, areas of high pressure, develop. These may persist for several weeks or even months over the same place, reversing the normal airflow and introducing surges of air of continental or arctic origin. They help to explain the huge variations from one year to the next that are a notable feature of the weather in places such as Britain and north-western North America.

The natural vegetation in these regions is woodland. It gradually gives way to steppe grassland towards the continental interior as rainfall levels decline away from the ocean. Winters are colder and drier, summers hotter. Towards the Equator, summer rainfall declines and temperatures increase, merging into a Mediterrean climate. Towards the poles a bleaker climate takes over where all seasons are colder.

In Europe, little remains of the natural vegetation, following centuries of intensive cultivation. This climate is particularly suitable for grain and root crops, hardy fruits, such as apples, pears and berries, and rearing animals. Such diverse agriculture, rarely disrupted by summers cold enough or dry enough to cause harvests to fail completely, is one factor that encouraged the explosive growth in population in north-western Europe during the last 500 years.

London's statistics are characteristic of this climate. Average temperatures never sink very low – the mean maximum daytime temperature in January is 7°C (45°F). Nor

TEMPERATE HARVESTS *Fields are ploughed along the contours of the land in the Palouse valley of Washington state (right). This minimises erosion in rainy winters. Fruit trees such as apple, pear and plum (below) thrive in the cool temperate climates of north-western and central Europe.*

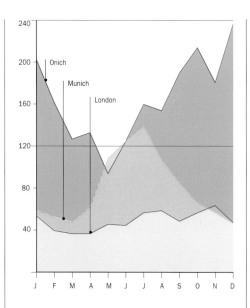

PEAKS AND TROUGHS *London's month-by-month rainfall shows few marked variations. The figures for Onich in the Scottish Highlands and Munich are much more striking. Onich, close to the ocean, peaks in December; Munich, in the heart of continental Europe, in July.*

do they rise very high – in July the mean maximum is 23°C (73°F). Winter temperatures do occasionally fall much lower than the average, but prolonged spells, lasting several days, with daytime temperatures below 0°C (32°F) are rare.

The average annual rainfall in London is 23 in (584 mm), well distributed through the year. The driest months are February and March with 1^1/$_2$ in (38 mm) each; November, the wettest month, has 2^1/$_2$ in (64 mm). Winter rains come chiefly from Atlantic fronts and depressions. These cyclonic rains are scantier in summer but are supplemented by showers and thunderstorms caused by convection – Sun-heated rising air.

Closer to the oceans annual rainfall rises, with a marked peak in autumn and winter, especially where hills and mountains give added impetus to the rain-making processes. Thus Fort William, in western Scotland, receives 79 in (2007 mm) a year, peaking in December. Travelling eastwards from the oceans, convective summer rains become dominant. At Munich, in south-eastern Germany, the annual rainfall is 34 in (864 mm), of which 68 per cent falls in the summer half of the year. Throughout the west-margin cool Temperate Zone, snow falls fairly often in the winter months and occasionally very heavily, but it rarely stays on the ground for long on the coastal lowlands.

Away from the oceans, cool temperate climates become more inhospitable. Winters are colder and longer, with frequent snowfalls and prolonged snow-cover. Summers are shorter, although they are still decidedly hot in some areas. The intermediate spring and autumn seasons are practically non-existent. In some places spring is distinguishable only because there is hot sunshine at the same time that mud and melting snow are making roads impassable while rivers and lakes are still icebound.

FLOODED AND FROZEN *Flood waters pour down the Carmanah River on Vancouver Island. The cool temperate west-margin climate is essentially a rainy one, feeding thousands of streams, rivers and lakes. In Russia, where winters are very cold, the Moskva River is usually frozen over for three or four months.*

Large populations exist quite happily in parts of Europe and North America where less extreme forms of this climate hold sway. Cities in these areas include Stockholm, St Petersburg and Moscow. Elsewhere, however, winters are so prolonged and the growing season so short that cultivation of the land is very difficult. Huge tracts of almost uninhabited coniferous forest stretch across vast portions of both Canada and Russia.

New York lies on the southern fringe of North America's cool temperate eastern margin. Thanks to the softening influence of the Atlantic, its winter temperature patterns are not all that different from London's. Mean maximum temperatures range from 4°C (39°F) in January to 28°C (82°F) in July. The winter is short if sometimes very snowy. Annual rainfall is 44 in (1118 mm), distributed evenly throughout the year.

However, at Buffalo at the opposite end of New York state, the pattern is much more extreme. Mean maximum temperatures vary from 0°C (32°F) in winter to 27°C (81°F) in summer. Rainfall is still plentiful, averaging 36 in (914 mm) a year, and evenly distributed. Winter snowfalls are among the heaviest in any well-populated area in the world.

In the European interior, Moscow offers still greater extremes. Mean daytime temperatures range from –6°C (21°F) in winter to 25°C (77°F) in summer. It is a drier climate, with 25 in (635 mm) of rainfall a year, peaking slightly in summer. Still farther east, in Ekaterinburg on the eastern fringe of the Urals, January afternoons have average temperatures of –15°C (5°F). July afternoons average 21°C (70°F). Annual rainfall is just 17 in (432 mm), most of which falls in summer.

THE FRIGID ZONE

Ice and snow and numbing cold have always made life in the Frigid Zone a battle for survival. Modern technology is changing this, but only scientists yet live on the very coldest part of our planet: the icebound interior of Antarctica.

Summer comes, and the vast expanses of tundra – stretching across northern Alaska and Canada, around the coast of Greenland and along northern Scandinavia and Russia – spring into life. For the rest of the year, they are Arctic wastelands, a band of bleak, barren landscape slotted between the lonely forests of the northernmost temperate latitudes and the perpetual snow and ice of the true polar clime. Thanks to the permanently frozen subsoil, no tree can

grow to relieve the monotony of the scene that undulates gently to the far horizon.

Then, for a few precious months from late May or early June, temperatures rise, eventually reaching around 5°C (41°F), and the tundra renews itself. Low, woody shrubs and mosses put on a spurt of growth.

Reindeer venture forth from the forests to the south, followed by wolves and other predators – but these animals return to the forests as soon as temperatures begin to fall in August. During the warmest weeks, birds arrive, though they, too, fly south again well before the autumn

SUMMER GRAZING *Wild reindeer graze on the lush grass of the short summer in Norwegian Lapland.*

LONE HUNTER *A glacier looms in the background as an Inuit seal hunter paddles his kayak in pursuit of prey off north-west Greenland. Inshore waters unfreeze during the summer.*

equinox in late September. Other animals are hardier. Musk-oxen, lemmings and arctic hares stay throughout the year. Unlike other creatures of cold climates, hibernation is no option for them. Winters are too long and harsh, and summers too short with food too scarce for them to develop the necessary reserves of fat or to squirrel away big enough hoards of food. Fortunately, however, snowfall is nearly always light and powdery, and it usually blows into clefts and hollows in the ground. Nosing around in the thin snowy mantle, they feed off the mosses and lichens that usually lie beneath it. The sea, too, provides a good source of food for many predators, notably the walrus and the polar bear.

For humans, life is an endless struggle against the odds. Among the traditional dwellers of the tundra, such as the Inuit (Eskimos) of North America and Greenland,

the Lapps of Scandinavia and the Chukchi of Siberia, fishing and hunting occupy most of the men's time, especially during the all-too-brief summer when they can build up stocks for the winter. But no one can survive the eight or nine-month freeze on stocks alone, so local people have to carry on seeking out food, chiefly by fishing, even in the very coldest months.

Many groups still lead a nomadic life. Their winter settlements consist of homes built of ice (igloos) or earth or a combination of the two. Long hunting expeditions during the milder months require tents made of animal skins. Transport in summer is usually by canoe, since only the top few feet of the ground thaw out, and the land becomes an impassable bog that overlies the deep-frozen subsoil known as permafrost. During the freezing months dog sleds come into their own, although in recent decades mechanised forms of transport, such as the snowmobile, have penetrated the Arctic and are now used by even the remotest communities.

Severe though the climate is, the cold does offer certain advantages. Viruses and bacteria are virtually inactive in the very low

temperatures, and airborne infections are almost unknown. Foodstuffs can be preserved merely by leaving them out in the cold. All in all, life in the tundra is hard but it is also perfectly sustainable. As for the cold, the best way for humans to deal with this is, as the Inuit say, to take care not to be cold. Their extremely warm, traditional fur garments are ample proof that they have mastered this art.

TUNDRA STATISTICS

Barrow Point on Alaska's Arctic shore is typical of coastal tundra sites. Mean maximum temperatures range from –25°C (–13°F) in February to 7°C (45°F) in July. Temperatures remain continuously below freezing from early October until late May. Even in mid-summer, night-time temperatures often drop below freezing point. On average there are only 40 frost-free nights during the year. Annual rainfall is low, at just $4^2/_5$ in (112 mm), with a marked late-summer peak.

Snowfall in the tundra is frequent but mostly light. Around the fringes of the Arctic Ocean, it is more common than rain even in summer. During the winter half of the year true blizzards sweep the plains from time to time. Dense swirling clouds of snow crystals cut visibility almost to zero, the falling snow mixed in with vast quantities of dry powdery snow that the wind lifts from the ground. A Russian traveller called Zenzinov described one such blizzard in the Russian tundra. Here the blizzards are known as 'purgas':

'We ran into a frightful purga on December 31 . . . It started soon after midday, in the form of a slight wind. Around us was the lifeless tundra, under an even blanket of snow. About one o'clock twilight began to descend. Everything was shut off from sight, as if a grey and muddy curtain had been drawn about us. The sky fused with the snow. It seemed as if our reindeer were suspended in the air, their legs moving but without making any headway. The snow was so dense that I could not even see the antlers of the deer drawing my own sled. I could only see their regularly moving

rumps. The wind grew stronger. It turned into a hurricane. Currents of snow sped past me, skimming the ground and striking the sled with a dry rustle. Many times I thought we had hopelessly lost our way. The snowstorm would hit me directly in the face, then from the right, from the left, and in the back . . . What if we had really lost our way? In the open tundra the snow would surely drift over us and bury us for good.'

POLAR WILDERNESSES

Humans have lived in the tundra for thousands of years. The polar regions of the Arctic and Antarctic, probably the most inhospitable of all environments on Earth, are among the few land areas on our planet that have no indigenous human population whatsoever – although even these regions have been invaded in recent decades by an assortment of scientists, explorers, military personnel and mineral prospectors.

In the Northern Hemisphere the polar regions include most of Greenland, much of the Canadian Arctic archipelago and some of the islands in the Russian Arctic. In the Southern Hemisphere (which has no tundra), they include the entire Antarctic continent – with the exception of the coastal fringe of the Antarctic Peninsula. Even in 'summer', there is not enough warmth in these regions to melt the snow and ice.

Many early explorers of the Antarctic were puzzled by the behaviour of the winds. At ground level, they were very light, or even non-existent, for long periods. But higher in the atmosphere, clouds moved briskly from west to east; the same high-level air currents carried along smoke from the grumbling Antarctic volcano Mount Erebus. This phenomenon is a direct consequence of the coldness of these latitudes. The density of air increases as its temperature drops, and the higher the

WINDS THAT BLOW UP HILL AND DOWN DALE

The morning sun shining on a valley side warms the slope and the air above it. The warm air rises, creating a gentle breeze flowing up the valley side. By midday, the sunshine is reaching the valley bottom and the up-slope breeze is at its strongest. At the same time, a new breeze is triggered, blowing up the length of the valley, from the lower reaches to the upper ones. This gains steadily in strength, reaching its peak in the late afternoon. These two breezes, one blowing up the valley sides, the other up the length of the valley, are both known as anabatic winds – from the Greek *ana*, 'up', and *bainein*, 'to go'. They are a feature of mountain regions on occasions when there is

MOUNTAIN BREEZES *The geography of mountains and valleys produces a complex network of winds which changes with the time of day.*

no other, stronger weather system in the vicinity to override them.

Around sunset or just after it, the breezes start to reverse direction, becoming katabatic winds – from *kata*, 'down'. The valley sides cool down; cool air is denser than warm air, and a down-slope breeze sets in. At this point, the lower part of the valley is

still warmer than the upper, so the up-valley breeze continues blowing for a while. Eventually, however, cool air from the down-slope breeze gathers in the valley bottom. The up-valley breeze ceases, and after a few hours is replaced by a down-valley one.

If the highlands around the valley are covered with snow, the katabatic

effect is particularly pronounced. After nightfall, air over the snow-clad heights cools down rapidly, increasing the supply of cold air flowing down the valley sides – even so, wind speeds rarely exceed more than a few miles per hour. The accumulation of cold, dense air in the valley bottoms is known as 'katabatic drainage', and the resulting 'katabatic lake' is often marked by wreaths of mist.

Mountain ranges such as the Alps sometimes act as a kind of wind dam. A stream of cold, dense air, blowing onto the range at right angles, is blocked, and a ridge of high pressure builds up on the mountains' windward side. On their lee side, a shallow but extensive area of low pressure forms. Eventually, the difference in pressure becomes so great that the cold air forces its way through gaps in the mountain range and rushes swiftly down the valleys on the far side – just like water topping a dam.

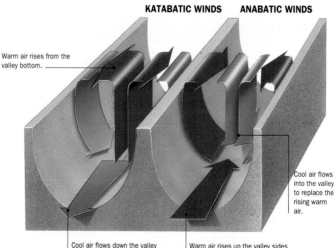

KATABATIC WINDS   ANABATIC WINDS

Warm air rises from the valley bottom.

Cool air flows into the valley to replace the rising warm air.

Cool air flows down the valley sides and the valley bottom.

Warm air rises up the valley sides and valley bottom.

SUMMER IN ANTARCTICA
Threatening-looking clouds hang over Paradise Bay. In fact, they are reflecting the colour of the sea and are not producing any rain or snow.

air's density, the larger the pressure exerted at the Earth's surface. Cold, dense air collects near the ground in both Arctic and Antarctic polar regions, forming a shallow dome of stagnant air. High above the ground, the winds continue swirling west to east, just as they do in lower latitudes.

This cold, dense air accounts for the huge anticyclone (high-pressure system) that hangs more or less permanently over the whole of Antarctica and the smaller 'highs' that regularly dominate weather charts of the Arctic region in winter and spring. They include an intense high-pressure system that sometimes settles over the Greenland ice cap and a large semipermanent anticyclone over Siberia. In the summer half of the year, an extensive but relatively weak anticyclone typically straddles the Arctic Ocean and the Canadian archipelago.

In Antarctica, the permanent high pressure keeps at bay mid-latitude depressions and the storms they bring. In the Northern Hemisphere, however, occasional travelling storms do make inroads into the Arctic Ocean. This happens chiefly in its Atlantic sector where the warm North Atlantic Drift, an extension of the Gulf Stream, flows northeastwards along the Norwegian coast and

SUMMER THAW *Even in mid-summer, most of Antarctica remains icebound, but the Antarctic Peninsula has a brief thaw and supports a few flowering plants.*

past the northern tip of Scandinavia – Atlantic depressions tend to follow the course of the current into the Arctic. A few storms also reach the North Pole, travelling northwards along the western side of Greenland,

following the course of the Irminger Current, another extension of the Gulf Stream.

Very occasionally, in both polar regions, truly ferocious gales spring up, which can be as violent as any other windstorms, apart from tornadoes. Their severity, allied to the extreme cold and the blinding, blowing snow, makes them deadly. When they occur, they can last for several days. One such storm ended Captain Robert Scott's ill-fated expedition on its return from the South Pole early in 1912.

These storms are caused by a combination of factors. When the Antarctic (or Greenland) anticyclone shifts slightly, or its intensity changes, an enormous mass of air must also move. But the moving air is confined to the lowest few hundred feet of the atmosphere – the less cold air above it acts as a sort of lid, as the heavier air below cannot rise up and displace it, and prevents any momentum being transferred upwards into the free atmosphere. The winds are now being controlled by the topography of the land or ice beneath, squeezed over hills and plateaus, funnelled through valleys and gorges.

On the edge of the Antarctic continent these winds accelerate through gaps on the edge of the plateau and then sweep down the steep slopes to the ice-choked seas below. Commonwealth Bay in George V Land has reported wind speeds of more than 200 mph (320 km/h) during one such storm. Unfortunately for the members of Scott's British Antarctic Expedition, they chose a route to the Pole that ran through the part of the continent most prone to these violent winds. Here, the Transantarctic Mountains rise abruptly from sea level to over 15 000 ft (about 4500 m). Blizzards roar down the slopes to McMurdo Sound and the ice shelf covering the Ross Sea.

At Cape Evans on McMurdo Sound, Scott's base camp, the team's meteorologist Sir George Simpson noted the dramatic contrasts in wind speed. Winds blew at 5 mph (8 km/h) or less for 22 per cent of the time, but approached or exceeded gale force for 30 per cent of the time. Scott's Norwegian rival, Roald Amundsen, was more fortunate in his choice of a base – at Framheim on the

SNOW DUNES *Eerily lit by low slanting sunlight, these Greenland snow ridges could be mistaken for sand dunes. They are aligned parallel with the prevailing wind and are technically known as 'sastrugi'.*

BEAMING UP *A sun pillar shoots upwards from the setting Sun over a Lapland horizon. Sun pillars are not unusual in Arctic and Antarctic latitudes but are rarely as bright as this.*

opposite side of the Ross Sea. Here, the coast shelves much more gently to the sea. Winds are light or non-existent for 42 per cent of the time; gales or near-gales blow for only 2 per cent of the time.

SUN AND ICE

The relatively high pressure of the polar regions means that precipitation is low. When snow does fall it is rarely heavy, since intensely cold air can hold only comparatively little moisture. Most blizzards involve vast quantities of snow being whipped up from the surface, rather than much new snow falling from the sky. Low levels of moisture also mean that there is rarely much thick cloud over the Antarctic and Greenland ice caps, although tenuous ice-crystal clouds often form in the lower part of the stratosphere. Halos around the Sun and other optical phenomena are often noticed as sunlight is refracted through the ice crystals.

In Antarctica, clear skies bring very high levels of sunshine in the summer half of the year when the Sun is continuously in the sky. But this has little influence on ground-level temperatures; the Sun never rises higher than 23.5° above the horizon, and most of its energy is reflected back into space from the surface of the snow. By contrast, summer in the Arctic region as whole, as opposed to the Greenland ice cap, is often overcast, misty and damp due to the moisture released by the very gradual melting of the snow and ice.

Temperatures in Antarctica mostly stay well below freezing point. At the Russian base Vostok, mean monthly figures range from a low of –70°C (–94°F) in July to a high of –46°C (–50°F) in January. The Antarctic Peninsula, extending towards the southern tip of South America, is positively balmy by comparison. The mean monthly figures for Deception Island, off its northern edge, range from –9°C (16°F) in July to 1°C (34°F) in January. Even in midwinter, the mercury rarely falls below –20°C (–4°F), and most summers record the odd day around 10°C (50°F). Between October and March, some precipitation on Deception Island actually falls as rain rather than snow. The total for both snow and rain amounts to the equivalent 22 in (559 mm) of rainfall.

ALL THE WORLD'S CLIMATES
From dense equatorial rain forest to snowy peaks, a range of climates is represented on the slopes of Mount Kenya.

Though its climate is still inhospitable, the Arctic does not have the extreme temperatures of the Antarctic plateau. For instance, Alert, on Canada's Ellesmere Island, in latitude 82.5°N, has a comparatively mild midwinter average temperature of –33°C (–27°F). July temperatures rise above freezing: 7°C (45°F) by day. The mercury once climbed as high as 20°C (68°F). Precipitation at Alert averages a rainfall equivalent of almost 6 in (152 mm) a year.

The nearest approach to the Antarctic deep-freeze is on the Greenland ice cap. A base called Eismitte, 10 000 ft (3000 m) above sea level, was manned for three years. The average monthly temperature ranged from –41°C (–42°F) in February to –13°C (9°F) in July. The temperature rose above freezing point on just one day in that period.

CLIMATES ON HIGH

Mount Kenya, a long-extinct volcano, rises from baking acacia-dotted grasslands in East Africa. Lying less than 1° south of the Equator, it climbs to 17 058 ft (5100 m) above sea level. At its base, the hot, humid, rainy conditions of an equatorial climate prevail. Then, up to about 10 500 ft (3200 m), comes a band of dense forest, with yellow-wood trees, cedars and huge stands of bamboo. Above that are moorlands sprinkled with giant groundsel, lobelia and heather. Crowning it are jagged, permanently snow-capped peaks, with glaciers creeping through the

valleys between them. The mountain is a perfect illustration of how altitude affects climate.

Broadly speaking, height above sea level affects the climate in four ways: temperatures decrease with altitude; windiness increases because the mountain slopes are exposed to the strong winds of the free atmosphere (at lower levels winds are slowed down by frictional effects); cloudiness and precipitation increase because of orographic uplift, though they sometimes decrease again on the very highest slopes because the air at these levels carries much less moisture than air at lower levels, thanks to the lower temperatures on the upper slopes.

In addition to these, sunlight becomes brighter because there are fewer haze particles, tiny particles of dirt or salt in the air that veil the sunlight, and because the atmosphere itself gradually becomes thinner. The brightness is what immediately strikes visitors to high mountains, especially when intensified by reflection from snow and ice. At the same time, more ultraviolet radiation gets through from the Sun. This is why it is easy to acquire a suntan on a skiing holiday – and why sun-screen products are vital, to counter the effects of ozone depletion.

In equatorial latitudes, high plateaus enjoy uniquely temperate climates. Temperatures are comfortable and vary little, if at all, through the year. Nairobi, for instance,

HIGH AND BLEAK *Snow-covered volcanic peaks tower over the Andean Altiplano where the climate is dry and cold, with marked differences between day and night-time temperatures.*

MILD AND STEADY *At 9250 ft (2820 m) above sea level, Quito enjoys a temperate climate. Lying close to the Equator, it also enjoys the consistency of the Equatorial Zone.*

lies on the Kenyan plateau some 6000 ft (1800 m) above sea level, about 75 miles (120 km) south of the Equator. Average maximum temperatures in the afternoon range from 21°C (70°F) in July and August to 26°C (79°F) in February; the mercury never climbs above 32°C (90°F). Daytime humidity levels are comfortably low, and rain falls regularly but not excessively throughout the year. In South America, the capitals of Colombia and Ecuador, Bogotá and Quito, have an even more equable climate. At Bogotá, 8600 ft (2600 m) above sea level, daytime temperatures average 18-20°C (64-68°F) throughout the year. Quito, although slightly higher, at 9250 ft (2820 m), is slightly warmer by day, with afternoon maximum temperatures averaging 21-23°C (70-73°F) in every month.

Snow-capped mountains give an idea of how cold it is on their upper slopes; they are also proof that there is enough precipitation to keep the snow-cover topped up. In places where the climate is predominantly dry – Central Asia, for example – there are mountainous areas where the temperature remains well below freezing for the greater part of the year, but there is not enough snow to keep the slopes covered. In other ranges, the snow line is much lower on one side than the other, because of the rain-shadow (or 'snow-shadow') effect. This is true in the southern Andes, where the snow-cover extends almost 1000 ft (300 m) lower on the Chilean side, with frequent and abundant precipitation, than it does on the Argentine side, with much sparser precipitation.

The lie of the land also affects climates at high altitude. Conditions will be different on a flat, open, grassy plateau, in a steep-sided valley between two mountain peaks and on a snow-covered slope facing away from the Sun. Some valleys act as sun-traps by day and frost hollows by night, while a broad valley running from east to west will often encompass huge contrasts, especially in spring, between the slope facing towards the Sun, which may be green and flower-bedecked, and the slope facing away, which may still be snowbound.

OUR CHANGING CLIMATE

4

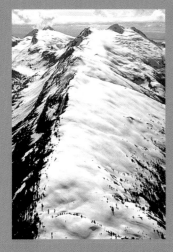

SNOWBOUND *Snow and ice are year-round phenomena in regions such as Alaska.*

ICE OVER NORTHERN NORTH AMERICA AND EUROPE, TUNDRA COVERING THE SOUTHERN PARTS OF THESE CONTINENTS; RIVERS FLOWING IN NORTH AFRICA WHERE THERE IS NOW DESERT; GLACIERS IN SOUTHERN AUSTRALIA: THESE MAY SEEM UNLIKELY NOW, BUT THE WORLD'S CLIMATE HAS BEEN THROUGH MANY CHANGES. NORMALLY THESE HAVE TAKEN PLACE SO SLOWLY THAT THEY WERE IMPERCEPTIBLE TO HUMANS, BUT TODAY THERE IS A NEW FACTOR, AS THE ACTIVITIES OF HUMANS THEMSELVES APPEAR TO BE HAVING AN IMPACT ON THE CLIMATE AND ITS RATE OF CHANGE. AS THE WORLD'S CLIMATE WARMS UP, AND THE OZONE LAYER BECOMES DEPLETED, SCIENTISTS DEBATE THE IMPLICATIONS OF THESE CHANGES.

GLOBAL WARMING *Natural gas is burnt off at an oilfield.*

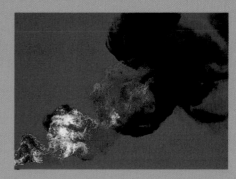

PAST CLIMATES

Wherever we live, our climate is changing, as it has always done. Many regions have experienced both tropical episodes and ice ages at various times, although most of these changes are very gradual measured against the length of a human life.

Earth's climate has never stood still. About 22 000 years ago, at a time when Cro-Magnon man was creating some of the earliest-known artistic masterpieces, such as the cave paintings of Lascaux in southern France, ice covered most of northern Europe and the British Isles. In North America, it spread over the eastern part of modern Canada and down into the northern states of what is now the USA.

Most of Europe south of the ice sheet had a harsh, cold climate similar to that of today's tundra extending along the northern fringe of North America, Scandinavia and Russia – though southern Europe's tundra-like belt had warmer summers because of the relatively high angle of the Sun in these latitudes. The climate of the Mediterranean region was not much different from that of present-day north-western Europe. Frequent winter rains fell on what is now the northern flank of the Sahara, enough to feed many substantial rivers flowing into the Mediterranean – their courses can still be seen in the normally dry gullies known as *wadis* that cut across parts of the desert. Even the equatorial tropics were cooler than they are now. In the Southern Hemisphere, glaciers spread out over Patagonia, New Zealand and south-eastern Australia, with small ice caps over the southern Andes and the Southern Alps of New Zealand's South Island.

Then, around 14 500 years ago, the ice started very slowly to retreat – the exact reason for this is still a subject of debate among scientists. By around 8000 BC, the Northern Hemisphere's climate had become warm enough for birch forests to spread northwards into Scandinavia and the northern parts of the British Isles, followed later by oaks and elms. Reindeer roamed the forests and Stone Age hunters went after them. The northern regions of North America saw similar changes in vegetation.

NEW OCCUPANTS *A forest now covers an area of Sweden that, 12 000 years ago, was buried deep under the huge Scandinavian ice sheet.*

ARCTIC SUMMER *In the past, tundra vegetation would have covered places as far south as modern Oregon in the USA and Austria in Europe.*

As the ice caps melted, sea levels rose, and the land bridge between Britain and mainland Europe was severed. So, too, was the bridge across the Bering Sea that had linked Asia to North America during the preceding Ice Age, allowing Mongoloid peoples, the ancestors of today's native Americans, to cross from Siberia.

CYCLES OF CHANGE

Climates in different parts of the globe's surface have always varied and always will vary. Some fluctuations, such as those associated with the ice ages, happen over thousands or even millions of years, some over a few decades. Sometimes they affect the whole planet; at other times they touch only a small portion of it. The changes that happen over very long periods are probably due to the changing distribution of land and sea resulting from 'plate tectonics' – or 'continental drift'. For example, geologists have found glacial debris in what is now Brazil. This region of South America once lay closer to the South Pole – as part of the ancient supercontinent of Gondwanaland – but over millions of years has drifted towards the Equator.

Over the centuries, scientists have put forward a number of theories about climate change. In 1796 the French astronomer, the Marquis de Laplace, suggested that the solar system was formed when a diffuse, rotating mass of dust and gas cooled and contracted, eventually condensing into the Sun and different planets. According to this 'nebular hypothesis', the Earth, along with the rest of the solar system, was still very slowly but surely cooling down. The global climate must therefore show a similar trend, although the rate of it would be imperceptible to human beings, with our relatively short life span. To back this up, there seemed to be plenty of evidence that many parts of the world had enjoyed

GLACIAL SCENE *The snows of Mount Cook, New Zealand, feed several glaciers, remnants of an ice cap that once covered much of South Island.*

a warmer climate at some time in the distant past – though a more rigorous examination of the evidence would later show that plenty of places had also endured much colder climates at intervals.

By about 100 years ago, when the keeping of systematic weather records was still very much in its infancy, scientists believed that the climate in any one place was more or less static over a long period, but with short-term fluctuations or cycles. It was at this time that the notion of 'averages' was conceived: if temperature and rainfall records were maintained for, say, 30 or 35 years, they would cover all the minor fluctuations. From these records it should be possible, experts believed, to explain everything anyone needed to know about the climate of a particular place. Even today, official climate records relate to standard 30 year periods – latterly 1961-90.

CORE TECHNOLOGY: HOW TO MEASURE PAST CLIMATES

For several decades, scientists have painstakingly reconstructed the vagaries of past climates by studying glacial deposits, pollen and dust deposits and tree rings. More recently, 'core technology' – a kind of climatic archaeology – has enabled them to build up an even clearer picture by boring into the Greenland and Antarctic ice caps and into soft sedimentary rock both on dry land and on the seabed. As they measure the varying levels of gases such as carbon dioxide, methane and rare isotopes of oxygen in each layer of the 'core' samples, they are able to unlock the secrets of the past. As with the more traditional approach, differing levels of pollen and other organic deposits in each layer, and the varying chemical composition of dust, have also been revealing.

COLD CORE *A scientist working at the South Pole labels and wraps part of an ice core, which will be used in research into climate change.*

Investigations are often lengthy. In the Greenland Ice Core Project, experts began boring in the 1980s and finally reached the bedrock only in the summer of 1992 – but it yielded a treasure trove of information going back 250 000 years. It also gave a clearer picture than similar investigations in the Antarctic, where some of the layers

are almost undetectable because precipitation there is so limited and because there is not enough of a contrast between summer and winter.

Information from this and another core, drilled by the US-Greenland Ice Sheet Project and completed in the summer of 1993, shows that the climate of the Northern Hemisphere

was far from stable during the last glacial period. Typically, there were sudden substantial warmings every 10 000 to 15 000 years, followed by a gradual fall in mean temperature lasting some 10 000 years. Superimposed on these slow general declines were smaller fluctuations lasting around 1000 years each. The coldest period of all seems to be associated with a drop in the salinity of the North Atlantic – though with this, as with much of the data yielded by the core samples, scientists have yet to establish a satisfactory theory to explain their findings.

At least, they now have reliable evidence to work on, particularly for the last 87 000 years. Both teams of experts drilled down some 10 000 ft (3000 m), obtaining information for the same period of 250 000 years. As far back as 87 000 years ago the records from each core are strikingly similar. Before that, there are marked discrepancies, which may have been caused by deformation in the ice at one or both of the sites.

Nowadays, scientists take a much more long-term view of things. Our planet, after all, has borne life of some sort for hundreds of millions of years, and during that period there have been several colder periods, loosely referred to as 'ice ages', with warmer interludes between. The geological evidence for this is overwhelming, and astronomers, botanists, zoologists, palaeontologists and anthropologists have added, and continue to add, information that confirms the geologists' findings. Historians, too, have brought important new insights, gleaned from ancient documents, into how climates have fluctuated over the last 1000 years or so.

ICE CAPS ON THE MARCH
Some of the most interesting climatic fluctuations have occurred in the last 2 to 3 million years – roughly corresponding to what geologists call the Quaternary period, the period to which we still belong.

These fluctuations have brought a series of ice ages, each lasting on average around 100 000 years, separated by comparatively short, warmer interludes lasting only 10 000 years. Each of the lengthy cold episodes is technically called a 'glacial', and each of the brief warmer spells an 'interglacial' – scientists believe that we are currently somewhere in the middle of an interglacial. For scientists, an 'ice age' is not one single glacial but a length of time, such as the last 2 million years or so, that sees repeated cycles of glacials and interglacials. Other such ice ages, with series of alternating glacials and interglacials, have occurred roughly every 200-250 million years throughout the geological history of our planet.

During a glacial, the polar ice sheets advance towards the Equator; during an interglacial they retreat. The latest research suggests that the chief causes of these cycles are changes in the shape of the orbit of the

Earth around the Sun, and changes in the tilt of the Earth on its axis. It is thought that these factors create slight variations in the total energy received at the Earth's surface from the Sun. They also affect how the energy is distributed across the globe.

Some experts also believe that the times when many of the Earth's mountain ranges were formed – known as orogenies, from the Greek *oros*, 'mountain' – also helped to trigger the different ice ages. Mountain formation is often accompanied by volcanic activity, and the erupting volcanoes would have thrown up vast quantities of dust into the atmosphere, reducing heat from the Sun and lowering temperatures on Earth. The present Quaternary Ice Age, for example, was preceded by the so-called Alpine Orogeny that created all the mountain ranges of southern Europe, north-west Africa and the Middle East. Each of these mountain-building periods would probably have been accompanied by more volcanic activity than usual.

The most recent glacial has different names in different parts of the world – usually taken from the place where the first evidence for it was found. In North America it is known as the Wisconsin glaciation, in Britain the Devensian, on the North German Plain the Weichsel and in the Alpine region the Würm.

LIFE WITH ICE

In Europe, the main ice sheets developed over Scandinavia and the Scottish Highlands around 75 000 years ago. The coldest period, when the ice advanced farthest, was between 26 000 and 14 500 years ago. The ice sheets then started to retreat, though it was not until 10 000 years ago that the last glacial period could be said to have ended.

At its height, ice covered a substantial part of northern Europe and the British Isles, with a separate ice cap centred on the Alps. In North America, the so-called Laurentide ice sheet covered eastern Canada and the northern USA, with a separate ice cap over the Rocky Mountains. With so much water locked up as ice, sea levels dropped dramatically. When the ice caps

MOROCCAN PAST *During the last glacial, the High Atlas Mountains fed several small glaciers, while the sea-level climate was cool and moist.*

were at their greatest extent, sea levels were about 400-460 ft (120-140 m) lower than they are today, exposing land bridges such as the one across the Bering Sea that permitted our prehistoric ancestors to migrate into previously unpopulated or sparsely populated islands and continents.

Polar climates prevailed over large swathes of the planet, although the effect in the Southern Hemisphere was much less marked than in the northern, because there is less land between the key latitudes 40° and 60°. As the polar climates expanded their territory, so the temperate and tropical belts were pushed towards the Equator and squeezed into tighter bands, as was the Equatorial Zone itself, which was cooler.

A steppe climate, with extremely cold winters, warmish summers and low rainfall, extended into eastern and south-eastern Europe. In southern Asia, the monsoon system was much weaker than at present, because cooler summers over the interior of Asia meant a less extensive summer low-pressure area. India and South-east Asia had much smaller monsoon rains; indeed northern India was probably semidesert. A gentler monsoon circulation also meant that the Ethiopian Highlands received less rain than they do nowadays. There was not enough rain to feed the headwaters of the River Nile, which therefore petered out in the southern fringes of the Sahara. The Nile as we know it is, in fact, a relatively young river, dating back only some 14 000 years. The hot deserts in both hemispheres pushed farther towards the Equator. The Equatorial Zone itself had higher rainfall. Lake Victoria in East Africa, for instance, was much larger than it is now, and its water level was some 600 ft (180 m) higher.

At the same time, in North America cold air over the Laurentide ice sheet created a semipermanent, high-pressure system, with easterly winds prevailing on its southern flank. Blowing in off the Atlantic, these brought abundant rain and snowfall to the

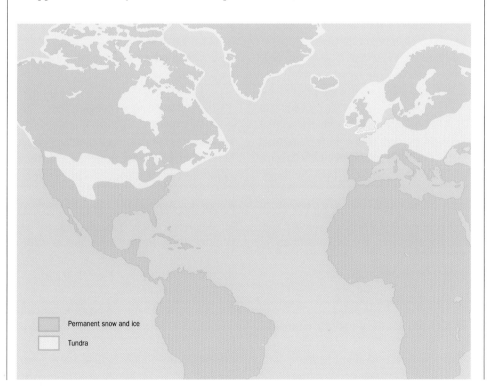

Permanent snow and ice

Tundra

WHERE THE GLACIERS WERE *Around 20 000 years ago ice sheets covered all of Canada, the northern USA, and much of the British Isles.*

eastern seaboard of the modern USA as far as the Appalachian ridge. Similarly, the Great Basin, the region of mountain ranges and broad valleys corresponding roughly to modern Nevada and parts of adjoining states, had a colder climate and therefore much higher rainfall than it does now. Extensive lakes formed, notably Lake Bonneville – of which the Great Salt Lake is a tiny remnant. Its water level was some 1000 ft (300 m) higher than the present shoreline of the Great Salt Lake.

RETREAT TO THE POLES

The retreat of the ice sheets was by no means smooth. Indeed, there was a dramatic though short-lived deterioration around 11 000 years ago, lasting maybe 200 or 300 years, known as the Younger Dryas. Scientists believe that it resulted from the collapse of the Laurentide ice sheet, which sent vast amounts of meltwater and an endless stream of icebergs into the Atlantic.

This reduced the temperature of the surface waters, which in turn disrupted weather patterns across much of the globe.

In Europe, ice advanced again, but only briefly – this was the last time that major glaciers existed anywhere in the British Isles, for example. Recent work has shown that the Younger Dryas ended extremely abruptly, perhaps within 20 years, probably because the supply of ice from Canada to the Atlantic had been exhausted. After that, the ice retreated rapidly, and the climate of regions bordering the North Atlantic became much warmer and less disturbed. Evidence suggests that the mean annual temperature in southern Greenland rose by some 7-8°C (13-14°F) in less than half a century.

The present interglacial period began around 10 000 years ago – or 8000 BC. Climates all over the globe started to take on more or less the patterns they have today. Warming continued between 8000 and 5500 BC, though much more slowly

ICE-SHEET REMNANTS
*Substantial glaciers still exist
on the slopes of Mount St
Elias, on the border of
Canada and Alaska.*

than at the end of the Younger Dryas. The ice sheets gradually retreated and forests moved in to fill the areas they had once covered. This process reached a peak – sometimes known as the 'climatic optimum' – between about 5500 and 3000 BC, a period that saw the rapid spread of agriculture across Europe and Asia as higher temperatures in more and more places made crop-growing possible, and the emergence of the early civilisations of the Near East.

Climates were mostly warmer than they are today. Mean temperatures in Europe and North America are estimated to have been about 2-4°C (3-7°F) higher than at present. In Britain, the climate was windier, cloudier and wetter, as well as warmer, than

today. Globally, the mid-latitude jet streams – the high-altitude airstreams that drive much of the Temperate Zone's weather – were probably stronger, and perhaps a few degrees north in the Northern Hemisphere and south in the Southern Hemisphere of their present positions. Hot deserts shifted once more towards the poles, pushing, for example, into large, previously fertile areas of North Africa. Rainfall levels declined around the Equator. This was also a period of high sea levels – some 30 ft (10 m) above their present level.

ICE SCAPE *During the Little Ice Age of the 16th and 17th centuries, cold winters were much more frequent than now throughout north-west Europe.*

Since then, there have been several oscillations both above and below the 20th-century average. These oscillations appear to have become more frequent in the last 1000 years, but the explanation for this is probably quite simple: we have much better information for that period.

WARM SPELLS, COLD SPELLS

In Europe, the advance of Roman civilisation roughly coincided with one of the warmer episodes, while the collapse of the Roman Empire occurred during a cooling in the climate. In the early Middle Ages, between 1100 and 1400, temperatures rose again in Europe. Mean annual temperatures were around 1°C (2°F) higher than in the 20th century, allowing vineyards to flourish in regions such as southern and central Britain and northern Germany.

During the 14th century the weather became cooler and more stormy as the polar ice cap started to advance south again, and several disastrous sea floods struck the Low Countries, north-west Germany and Denmark as storms swept through the North Sea. One of the worst of these floods, which may have taken some 30 000 lives, is known as the Great Drowning and happened in January 1362.

A colder phase – the Little Ice Age – lasted very roughly from 1550 until 1850. In Europe mean temperatures dropped 2-3°C (3-5°F) from their levels in the early Middle Ages. There were many severe winters and cool, rainy summers. These led to failed harvests, which resulted in great hardship and occasional famine. Many historians believe that these climatic events played a major part in the revolutionary politics of the late 18th and early 19th century, especially in France. The 1780s, the decade of the French Revolution, was a particularly cold decade in Europe.

Evidence for a deterioration of the climate in other parts of the world is surprisingly limited. However, the population of Iceland fell substantially. In the North Atlantic, sea ice spread farther south than at any time since the Younger Dryas, cutting off the Greenlanders' supply and trading routes, while winter pack ice reached the eastern coast of Iceland.

In the last 100 years, the main fluctuations in the climate of Europe have included a marked warming between 1895 and 1940, then a cooling between 1940 and 1970. Since then the climate has warmed up again, especially from the mid-1980s onwards. These phases have their parallels in other parts of the Northern Hemisphere, including the USA and Canada, although the exact dates at which they began and ended have varied from region to region.

HOW THE WORLD'S CLIMATE IS CHANGING

Climate change is usually very slow, but human intervention may be altering that. Increasing carbon-dioxide emissions, and the depletion of stratospheric ozone above the polar regions, may have triggered climate changes across the world.

The world's climate was changing, and on a potentially dramatic scale: by the mid-1970s, a number of scientists were agreed on that. There was less agreement about the direction of change. In 1973-4, a team of climate scientists caused a stir when they suggested a strong possibility that the ice caps would expand rapidly in the 21st century – a return of the glaciers. Other learned papers published around the same time predicted the precise opposite. In August 1975, the climatologist

W.S. Broecker wrote an article for the journal *Science*: 'Climate Change: Are We on the Brink of a Pronounced Global Warming?' A year later the same journal published a paper by P.E Damon and S.M. Kunen called 'Global Cooling? No. Southern Hemisphere Warming Trends may Indicate Onset of the CO_2 "Greenhouse" Effect'.

In February 1978, the US Pentagon-funded National Defense University conducted a survey among climate experts around the world. It was trying to gauge any kind of emerging consensus. In fact, there was little. At one extreme, experts were predicting a 10 per cent chance that

WORLD PROBLEM *A coal-fired power station burns large quantities of coal every day, contributing to the rising CO_2 levels in the atmosphere.*

SMOG BLANKET *A bank of pollution – probably a mix of carbon monoxide, nitrogen oxides and ozone – fills the streets of San Diego.*

mean temperatures across the globe would rise by 0.6°C (1.1°F) between 1970 and 2000. At the other extreme, they predicted a 10 per cent chance that temperatures would fall by 0.3°C (0.5°F). Averaged out, these came to a prediction that global temperatures would rise by 0.1°C (0.2°F).

The experts were agreed on one thing: that increasing levels of carbon dioxide in the Earth's atmosphere, due chiefly to industrial emissions and motor-vehicle fumes, would tend to produce global warming. Most, however, believed that other factors, such as volcanic activity and natural cooling following a mini-peak in mean temperatures that occurred in the early part of the 20th century, would counterbalance it.

Several important things then happened between 1975 and 1990 that changed their views. First, the trend towards cooler temperatures worldwide, which had been evident since about 1940, ceased and went into reverse. There was now no doubt that the world's climate was actually warming. At the same time, the revolution in computer technology gave climatologists far more powerful tools to assess existing evidence of climate change. More powerful computers also enabled them to make more useful predictions about how global and regional climates might change over coming decades.

Finally, continuing research into the stratospheric ozone layer – the layer 10-20 miles (16-32 km) above the Earth's surface that screens out much of the ultraviolet radiation coming from the Sun – revealed that human activity was damaging ozone concentrations above the Antarctic in spring and early summer. Here, in other words, was evidence of one way in which man was damaging his environment and affecting world climate patterns. All these factors came together to thrust climatology, a hitherto rather boffinish science, into the political and media limelight.

ENERGY IN, ENERGY OUT

Human beings are able to live comfortably in the lowest few hundred feet of the atmosphere because they can rely on temperature levels there remaining more or less static – at least, when averaged out over several years. This long-term equilibrium results from a balance between heat energy coming in from the Sun, on the one hand, and, on the other, energy radiated back out again from the surface of the Earth into space.

Generally speaking, the hotter the source of radiation, the shorter the wavelength of most of the energy radiated by it. As the Sun is considerably hotter than the Earth, the energy it radiates has a much shorter wavelength than that radiated by the Earth. This short-wave radiation is able to penetrate the atmosphere more easily. While much of the incoming solar radiation gets through to ground level, some of the long-wave radiation from the Earth is absorbed by various

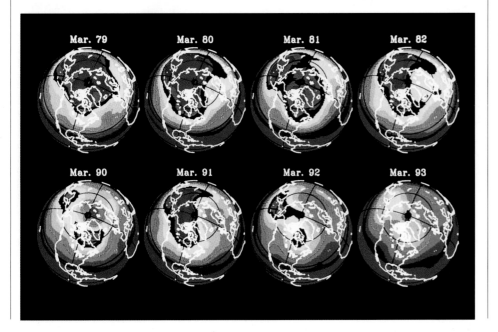

OZONE DEPLETION *Red marks the highest concentrations of ozone; blue and purple the lowest. The change from 1979 to 1993 is dramatic.*

BURNING ISSUE *Every time rain forest is cleared by burning, carbon dioxide is released into the atmosphere.*

gases in the air, especially carbon-dioxide, water vapour, methane and ozone. It is then re-radiated and a proportion bounced back towards the ground. In effect, some heat energy is trapped in the lower atmosphere, rather as heat builds up in a greenhouse on a sunny day, which is why this process is known as the 'greenhouse' effect. The gases in the air that absorb the energy are sometimes known as 'greenhouse gases'.

There is nothing alarming about this natural greenhouse effect. On the contrary, it enables us to survive, since without it global temperatures would be much lower than they are. Most atmospheric scientists believe that it warms our planet by some 30-35°C (55-65°F). In its absence, the mean global temperature would probably be –20° to –25°C (–4° to –13°F) – the Earth would be ice-bound and uninhabitable.

Mankind cannot significantly change the amount of water vapour – the most important greenhouse gas – in the atmosphere,

but we can change the proportion of carbon dioxide. In fact, we have been increasing the quantity of carbon dioxide in the air we breathe ever since the first human communities set fire to trees to make clearings in forests. For millennia these changes in carbon-dioxide levels were trivial. But

---

THREAT FROM THE HEIGHTS

Global warming poses a threat to mountain dwellers as well as those in low-lying areas. As glaciers shrink in ranges such as the European Alps, meltwater accumulates in the heights held back by natural rubble dams. But the ice acted as a kind of cement holding the dams together. It does not take much for a dam to break, sending a lethal avalanche of rocks and water tumbling into the valley below.

---

since the beginning of the Industrial Revolution in Europe, some 200 years ago, there has been a steady and continuous rise in carbon-dioxide levels, thanks to the burning of fossil fuels such as oil, natural gas and coal in industrial processes and in motor vehicles. As a result, concentrations

of carbon dioxide are now approximately 25 per cent higher than they were in 1800.

In the last 60 years we have compounded matters by manufacturing a completely new group of gases called chlorofluorocarbons or CFCs, for use as propellants in aerosol sprays, in packaging materials such as expanded polystyrene, and in commercial and domestic refrigeration units. These CFCs are also greenhouse gases, although they are better known for their damaging effect on the ozone layer.

Industrial countries have been – and still are – the biggest contributors to the rising levels of greenhouse gases in the atmosphere. The USA emits ten times as much carbon dioxide as Britain or France or Italy, and 100 times as much as Bangladesh. Put another way, the average US citizen contributes twice as much carbon dioxide as the average Briton or Australian, and 50 times as much as the average Bangladeshi. Emissions of greenhouse gases are no longer rising steadily; they are accelerating. At the present rate of industrial development around the world, carbon-dioxide levels are predicted to double their 1800 levels by the year 2025.

Methane is another powerful greenhouse gas that is increasing as more land is given over to agriculture. It is given off from farmyard animals, rice paddy fields and nitrogen fertilisers. Levels of natural methane are also starting to rise from the tundra regions around the polar ice caps, and as the ice sheets continue contracting more tundra will be exposed and so give off more methane.

Most atmospheric physicists agree that a major growth in greenhouse gases in the atmosphere will result in a major rise in the overall average temperature of the entire system of Earth, ocean and atmosphere. However, it is almost impossible – even with the latest computer technology – to predict how the climate of a particular continent

VINTAGE CROP *If global warming continues, vineyards may become a more common sight in the English countryside.*

will change in the long term, still less what the effect would be on an individual country.

As the temperature climbs, a number of 'feedback' effects may come into play. For example, the warmer the atmosphere becomes, the more water vapour it can contain. The likely increase in cloud cover will divert some of the Sun's radiation back into space, producing a cooling effect. Equally, however, water vapour is itself a greenhouse gas and any increase in moisture will therefore also have a warming effect. Furthermore, any change in the energy balance of our planet will almost certainly change the global wind patterns, which in turn will change ocean currents. Some land areas would be particularly vulnerable to such a turn of events.

WARNINGS OF WARMING

The first serious predictions of future global warming were made in 1987-8 and generated a good deal of alarm. One result was that an international panel of experts – the International Panel on Climate Change (IPCC) – was established. It was asked to coordinate research into the planet's changing climate and to present reports on the latest findings at regular intervals.

Its first report was published in 1990. It stated that, if emissions of carbon dioxide and other greenhouse gases continued to grow at the current rate, the average global temperature would probably increase by about 2°C (3°F) by the year 2050.

By the time the second report was published in 1992, prediction models had been improved considerably, taking into account some of the feedback effects. As a result, the predicted warming for the middle of the 21st century was reduced to between 1° and 1.5°C (2° and 2.5°F). As knowledge

continues to grow during the next few decades, the predictions will no doubt change several times, possibly in different directions. A further report, published in 1996, contained an important statement explaining that the majority of the panel-members were finally persuaded that mankind's contribution to global warming was now discernible. However, a minority of the scientists still disagreed.

Global warming results in more than just rising temperatures. Another effect is the gradual melting of the polar ice caps. In particular, it might destabilise and give rise to the eventual break-up of the West Antarctic Ice Shelf. Were this to happen, enormous quantities of very cold fresh water would be injected into the surface layers of the world's oceans. This would raise the sea level and perhaps cause sudden and dramatic changes in circulation patterns in both the atmosphere and the oceans. At the moment, the balance of opinion is that the Antarctic ice shelves are safe for at least a century, and global sea level is not expected to rise by more than 18 in (46 cm) during the next 50 years. But opinions can change.

Global warming does not mean that all parts of the world will become progressively warmer. On the contrary, a few

MELTDOWN *Icebergs break off the ice shelf and drift away from Antarctica. Global warming may accelerate this process, destabilising the ice shelves.*

NATURAL POWER *A huge wind farm at Gorgonio Pass, near Palm Springs, California, and a solar furnace in southern France (above) generate electricity from renewable sources of power.*

regions may actually become colder, at least temporarily, due to factors such as changes in wind and ocean circulation patterns, while changes in rainfall patterns are likely to be very complex. In Britain, newspaper features in the early 1990s suggested that the country's climate would become more Mediterranean in character, with hot summers, mild winters, citrus orchards and vineyards, reduced heating bills and teeming holiday beaches. Such a change, if it happened, would also, however, have its down sides: the rising sea level would result in washed-out beaches; lowlands would be flooded; hitherto unknown pests and diseases would appear; summers would be plagued by photochemical smog (produced when sunlight reacts with vehicle exhaust to produce ozone and other toxic gases), and,

instead of lower heating bills, there would be the snag of large air-conditioning ones.

What should we do about possible climate change in the 21st century? Answers to this question are shrouded in controversy. Pressure groups and vested interests vie for the attention of government ministers. For governments it is hard to make balanced decisions, even when they have the will to do so, because the scientists' ability to predict the changes is so limited. One thing is certain, however: that the atmosphere takes a long time – many decades –to respond to changes in emissions of greenhouse gases. We are currently reaping the effects of gases emitted maybe 50 years ago. Climatic changes caused by mankind's activities during the intervening decades are still in the pipeline. Whatever

they are, they will appear over the next 50 years or so, and they cannot be stopped.

Nonetheless, there are certain things that can be done for the benefit of future generations. Changing to renewable energy sources such as wind and solar power when they become competitive, ending the unnecessary clearing of tropical rain forests, insulating buildings and improving the efficiency of transport systems – all these would help to reduce emissions of greenhouse gases. Increased spending on research into renewable energy sources would help and would cost comparatively little in the long run, especially when factors such as world population growth are borne in mind. At the moment, Earth's population is doubling once every 35 to 40 years. More people means more emissions of greenhouse gases, so curbing these levels would help to keep the problem more under control.

THE PROS AND CONS OF OZONE

Ozone is a confusing gas. The ozone layer in the high atmosphere is beneficial, because it protects us from harmful ultraviolet (UV) radiation coming from the Sun. On the other hand, ozone in the lowest layer of the atmosphere – where we live – causes breathing difficulties and other health problems. The stratospheric ozone layer is a natural phenomenon, but low-level ozone is a pollutant resulting from the action of strong sunlight on the exhaust gases of motor vehicles.

To confuse matters further, ozone is actually a form of oxygen – the most vital life-sustaining constituent in the atmosphere. But it is a comparatively rare form, comprising three atoms of oxygen instead of the usual two. Thus it is referred to in shorthand as O_3, whereas ordinary oxygen with two atoms is written as O_2. Roughly 20 per cent of the atmosphere is oxygen, but ozone forms less than one-millionth of it, and nearly all of that is in the high atmosphere, some 30-40 miles (50-65 km) above the ground.

The stratospheric ozone layer prevents nearly all the very damaging UV-C (shortest) wavelengths from getting through to the ground, and it removes some 80 per cent of the less damaging UV-B wavelengths. Ultraviolet radiation is harmful because it accelerates the wrinkling and aging of skin, causes sunburn and contributes to snow blindness. It can also damage our eyes and is responsible for some melanomas (skin cancers). Indeed, in sunny climates colonised by white-skinned peoples, such as California,

PROTEST *The measured warnings from scientists have prompted high-profile demonstrations by activists.*

South Africa and Australia, between 25 and 50 per cent of all cancer deaths among Caucasians are from melanomas induced by the amounts of UV-C radiation that manage to penetrate the ozone screen.

The ozone layer is produced by the effect of sunlight on ordinary oxygen. It needs to be constantly renewed because in the course of time the ozone naturally breaks down into the more usual diatomic oxygen (O_2). Other chemicals found in the atmosphere also break it down, as do some artificial chemicals. Chlorofluorocarbons, CFCs, are particularly lethal to O_3 under the influence of sunlight when the air temperature is low.

Stratospheric ozone will only remain there if a balance is maintained between generating and destroying the gas. Ozone depletion has been measured above the Antarctic since the 1970s, and generally appears to have accelerated since the mid-1980s due to the effect of CFCs used in the past. At first, it seemed that conditions in the Northern Hemisphere were not right for an ozone hole to develop above the Arctic. But observations revealed substantial losses above northern Europe during the early springs of 1991, 1993 and 1996.

Governments reacted quickly to the threat to the world's ozone layer. They had set up a panel of experts as early as 1977,

UNWELCOME CHANGE *In the Northern Hemisphere between 1992 and 1993, levels of chlorine monoxide (ClO), a by-product of CFCs that scavenges ozone, increased, while ozone concentrations decreased.*

and a plan known as the Montreal Protocol was agreed in 1985. The most important result of this has been the rapid phasing out of CFCs. However, the atmosphere responds very slowly to these changes, and assuming we completely rid the planet of CFCs by the year 2000, ozone concentrations would not return to 1990 levels until 2060.

NATURAL OR MAN-MADE?

Climate change over long periods of time is a natural phenomenon. Year-on-year fluctuations are also part of the normal scheme of things. Both these factors make it hard to disentangle natural changes from those occurring as a result of human activity. Hasty conclusions have to be avoided. The global-warming debate of the late 1980s took place against the background of a series of very hot summers in the USA. This was almost certainly coincidence, though it helped to focus attention on the debate.

In all parts of the world, gradual climatic trends are masked by much larger fluctuations from year to year. Individual hot summers or warm winters are not evidence of a warming trend; cold snowy winters or cool rainy summers are not evidence of its absence. In the end, only time and the efforts of climate experts, refining their studies of the statistics, calculating their averages and running their computer models, will confirm conclusively whether or not global warming as a result of human activity is actually happening.

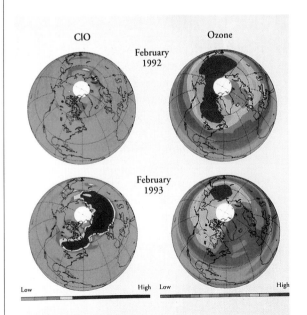

PICTURE CREDITS